# AMERICA
## AS A
# MILITARY POWER

# AMERICA
# AS A
# MILITARY POWER

## From the American Revolution
## to the Civil War

JEREMY BLACK

Studies in Military History and International Affairs

Westport, Connecticut
London

*4858854q*

**Library of Congress Cataloging-in-Publication Data**

Black, Jeremy.
   America as a military power : from the American revolution to the Civil War / Jeremy Black.
      p.   cm. — (Studies in military history and international affairs)
     Includes bibliographical references (p.   ) and index.
     ISBN 0–275–97298–4 (alk. paper)—ISBN 0–275–97706–4 (pbk. : alk. paper)
     1. United States—History, Military—To 1900.  2. United States—Military relations.  3. United States—Foreign public opinion, British.  4. Public opinion—Great Britain.  I. Title. II. Series.
     E181.B674   2002
     355'.00973'09033—dc21      2001059079

British Library Cataloguing in Publication Data is available.

Library of Congress Catalog Card Number: 2001059079
ISBN: 0–275–97298–4
     0–275–97706–4 (pbk.)
ISSN: 1537–4432

First published in 2002

Praeger Publishers, 88 Post Road West, Westport, CT 06881
An imprint of Greenwood Publishing Group, Inc.
www.praeger.com

Printed in the United States of America

The paper used in this book complies with the Permanent Paper Standard issued by the National Information Standards Organization (Z39.48–1984).

10 9 8 7 6 5 4 3 2 1

For Roger Kain,
a much-appreciated friend and fellow scholar.

# Contents

★

# Preface

The purpose of this book is a bold one, and it is only possible thanks to the excellent work already produced by others. I want to consider American military history in a fascinating period—from the struggle for independence to the end of the Civil War, but to do so from a particular angle, that of a foreigner, with all the drawbacks that that entails. In doing so, I am not in any way querying the value of American scholarship on the subject, but simply suggesting that it would be valuable to re-examine what is generally presented as American military exceptionalism from a foreign viewpoint. American exceptionalism is understood according to the distinctive combination of political, social, intellectual, and physical factors, including potential threats, that shaped and were shaped by the greater American culture.

The British viewpoint is especially valuable for three reasons: the British fought two wars with the Americans, contemporary British commentators followed American developments with interest, and Britain, like the United States, had no conscription. Neither country conformed to the autocratic model of the Continental European state nor to their large standing army. Instead, both Britain and the United States had representative assemblies and small standing (permanent) armies. The particular dimension I offer is that of the contextualization of American military developments and wars. This enables both to be considered by comparing them with those elsewhere in the Western world. I have written extensively on military history, British, European, and further afield, before, during and after this period. Hopefully others will pursue this approach to offer full-scale comparative studies as well as a history of America in this period from the perspective of military and related issues.

It is very pleasant to record the friendship and hospitality I have met with on my visits to the United States over more than thirty years. During the period when I was writing this book, I benefited from invitations to lecture at Adelphi and Appalachian State Universities, to the Continuing Education Programs of the Universities of Oxford and Virginia, and at Radley College. I would like to thank Ian Bunker for taking me to the battlefield at Guilford Court House, Ron Fritze for taking me to that at San Jacinto, Stan Carpenter for taking me to those at Bull Run and Antietam and to military sites on the eastern shore of the Chesapeake, and my wife, Sarah, for taking me to Chancellorsville and Fredericksburg on a great family holiday in Virginia. Heather Staines has proved an encouraging commissioning editor, and Frank Saunders an effective production counterpart. I have benefited from the comments of Gary Gallagher, Ricardo Herrera, Wayne Lee, Peter Onuf, Donald Ratcliffe, David Skaggs, William Skelton, Armstrong Starkey, Bill Skelton, Howard Temperley, Bruce Vandervort, Harry Ward, Sam Watson, and Neil York on part or all of earlier drafts. Last, I would like to record my great enjoyment of America and its wonderful, lively people.

# Abbreviations

| | |
|---|---|
| BL. Add. | London, British Library, Additional Manuscripts |
| DRO. 152M. | Exeter, Devon Record Office, Sidmouth papers |
| FO | Foreign Office papers |
| *GW* | *The Papers of George Washington. Revolutionary War Series* |
| PRO | London, Public Record Office |
| WO | War Office papers |

Unless otherwise stated, all books cited are published in London.

# 1

# Introduction

American military history can be divided into four periods. The first, lasting until circa 1530, was the longest, but the least studied and most obscure: pre-contact (i.e., European contact) warfare. It is unreasonably neglected both in accounts of global military history and in those of American military history. Second, comes the second longest period, from circa 1530 to 1775, that in which the European colonial powers were a growing presence, although they still only affected, directly or indirectly, a minor portion of what was to be the United States. In this period, there were three types of warfare, although they frequently overlapped. Native versus Native warfare continued, although it was affected by the spread of firearms and the horse, both of which had been introduced by the Europeans. Native versus European warfare and European versus European conflict were both new to North America, although they were restricted in scope, and cannot be considered in isolation from the trans-Atlantic commitments, drives and resources of the European powers.

The third period, the subject of this book, began in 1775 when conflict broke out between the government of the dominant European colonial power in North America, Britain, and a significant portion of its European population in the colonies. This begins the history of modern American warfare, and the American state itself was formed in 1776 with the Declaration of Independence.

The period 1775–1865 is defined in contrast not only to what came earlier but also to what followed. There, the divide is between a state that had devoted its military resources to conflict with neighbors (Native Americans, War of 1812 with Britain largely fought in North America, Mexicans) or to civil warfare, and, increasingly from 1865, the imperial America that was able to project its power convincingly across the globe as befitted the world's leading economic power. The ability to conquer both Cuba and the Philippines, or at least their centres, from Spain, in 1898, both emulated the British achievement in 1762 and was a striking display of strength. It was followed by America's major role in the last stage of World War I, her central role in World War II, and her dominant role in the Cold War and in the post–Cold War world.

It is impossible to forget this history when considering the 1775–1865 period, and it is tempting to search for continuities, not least in terms of a supposed and distinctive American way of war. There were of course continuities, but this approach can only be so helpful. It is, in addition, necessary to treat the period 1775–1865 in its own terms and to search for its specificities. That accords in particular with current interest in the role of what have been termed strategic cultures and, more generally, in the particular assumptions about warfare and military capability in different states. To cite a recent study of American naval development:

The thesis that emerges . . . is simple: changing the intellectual construction of peace and war decisively shapes the construction of military power. Predictions about American acquisition of military power must be based not on an analysis of the objective interests of political actors, but on an examination of dominant images of foreign policy and warfare and on an understanding of the intellectual and cultural forces shaping the construction of those images.[1]

It is also valuable to adopt a lateral approach and consider events in America in terms of comparable developments elsewhere. That is the approach in this book. For each chapter, there is a comparison with the most relevant developments elsewhere. This plays a central role in the analysis. Thus, warfare in America in 1775–1865 is discussed in the light of warfare elsewhere in the Western world in this period.[2] This world is understood as Europe and Latin America, while American expansion at the expense of Native Americans can be considered alongside other aspects of the expansion of Western states at the expense of non-Western peoples in this period.

Some conflicts can be readily compared and contrasted with wars in America. Thus, the French Revolutionary Wars (1792–1802) can be discussed alongside the American War of Independence (1775–83). Similarly, the Wars of German Unification (1864, 1866, 1870–71) can be discussed alongside the Civil War (1861–65). Other comparisons are less easy. The "War of 1812" with Britain (1812–15) was very different to the contemporary Napoleonic Wars in Europe (1803–15), or, indeed, to Britain's role in them. The Mexican-American War of 1846–48 was different to the warfare in Europe in 1848–49, much of which involved the suppression of nationalist rebellions. Nevertheless, it is still instructive to probe comparisons and contrasts, looking, for example, at similarities between the Mexican and the Crimean Wars (1853–56).

In so doing, it is important to appreciate the variety of military circumstances and developments in the Western world, not least within Europe. It is all too easy to concentrate on a central narrative—from the Prussia of Frederick the Great (1740–86), via the France of the Revolutionary and Napoleonic Wars (1792–1815), to the Prussia of the Wars of German Unification (1864–71)—and to treat these armies and conflicts as the paradigm or essential form of European conflict, and thus the basis of comparison with America. This would be wrong. Instead, there was both variety and no linear continuum of "progress" towards warfare in the modern world. Thus, American developments can be understood as an aspect of a diverse Western military and warfare, rather than being simply contrasted with them. It is also helpful to consider American developments in light of the concepts that have played a major role in military history, in particular that of a technologically-driven narrative that focuses on weaponry.

As this book is designed to work for those unfamiliar with the subject, each chapter devotes considerable space to a narrative of developments within America. Hopefully, that will also provide readers with encouragement to pursue particular aspects in greater detail and thus to make their own reflections on the fascinating question of American exceptionalism.[3]

## NOTES

1. E. Rhodes, "Constructing Peace and War: An Analysis of the Power of Ideas to Shape American Military Power," *Millennium: Journal of International Studies*, 24 (1995), p. 55.

2. For the background, J.M. Black, *European Warfare 1660–1815* (New Haven, 1994).

3. H.R. Guggisberg, "American Exceptionalism as National History?" in E. Glaser and H. Wellenreuther (eds.), *Bridging the Atlantic: The Question of American Exceptionalism in Perspective* (Cambridge, 2002), pp. 265–76.

# 2

# War of Independence

It is appropriate to devote considerable space in any study of American military history to the War of Independence (1775–83) because this led to the successful creation of the new state and was the first war fought by this state. That said, it is, nevertheless, the case that the importance of the conflict is sometimes exaggerated in military history: a crucial outcome is not necessarily the product of exceptional causes. First, the war is popularly taken to mark the beginning of American military history, when it was rather a transforming stage in conflict in North America; and, second, and more significantly, the war is seen as a move towards military modernity and a turning point in global military history. Thus, for example, the influential Arnold Modern Wars series began with Stephen Conway's *The War of American Independence 1775–1783* (1995). He presented the war "not as the last of the old order, but the first of the new."[1] In particular, scholars emphasise the degree of popular mobilization that was employed on the American side in order to suggest that the conflict was a people's war and therefore different from what had come before.

Treating the War of Independence as a people's war, which indeed accorded with some contemporary claims, simultaneously gives the struggle virtue and purpose. Furthermore, such a description ensures that the war can be seen as marking a new stage in military history, a stage that also readily explains the result in the shape of the triumph of the American people over a redundant political system and anachronistic military. Thus, the importance of the war is not simply measured by the creation of the United States.

Before considering the claims of modernity, it is necessary to offer a warning about the impact of stereotyping and then appropriate to offer a narrative. Stereotyping began before the war, became insistent during it, and has remained influential since. Paul Langford has pointed out:

... the stereotypes of England as the home of the aristocratic gentleman and America as that of the man of the people became ever more entrenched. Playing this game of stereotypes or ... fighting this war of manner reinforced the variety of two societies, both in some respects quite insecure, both undergoing rapid change and both struggling to make their traditions and aspirations fit the requirements of unprecedented growth.[2]

In contrast, American stereotyping focused on Britain as anachronistic and static.

The narrative is important not simply in order to provide an account of what happened, but also because the selection of what to include, and thus discuss, itself reflects assumptions about the conflict and what was important in it. How much weight, for example, should be placed on other global commitments in order to better understand the range of problems and priorities facing Britain, and therefore to contextualize and qualify America's role in Britain's defeat? How much weight should be placed on the American failure to conquer Canada, in other words on the failure to unite British North America in a new independent state?

Neither of these wider questions attract particular interest in conventional American treatments of the war. Instead, there is an emphasis on the conflict within the Thirteen Colonies. Even that, however, poses major choices. Chronological emphasis is one such. At one extreme, the war after the surrender of a British army at Yorktown in October 1781, in particular the abandonment of George Washington's plan to capture New York in 1782 and the unsuccessful American siege of Savannah that year, is commonly ignored. Even within the conventional narrative—Lexington to Yorktown—there is still a question whether insufficient attention is devoted to the struggle after the battle of Monmouth Court House in June 1778, with the exception of Yorktown, and therefore whether the war in the South, which was most intense in these years, is underrated in the general accounts (there is important specialist literature on the southern campaigns). Furthermore, the central narrative of battle minimises other military operations and other forms of conflict and confrontation. All of these deficiencies will doubtless be found in the following account, but these problems are worth stressing because part of the issue of analysis focuses on the question of what requires explanation.

## BACKGROUND

The background in America was scarcely that of peaceful development over the previous century. Indeed the American revolution took place against the background of war: the French and Indian War (1754–63). Conflict over the century prior to 1775 can be classified in terms of warfare with other European powers and with Native Americans, and, also, civil conflict, although there was a considerable overlap in the first two categories. All three required military efforts by the settlers. Thus, for example in 1690, an expedition of eight ships and 700 men sent by the General Court of Massachusetts captured Port Royal in Acadia (now Nova Scotia), but, the same year, an expedition of 32 New England ships and 2,200 troops failed to drive the French from the St. Lawrence. Carolina volunteers unsuccessfully attacked St. Augustine in 1702, 1728, and 1740. In 1745, 3,000 Massachusetts militia joined with British warships to capture Louisbourg. Nine thousand Americans joined 8,400 British regulars in the unsuccessful attack on Carillon (Ticonderoga) in 1758.

Conflict with Native Americans was not continuous, but it was frequent and it encouraged Americans in and near frontier areas to remain ready for fighting. Thus, in 1761, Carolina Rangers joined British regulars and allied Natives to invade Cherokee territory. In 1774, 1,500 Virginia militia advanced against the Shawnee who had attacked settlers in their territory and ambushed a volunteer force that went to their assistance. Conflict between the settlers was less common, but was not unknown. In 1676, Sir William Berkeley, the Governor of Virginia, called out the militia to resist Bacon's Rebellion, only to find many of the militia among the rebels. The rebellion only collapsed when Bacon died.[3] Just over a decade later, royal authority was overthrown as part of the "Glorious Revolution" that saw the Catholic James II driven from Britain in 1688–89. As late as 1771, a protest movement in North Carolina known as the "Regulators" fought a pitched battle against their own colonial militia under the command of the royal governor.

Americans were better prepared, not least psychologically, for conflict than Britons, although such a bald statement conceals a wide variety in circumstances. Nevertheless, this very readiness was important to American military history. The militia tradition still meant much in the American colonies, in contrast to Britain where the mid-eighteenth century interest in militia did not extend to ensuring that they were combat effective. The militia of the American colonies were not simply a local defence force, but also a strike force of considerable effectiveness. Thus, the invasion of Canada launched by the revolutionaries in 1775 was not a new initiative, but a continuation of a well-established pattern in which New England forces attacked targets in Canada. Unlike in the French and Indian War (1754–63), however, they did so without the co-operation of British regulars. On the contrary, one-time allies were now enemies.

In the Thirteen Colonies, in the 1760s and early 1770s, disagreements over the nature of the British imperial system and the colonial bond arose from the interaction of fiscal and regulatory pressure from the imperial state with more liberal constitutional ideas and political practices in the colonies. This created a volatile atmosphere as British ministries responded with wavering acts of firmness. Massachusetts was a centre of opposition, and the landing of troops in Boston in 1768 helped to increase tension. Policing the situation involved the use of military force. The "Boston Massacre" of 5 March 1770, in which five

Bostonians were killed, was seen by many Americans as proof of the militari-zation and corruption of British authority in the colonies, although it accorded with conventional British policing techniques in crisis situations, as seen in the Porteous disturbances in Edinburgh in 1736 and the St. George's Fields "Mas-sacre" in London in 1768.[4]

Disagreements over the colonial bond cut to the core of the nature of the British empire, which was that of a reciprocal profitability controlled by the British state, as expressed through the sovereignty of Parliament. This system, enshrined in the Navigation Acts, was publicly condemned in the American colonies, with attacks on the consumption of tea, and thus on the profitability of the East India Company. From 1770 the Sons of Liberty sought to prevent the drinking of British tea. When the North ministry passed a Tea Act in 1773, allowing the company to sell its tea directly to consignees in America, a measure designed to cut the cost of tea in America, this was condemned by patriot activists unwilling to accept Parliament's right to affect American taxation. In the Boston Tea Party of 16 December 1773, ten thousand pounds worth of tea was seized from three ships in Boston Harbor by the Sons of Liberty led by Samuel Adams and thrown into the water.

## THE EARLY STAGES OF THE WAR

Disorder encouraged governmental reliance on the army. The Boston Tea Party led to tough action against Massachusetts, including the dispatch of more troops. General Thomas Gage, the Commander-in-Chief in America, was ap-pointed Governor of the colony, and instructed to use force in order to restore royal authority. The British response to the crisis in Massachusetts led to the outbreak of war, as Gage sought to prevent an accumulation of arms that might serve as the basis for concerted armed opposition. On 19 April 1775, en route to seize a cache of arms reportedly stored at Concord, the British found about seventy militia drawn up in two lines in the village of Lexington. Heavily out-numbered, the militia began to disperse, but a shot was fired and the British fired two volleys in response, thereby scattering the militia. The British pressed on to Concord but their withdrawal to Boston in the face of opposition was a difficult one. The shedding of blood outraged New England, and a substantial force, largely dependent on their personal arms, soon lay siege to the British in Boston.[5] The sea route was open both as a path of communication and as the basis for a strategic dimension, but in political terms the outbreak of conflict helped unify radicals and moderates against British authority. Popular enthusi-asm for war rose dramatically, particularly as the radicals disseminated tales of British atrocities during the retreat from Concord. The ability of the patriot movement to dominate rapidly the telling of the story of Concord was a key to the spread of popular resistance.

Elsewhere in the Thirteen Colonies, British authority collapsed: governors were provided with no military assistance due to a concentration of troops in

Massachusetts. Local committees of correspondence seized authority. As in much of Scotland in 1745 at the outset of the Jacobite rising against the authority of George II, the small size of the British regular army ensured that it could not be spread widely enough to preserve royal authority. The lack of local allies at this stage willing to fight the Patriots was thus crucial, and where local support did exist, as in Virginia and North Carolina, it quickly fell apart when expected or sufficient British backing did not materialize. The situation paralleled that in the South in 1861: many did not wish to secede but they were overawed. On 14 June 1775, Congress decided to raise the Continental Army and, the following day, appointed George Washington commander of "all the continental forces, raised, or to be raised, for the defense of American liberty." Washington (1732–99) had served in the Virginia forces in the French and Indian War, taking part in advances against the French in 1754, 1755, and 1758, although he had no major command experience.

Military operations focused on Boston, the centre of power in New England and the British base in the Thirteen Colonies. The British responded to the build-up of patriot strength not by using amphibious expeditions to maintain royal authority along the eastern seaboard, a policy that would have taken advantage of their naval strength and widened the area of struggle, but, instead, by employing their troops in a concentrated manner against a clear target. The availability of an alternative strategy for the British is worth noting as it is too easy to assess respective capability only in terms of the strategy that was followed.

On the night of 16 June 1775, the patriots marched to Breed's Hill on the Charlestown peninsula and began to fortify the position. It commanded the heights above Boston, although the subsequent battle was named after the more prominent hill behind Breed's Hill, Bunker Hill. Gage, who had command of the harbor, decided on a landing at high tide on the afternoon of 17 June, followed by an attack on the American entrenchments. However, once his forces had landed, Gage moved ponderously, spending about two hours deploying his men before launching a frontal attack on the American positions which had not been damaged to any significant extent by the British artillery. A deployment in disciplined order was the standard Western military method of the period. The Americans waited until the advancing troops were almost upon them before shattering their first two attacks with heavy musket fire. An attempt to turn the American flank was repelled. The Americans, however, were running short of ammunition, and a third British attack took the American redoubt. Nevertheless, the exhausted British, harassed by sharpshooters, were unable to stop the Americans from retreating.

The British failure to win a striking success at Bunker Hill did not mean that the rebellion could not be suppressed. The British had been defeated at Prestonpans, the first battle of the '45, but had still suppressed the Jacobite rising the following year at Culloden. Bunker Hill was still a major blow. British casualties were heavy, and they had been lost without leading to a decisive victory. Instead, the battle induced caution in the British army. Having lost the strategic initiative, so that their troops did no more than control the ground they stood on in Boston, the British were unable to prevent the development and consolidation of the revolution. British operational and tactical capabilities were now also at issue.

As with other revolutions, the eventual limits of action by the revolutionaries were unclear. Political, economic and military factors provided reasons for spreading the revolution to Britain's other colonies. However, disaffection was contained in the British colonies in the West Indies, and support there for change ebbed after the 1776 slave revolt on Jamaica. Despite the presence of American privateers, the revolutionaries lacked the naval lift to project power to the West Indies.[6]

Similarly, there was no organised and powerful American naval force capable of providing support for action against Newfoundland or Nova Scotia. Thus, in the now hostile presence of British naval power, the Americans could not repeat earlier expeditions against, then French-held, Nova Scotia, Cape Breton Island or the St. Lawrence. This was to be demonstrated in 1779. A British force from Nova Scotia established a post at Castine, on Penobscot Bay, on the coast of what was then Massachusetts and is now Maine. It was designed to deny the Americans both a naval base from which they might threaten Halifax and timber supplies from the area. A force of 1,000 Massachusetts militia, supported by a fleet, sailed to Castine where they began a slow siege of the British position. However, within a month, a British squadron arrived. Rather than fighting, all but two of the ships in the far larger American fleet fled up the Penobscot River, where they were beached and set alight. The other two ships did not escape. The American soldiers and sailors fled into the woods. Castine was held by the British for the remainder of the war.

The American debacle, which effectively knocked Massachusetts out of the war financially and for which the naval commander was court-martialled and summarily dismissed, indicated that the Americans were not as successful at amphibious operations as the more experienced British could be, and that in offensive operations their militia was not necessarily an impressive force. The American force could certainly have fought better in 1779, but the campaign indicated the strategic limitation flowing from British naval power. The successful 1847 American amphibious attack on Veracruz offers an instructive contrast. Amphibious operations were about capability as well as opportunity, and this capability required infrastructure and training, in both of which the Americans were deficient in the 1770s.

However, Canada was vulnerable to American attack overland. Although, in the French and Indian War, the French base at Québec had fallen in 1759 to an expedition transported by water to and up the St. Lawrence, the British in 1758 had launched their main attack against Canada overland, along the Lake Champlain axis, and in 1759 and 1760 had also advanced on this axis. This axis was open to the Americans in 1775, not least because the peacetime deployment of the British army had not prepared it for operational planning for war with a widespread American rebellion. Crown Point and Ticonderoga, the main British positions that blocked the Lake Champlain axis, fell in May 1775. They had had a combined garrison of fewer than sixty men. Later in the year, the main American invasion force, 2,000 strong under Richard Montgomery, advanced along that axis, but was delayed for seven weeks besieging St. Johns, a fort on the Richelieu river. This lengthy siege, in cold and wet conditions, demoralized Montgomery's force, already affected by disease and threatened by the arrival of winter and the expiring of enlistments. The siege also displayed the potential strength of the defensive: the British did not surrender until they had only three days' provisions left.

Defensive strength was a factor throughout the war, but one that was lessened by the "demilitarized" character of most of the Thirteen Colonies: existing fortifications were concentrated facing Native Americans and what had been French Canada, rather than being scattered across the heavily populated coastal littoral in which most of the conflict took place. This put a premium on battle, rather than siege, although so also did the extent to which American forces were not prepared for major sieges. There was no episode in the war comparable in scale to British operations against Québec in 1759 or Havana in 1762.

In this respect, the American War of Independence might appear to contrast with conflict elsewhere in the Western world. However, this argument has to be employed with care. Fortified positions did play a major role in the conflict. This was true both with sieges, such as Québec in 1775, Fort Washington in 1776, the Delaware River defence network in 1777, Savannah in 1779, Charleston in 1780, and Yorktown in 1781, and also with positions that were not besieged but that helped to define operational possibilities, for example the role of the British occupation of New York from 1776 on the conflict in the middle colonies. The Americans used field fortifications at Saratoga. Much of the American strategy in the war was determined by their repeatedly proven inability to defend their own fortified positions and by their shifting ability to confront the British in a defended, fortified position. The sieges of Boston and Québec were made possible by the unpreparedness of Britain for war. When subsequently incapable of threatening a fortified British force, the Americans tried to choose battlefields with great care. The great achievement of Washington (and the French) at Yorktown was the capability of laying effective siege to a prepared British army.

After the fall of St. Johns, Montgomery marched on Montréal. The outnumbered British Governor, Guy Carleton, fled to Québec, leaving Montréal to surrender. Meanwhile, another American force under Benedict Arnold had been sent across Maine to the St. Lawrence. They were handicapped by rain, food shortages, strong currents on the rivers, and rough trails across the intervening carrying places. Several hundred men turned back, but the ability of Arnold to get through indicates that the terrain in non-cultivated parts of North America was not as impassable as might be suggested. Such operations also played an important role in cultivating an American warrior-image of being at one with, and able to use, American terrain, an image that, in fact, was really only appropriate for Native Americans and a small number of frontier militiamen. In 1690, in contrast, a diversionary attack overland under Colonel Winthrop, designed to support the New England amphibious operation against Québec, had not advanced beyond Lake George.

In 1775, the combined American force besieged Québec, but the British refused to sally out and risk defeat in the field, as the Americans had hoped. The Americans did not receive the support from Canada that they had expected. Bitter weather and terms of service due to end with the year led to a night-time attack on Québec that went disastrously wrong. The following year, the Americans were driven from Canada by British reinforcements that had arrived by sea. The failure of this expedition, the boldest American campaign in the war, is a reminder of the "frictions" of war, not least distance. It also illustrates the problems of operating without popular support. As such, the campaign serves as a reminder of the difficulties of mounting an offensive during the war. As the British were responsible for most offensives, it is easy to ascribe problems with the latter to deficiencies in British war-making. However, the failure of the American invasion of Canada suggests that a different interpretation is appropriate, and that the focus should be on the problems of mounting offensives. It is also worth pointing out that Québec was a difficult target. It had fallen to the British in 1629 and 1759, but the 1690 and 1711 British expeditions had failed, although in the latter case that was due to a night-time error in navigation in the St. Lawrence estuary that had led to the loss of eight transport ships and nearly 900 men.[7]

## THE 1776 CAMPAIGN

In 1776, the British government hoped that, by mounting what was then the largest trans-oceanic expedition ever sent from the British Isles, it would be possible to overawe the Americans. There was still, however, a failure to appreciate the scale of the revolution, and the extent to which they were confronting a nation in arms, and there were not enough British troops. Nevertheless, the ability to send so many troops reflected the role of counterfactuals. Unlike during the French and Indian War, or the War of 1812 prior to Napoleon's enforced abdication in April 1814, Britain was at peace in Europe in 1776 and thus in a position to focus attention and resources on the counter-revolution. Again this contrasted with the situation during the struggles with the Jacobites in 1745–46 and with Irish revolutionaries in 1798; although in each case the British were successful. Thus the challenge facing the Americans was particularly difficult. It was also unclear that the French would move from support for them, in the shape of arms supplies, to direct involvement in the war, and, indeed, they were not to do so until 1778.

The British plan focused on combining separate forces: one army would clear Canada, and then advance to the Hudson, linking up with another army that would secure New York City and then march north. This would cut off New

England, the hotbed of disaffection and sedition, from what appeared to be more loyal middle and southern colonies. Based on various falsehoods, this strategy, nevertheless, could have succeeded had a James Wolfe (the commander responsible for the capture of Québec in 1759) or Duke of Wellington been found to command the British army; because a successful campaign against the revolutionary army required rapidity of movement, flexibility of action, and boldness of execution, and a general of that calibre could have provided them.

The sequence of successful British attacks in 1776 followed the early months of the year in which the Patriots strengthened their position in the absence of any effective British field army. The principal Loyalist initiative, a rising in North Carolina, was defeated by the local militia at Moore's Creek Bridge on 27 February. Elsewhere, the militia was used to strengthen the new revolutionary establishment and to harry or intimidate its opponents. The understanding that had allowed British warships off New York to continue to receive provisions from the city was ended in early February. The following month, the British withdrew from Boston in order to refit at Halifax.

Under General William Howe, the reinforced army then landed on Staten Island on 3 July 1776. This began a second stage in the war that was more widespread, bitter and sustained than had at first seemed likely, the stage of the British counter-attack. The following day, the Americans declared independence. On 22 August, Howe made an unopposed landing at Gravesend Bay, Long Island. Naval strength gave him the ability to choose where he should launch amphibious attacks. George Washington's forces were scattered throughout the area. Against his better judgement, Washington's deployment was determined by political considerations. New York City was impossible to hold with the forces Washington had, and facing the power of the British navy, which quickly proved its ability to land troops at will. Rather than concentrating his forces, he placed them all over the harbor area, each section too small to do anything other than hinder a British landing. If the winds had been favorable, the navy could have swept up the East River and controlled the narrows between the Bronx and Long Island. Instead, Washington was able to retreat after his defeat on Long Island on 27 August, a defeat that reflected British skill in outflanking and rolling up his position.[8]

On 11 September 1776, the sole meeting between officially appointed representatives of the two sides before the final peace negotiations occurred. The Declaration of Independence proved to be the stumbling block. Howe declared that it prevented him from negotiating and that he could not acknowledge Congress because it was not recognized by the king. The American delegates stressed the importance of independence, Edward Rutledge claiming that Britain would gain greater advantages from an alliance with an independent America than she had hitherto done from her colonies. His perspicacious observation underlined the emptiness of Howe's negotiating position. As with most governments dealing with rebellions, it was difficult to put aside past relationships and the constitutional perspective, and the British did not rise to this challenge.

Instead, they invaded Manhattan and, after a check at Harlem Heights on 16 September, drove the Americans from the island. As the American position deteriorated, the British advanced, driving across to the Delaware, although suggestions of a further advance to Philadelphia were not heeded. An amphibious force seized Newport, Rhode Island. The end of the war and, presumably, the revolution appeared to be in sight.

British confidence was to be challenged by Washington's riposte at Trenton on 25–26 December. This was a triumph for bold generalship, while the successful simultaneous attack by two columns revealed the American ability to mount well-conducted operations.[9] Most of New Jersey was then abandoned by Howe, and, having lost the initiative, the British adopted a defensive posture. Trenton, and another victory at Princeton, revived Washington's army, Congress, and the Revolution as a whole. They spoiled Howe's conciliatory efforts, and made the British offer of pardon far less worthwhile. The battles round New York had suggested that American forces could not face regulars with confidence, but the operations in New Jersey revealed British vulnerability when in units of less than army size.

## THE 1777 CAMPAIGN

At the start of 1777, it seemed reasonable to predict that Howe would be able to seize Philadelphia that year, but the prospect of conquering America with his army was now less likely. Small forces of regulars could not count on victory, and the British were to have to hope first for a decisive defeat of Washington's army and, second, for the creation of effective Loyalist forces. Nevertheless, the British position was considerably better than it had been a year earlier, and 1777 was also the last year in which the British fought only the Patriots and did not have to worry about French naval power. However, it was also a year in which British generals mismanaged the war. As with 1776, the Americans essentially responded to British moves; faced with serious manpower and supply problems, they did not take the initiative. The British deployed two armies: one under Burgoyne, operating south from Canada, and the other under Howe, who sailed from New York in order to advance on Philadelphia from the Chesapeake. He did not feel confident about any advance overland through New Jersey.

Any campaign conducted under such circumstances by two independently-operating forces faced difficulties. There were really two totally uncoordinated campaigns, without overall unity of command or a clearly defined master strategy. In addition, the situation challenged Eurocentric military thinking, centered as it was on a well-known topography, with roads, strategic rivers and towns. In part, this thinking was irrelevant in the New World, as was the concept of operating on interior lines. The latter notion was of limited value in America, where, in large part, the conflict was a war without fronts. New World geography, recruitment, and logistics all created a hybrid Euro-American style of war similar on the surface to European warfare, yet, at the same time, very different.

To turn back to the example of the conquest of Canada, the British had successfully coordinated their advances on Montréal in 1760, but, the previous two years, it had proved impossible for the separate advancing British forces to provide mutual support. This was also to be true of American attacks on Canada in the War of 1812, and of operations by both sides in the Civil War.

The two major British offensives in 1777 exemplified the contrasts in operational circumstances and possibilities. Howe used Britain's naval strength to advance on Philadelphia without having to fight his way across New Jersey. Having landed at Head of Elk, Howe then managed a conventional advance on the city, outmanoeuvring and defeating Washington at Brandywine Creek on 11 September, and entering Philadelphia on the 26th. There were serious deficiencies in Howe's strategic planning: he did not open his campaign against Philadelphia until late in the summer and then after having failed to engage Washington earlier in the year. This ensured that no matter how successful he was Howe could not exploit his victory with winter approaching.

General John Burgoyne faced a very different task in his advance south to the Hudson. Ticonderoga fell easily, but he found the subsequent advance from Fort Ann to Fort Edward very difficult. Employing a method used in this area by the Native Americans in the French and Indian War, the Americans felled trees in order to block the creeks and make roadbuilding difficult. The already wet soil was turned into swamps as the side creeks overflowed their banks. Burgoyne took a long time to build bridges and a plank road across the resulting morass. If the British troops were tired, their opponents, however, were also in a poor state, affected by low morale and desertion, and uncertain how best to respond to Burgoyne's advance. Instead of resisting, they fell back. Indeed, one of the most insistent themes in the correspondence of the generals on both sides in 1777 was the weakness of their forces, a theme that was to grow stronger as the war progressed. Major-General Philip Schuyler wrote from Albany on 5 July 1777 about Ticonderoga: "Should an accident befal us in that quarter and the troops be lost we shall be in a disagreeable situation, with little else besides militia; with not a single piece of heavy or light artillery, and not one artillery man . . . we have no cartridge paper."[10]

Once he had reached the Hudson, Burgoyne was unable to replenish his supplies or to win local support. He was also faced by a growing American force, including reinforcements sent by Washington. Unable to obtain sufficient supplies to remain on the upper Hudson, Burgoyne had the choice of advancing or retiring. Optimism, over-confidence, and conceit led him to the former, his army crossing the Hudson on a bridge of rafts on 13 and 14 September. A defence can be made of his conduct until this point. All war involves risk and to have not pressed on, having taken Ticonderoga so easily, and when in command of one of the only three British forces able to mount an offensive, would have been to make no contribution to what appeared likely to be a decisive campaign. However, Burgoyne also underrated the risks of advancing, not least because he was well aware of his lack of accurate information. On 19 September, Burgoyne advanced on the American positions at Freeman's Farm only to meet stiff opposition and to lose troops, especially officers, to American snipers. The Americans fell back when their position was turned, but British losses were heavier. A second attack, on 7 October, was similarly unsuccessful, and, when Burgoyne attempted to retreat, he discovered the route blocked.[11]

On 17 October 1777, Burgoyne surrendered. He had discovered the folly of underestimating his opponents. Furthermore, his approach to forest operations had been insufficiently flexible, the heavy baggage train was a particular mistake, there was too few light infantry, and reliance on Native Americans had proved unwarranted, and counterproductive as their presence had helped increase militia numbers. Most of the fighting on the American side was done by men detached from Washington's army under Arnold, who was probably the best operational combat commander in either army. The notion that the militia or Morgan's sharpshooting riflemen won the battle is a hoary old tradition no longer accepted by modern scholars; but one that again reflects the emphasis on volunteerism and the strength of sturdy amateurism in the American military myth. Saratoga powerfully contributed to this myth over the following century. It was seen as a victory for a distinctly American way of fighting. It was, indeed, the case that, earlier in the campaign, militia forces defeated a British detachment at Bennington, which was a major blow to the campaign. Furthermore, Gates' force of Continentals at Saratoga was only enabled to stand and fight because of the large numbers of militia who had rallied to their support.

In strategic terms, Saratoga was a warning to the British of the folly of thinking that the Americans had really only one important field army, and, consequently, that its defeat would signal the effective end of the conflict. When Burgoyne's advance had first been considered, it had been assumed that the sole significant risk would be if Washington moved against him. Instead, Burgoyne had been defeated while the bulk of Washington's army had been deployed against Howe. Saratoga showed that a field army could rapidly coalesce around a Continental core if the militia were sufficiently aroused.

Saratoga had a major impact in America and Europe, raising the morale and prestige of the Revolution. By helping to demonstrate American resilience, the campaign led France closer to intervention. Saratoga also ensured that, thereafter, British forces based in Canada would be no more than a modest diversion to the American war-effort. Saratoga marked the end of any prospect of cutting off New England from the rest of America. Had such a policy succeeded, it would have harmed the economy and logistics of the Revolution. Washington's army depended in part on supplies from New England, especially Connecticut, while Pennsylvania provided grain to New England.

The possibility of isolating New England was thrown away in 1777: had Burgoyne retreated, he would have been in a position to threaten the upper Hudson again. The capture of Philadelphia did not therefore have the dramatic consequences Howe had anticipated. This was due not only to Saratoga but also because the notion that the capture would necessarily have such consequences was flawed. Had Philadelphia fallen a year earlier, against the background of the collapse of the American position in the middle colonies, the situation might have been very different; but, in 1777, the fall of the city might have been decisive only had it been accompanied by a repetition of the position a year earlier: the collapse of the major American force in the field, and possibly not even then.

This point can be regarded in several ways, one of which apparently demonstrates American exceptionalism, a salutary consideration when considering the wider nature of the debate about exceptionalism. It could be argued that the loss of Philadelphia was less important than that of a European capital, not only because, as a capital, Philadelphia was held in no special regard by Americans, but also because the Revolution was primarily fought to uphold ideas and ideals and, therefore, European standards were not applicable. This was apparently further demonstrated in 1814 when the British burnt Washington, a source of embarrassment, but not crucial to the course of the War of 1812. Conversely, it could be suggested that the American war was not uniquely motivated by ideas and ideals (and not therefore bound to follow different "rules"), and it can be pointed out that the loss of a capital did not mean the end of a war in Europe. Maria Theresa had been prepared to fight on had she lost Vienna in 1741, Philip V survived the temporary loss of Madrid in 1706 and 1710, Frederick the Great that of Berlin in 1760, and Alexander I of Moscow in 1812, while the Spaniards fought on against Napoleon although the French occupied Madrid in 1808–13.

Thanks to George Washington's caution, Burgoyne's miscalculations, and the fighting skills and spirit of the American soldiers, there had been no decisive British victory in 1777. Washington chose to fight only when in a good defensive position at Brandywine and when, at Germantown, an attack seemed propitious. Neither encounter lived up to expectations, and Washington was forced from the field, just as elsewhere that year the Americans revealed deficiencies: in the defence of Ticonderoga and the Hudson forts, in the failure to organize a successful attack on Rhode Island, and in the more serious inability to supply Washington's army. However, in both battles, as in the Saratoga campaign, the fighting spirit and skills of the American soldiers had been complemented by enough leadership under pressure and tactical flexibility to create a formidable military challenge to the British. By the Hudson, the terrain, Burgoyne's folly and American numerical superiority had brought a clear victory. Near Philadelphia, the outcome had been less happy for the Americans, but they had fought well enough to deny Howe what he needed, a clearly successful conclusion to the campaign that could convince opinion in America, Britain, and France that the British were winning and would triumph. British politicians were already discussing the abandonment of overland offensive operations in favour of amphibious attacks and a blockade, a course that appeared necessary to some if France intervened.

## THE 1778 CAMPAIGN

This intervention followed from the signing, on 6 February 1778, of a treaty of alliance, although Anglo-French hostilities did not begin until 16 June. French entry into the war pushed naval considerations to the forefront, as France was the second strongest naval power in the world (after Britain), and French entry also brought about a shift of geographical focus in the war to encompass the West Indies and even India. The war in North America took a second place for the British, below the struggle with France, which centred on the security of the British Isles against invasion and the fate of the profitable colonies in the West Indies.[12] This shift in strategy was marked most clearly in North America by the fact that British troops largely stopped coming. Since Lexington, British forces had been reinforced with fresh recruits to replenish existing units and with new units. From 1778, this flow was drastically cut, while the army in North America was expected to serve as the source for forces to be sent to the West Indies.

Even before French entry appeared inevitable, it was already clear that a major change was required in British policy. The plans of 1777 had failed not only at Saratoga, but in Pennsylvania where the British position was now exposed to an increasingly stronger American army. At the start of 1778, the British controlled more of America than they had done at any stage since the beginning of the conflict, but the fall of Philadelphia had not been followed by an explosion of Loyalist military activity, and the presence of Howe and much of the army near the city suggested that it could only be retained if such large forces were deployed that Britain's offensive capability elsewhere would be drastically reduced. In short, Philadelphia might become another Boston. Such a strategy could have worked only if American morale and resilience had collapsed after the fall of major cities or if there had been a Loyalist resurgence capable of taking over the defence of such cities, but neither had occurred.

There was no attempt to revive the "Hudson" strategy of 1777. Canada was no longer to be the base for substantial invading forces; and the British moved onto the defensive in the middle colonies except for some coastal raiding. Instead, there was revived interest in a campaign in the South. Unlike Philadelphia, Savannah or Charleston would be readily accessible to the sea and were far distant from the main American army.[13]

At the same time, there was a major British peace offensive. In February 1778, Parliament agreed to renounce the right to tax America except for the regulation of trade, and a commission, headed by the Earl of Carlisle, was appointed to negotiate the end of the war. They were to be allowed to address the Revolutionaries "by any style or title which may describe them," a concession not made in 1776 and to accept as part of the peace settlement the withdrawal of all British forces and direct American representation in the Commons, but "open and avowed independence" was unacceptable. Such a policy, however, was now too late.

The dispatch of the Peace Commissioners marked a new stage in the conflict. The ministry and, more crucially, George III had been forced to accept both that the war would be ended by negotiation—that a war of conquest, a decisive victory followed by an American collapse, was unlikely—and that the imperial relationship would be substantially altered. Although there was still a determination to keep America in the empire, not least in order to separate her from France, this was now a lesser priority than the war with France.

Howe was replaced by General Sir Henry Clinton, who was to be responsible for executing the southern strategy, but he was to find that he lacked sufficient troops to undertake a sustained offensive against Washington in the middle colonies, and also could not guarantee the naval superiority necessary to ensure the safety of his dispersed operations. Meanwhile, Washington had built up his army, exemplifying the process that the Americans were to demonstrate on a number of occasions: creating a tested force out of adversity. Washington's army wintered in 1777–78 at Valley Forge, eighteen miles northwest of Philadelphia. He hoped that the rich Pennsylvania countryside would provide his men with food and forage, since what passed as Continental Army logistics were weak at best, and New Jersey was bare.

As over previous winters, Washington's army largely dissolved, leaving only a hardcore of officers and men who were, by now, attaining the status of veterans; learning war through war. They had an arduous time, cold and short of supplies, but it was important for the training of the Continentals so that they could confront the British on the battlefield without having to rely on defensive positions, as at Bunker Hill, on Long Island and at Brandywine, or on surprise, as at Trenton and Germantown. Under the self-styled Baron von Steuben, a German soldier of fortune who had served, although not at the high rank he claimed, in the army of Frederick the Great of Prussia, then regarded as the best in Europe, they were drilled in bayonet practice and in battlefield manoeuvres. Most European officers tried to impose their training on Americans, but Steuben, appointed acting Inspector General, realizing that Americans were not Prussians, reworked Frederickian drill to fit American needs. He was prepared to explain manoeuvres, and to answer questions. Drill was important, but the key factor was that, by the spring of 1778, Washington had a corps, albeit small, of junior-grade officers, NCOs, and men who had been blooded in combat and toughened by strenuous toil. It was, however, short of supplies and men.

Washington focused on the Continental Army and was unwilling to see militiamen as a substitute for Continentals. However, the American ideological-political preference for militia over a trained army, which was strengthened by hostility to British regulars, continued throughout the war. It created numerous problems for Washington, and made it difficult to complete the Continental regiments.

This tension between Continentals and militia was to play a major role in the American memorialization of the war. Charles Royster has pointed out that

Americans' celebration of the victory at Yorktown exemplifies the contrast between the employment of military professionalism and the praise of national prowess and communal patriotism. The army was often avoided, forgotten, even scorned; yet military success proved the nation's righteousness and might. George Washington never lost sight of the tenuousness of the military combinations that made the capture of Cornwallis's army possible. But after the victory, most people seemed to treat it as a providential yet inevitable confirmation of Americans' virtuous strength.[14]

This account of Yorktown was an aspect of the mythic character of American collective history and public history that was a poor guide to history and to military capability.

The major battle in 1778, at Monmouth Court House (28 June), saw improved American fighting quality. American regulars could be regarded as seeing off British regulars withdrawing from Philadelphia; not retreating in disorder as in previous engagements. Indeed, at the end of the battle, Washington ordered an advance against Clinton's retiring force, but his men were too tired and hot to comply, while Clinton's position was reasonably strong. He was able to get his army back to New York City and Staten Island.

At the end of the year, a British amphibious force captured Savannah. The American position at that stage was not without severe difficulties. Poor pay and inadequate supplies continued to hit enlistments and many units were below strength: in September 1778, the fifteen Virginia regiments in Continental service were consolidated into eleven.

However, in the winter of 1778–79, Washington was able to keep the largest American force-in-being of any winter of the war thanks to improvements in the supply system the previous year. This owed much to the abandonment of inland offensive operations by the British which might have threatened the newly-created system of magazines along the main lines of communications. Jeremiah Wadsworth improved the commissariat and Nathanael Greene the quartermaster's department. Washington was keen to keep his army together in order not to have to face the problem of re-enlistments. Nevertheless, the extension of the war to the South caused new problems.

Similarly, in the 1790s, the improvement in the administrative structures of the armies of Revolutionary France made by Lazare Carnot, head of the military section of the Committee of Public Safety, made it easier to keep the armies in being and enhanced their operational ability. Unlike the Americans, however, the French were helped by their ability to advance into conquered areas where they could transfer the burdens of supporting the war to the local population, albeit at the cost of bitter opposition and of popular uprisings. The cause of Revolution became the practice of repression. Furthermore, both central reorganization and local exaction failed to overcome supply problems. They continued to affect French operations. For example, an absence of pay and new clothing hit France's Army of Italy in 1799, exacerbating desertion and disease.[15] The British forces in North America encountered supply difficulties, but they were less serious, in part thanks to their relatively small number, certainly compared to the armies of Revolutionary France, and to the wealth of Britain.[16]

Despite the difficulties the American forces faced, there was a growing confidence on the American side about the likely military outcome of the war, which can be seen in the letters of delegates to Congress. This confidence owed much to international recognition. French entry into the war was likely to be followed by that of Spain, as indeed happened in 1779; British control of the sea had been challenged successfully. The withdrawal from Philadelphia represented a retreat from the high-water mark of British advance.

## 1779–80

1779, however, was a year of disappointment for America. Washington appeared to be able to do little more than avoid battle and wait for the French, a strategy that left the initiative for most of the year with the British. This, however, was strategically sound. Resting on the strategic defensive, Washington wished to avoid battle, and was able to do so while continuing to challenge the British position in the middle colonies. He was also affected by serious supply problems. On 22 May, Washington outlined his problems in a circular to the states: the weakness of his army, increasingly dramatic currency depreciation, and lethargy and disaffection among the population. British amphibious raids inflicted serious damage, but a bold night attack led to the capture of the British position at Stony Point on the Hudson on 15 July. However, in the face of a British advance, Washington ordered Stony Point's works destroyed and the position abandoned.

French commitments in the West Indies limited their role further north, and is a reminder of the need not to place America in the central place of the strategies of the combatants. Most of the campaigning in 1779 was in the South. The arrival of the British at Savannah led to an upsurge of Loyalist activity but this was contained by the militia at Kettle Creek on 14 February: the casualty figures—twenty Loyalists and seven Patriots killed—are a reminder that "battles" were often small-scale. In addition, the Georgia militia defeated a force of Creeks on the Ogeechee. The British, under General Augustine Prevost, invaded South Carolina and marched on Charleston. Summoning the town, he was offered its occupation by John Rutledge, Governor of South Carolina, in return for a guarantee of the neutrality of the harbor and the rest of the state for the remainder of the war, proposals that scarcely imply a bellicose spirit, and that suggest that negotiation from a position of strength was not a policy without hope.

Prevost foolishly insisted on unconditional surrender and then had to withdraw on the approach of a relief force under Benjamin Lincoln. In September, Lincoln advanced to besiege Savannah in conjunction with a French amphibious force. After bombardment had failed to obtain surrender, a storming attack was launched on the morning of 9 October. Thanks to a deserter, the British were forewarned, the attacking columns did not coordinate their operations, and, despite the bravery of the South Carolina Continentals and the French, they were repulsed with heavy losses.

In 1780, the British hit back in the South. Washington had anticipated this and had advised a building up of American defences in the region, but the response to the British arrival off Charleston was poor. Lincoln neither obstructed their advance nor moved his army away from Charleston, unlike Washington's conduct at New York in 1776 and Philadelphia in 1777. There was considerable political pressure to hold Charleston and this played a key role in helping trap Lincoln in the city. As a reminder of the decentralised nature of the American war-effort, pressure came from local politicians. In a series of bold moves, the British were able to block access to the city and then open a heavy bombardment including hot shot designed to cause fires.

By now, the population, their wooden houses aflame, were in favour of peace on any terms. On 12 May 1780, the American force, about 5,500 Continental soldiers, militia and armed citizens, surrendered. The Americans also lost most of what was left of the Continental Navy, which had been foolishly left there and employed only in static defence. Lincoln had spent a day working on the fortifications in order to lift American morale, but he was an unenergetic general, and the defence was irresolute and unimaginative and, on the whole, lacked the brave fighting spirit that the Americans displayed on so many occasions during the war. Exceptions, such as the sortie on 23 April, were rare.

The British then gained control over most of South Carolina, but were challenged by Major-General Horatio Gates who was appointed by Congress to succeed Lincoln as commander of the Southern Department. His army comprised new Continental levies, militia, and those who had escaped capture at Charleston, as well as those who had not arrived in time to relieve the city, but it was short of supplies and required time for organisation into an effective fighting force. The problem of creating a coherent force was one that repeatedly confronted the Revolutionaries.

Gates, however, rejected cautious advice. Under pressure to act from local military and political leaders, he also believed it necessary to advance before the British could move into North Carolina and was aware that it was important to repair the effects of Charleston and counter the recent drop in morale. Food was collected by the use of threats and violence, but sufficient supplies did not arrive and the troops were forced to eat green corn and peaches. To Gates's surprise, at Camden on 16 August, he encountered a British force under Charles, 2nd Earl Cornwallis. In the resulting battle, the militia did not fight well. Many fled without firing a shot, discarding their arms and equipment. Their panicky retreat unravelled the American front, although, as a reminder of the variety in fighting quality, the Delaware and Maryland Continentals on the right fought bravely, and nearly broke the British left. They were, however, exposed by the flight of the militia, enveloped by the British, and attacked in the flank by cavalry. The Continentals broke under the fearsome pressure. The Americans suffered about 800 dead and wounded as well as having 1,000 prisoners taken and the loss of their supplies. A terrified Gates fled the field.

The battle throws considerable light on the respective fighting merit of regulars and militia. The 1,400 Delaware and Maryland Continentals were hardened veterans many of whom had seen combat from the battle of Long Island on. Their commander, the self-styled "Baron" Johann de Kalb, was a good officer and a veteran of European wars (rising to be a Lieutenant-Colonel in the French army) who had been sent by Washington. He was killed in the battle. Gates's foolish advance reflected the general pressure on commanders to achieve results, not least in order to hold their forces together. This serves as a commentary on Washington's more skilful caution.

Local American forces were able to prevent Cornwallis from turning his victory into control over the South. Loyalists were defeated at Ramsour's Mill, and a number of bitter engagements between Loyalists and Patriots revealed that the South Carolina backcountry was far from settled. Patriot frontiersmen wiped out a force of Loyalist militia under Patrick Ferguson at King's Mountain on 7 October. They exploited the wooded cover to harry Ferguson's men, who resorted to bayonet charges but were unable to break the encirclement. The southern militia and frontiersmen were more mobile than their northern counterparts, as they rode rather than walked. The frontiersmen also carried rifles. It is important to remember that Loyalist units are part of the American military tradition. They were Americans fighting for their view of America and many took high casualty rates. It is scarcely more appropriate to exclude them from the narrative of American military history than it would be to exclude Native Americans or Confederates.

Gates meanwhile had been dismissed by Congress on 5 October 1780: after Camden, there was clearly need for a fresh face in the south and, in addition, Gates's position had been undermined by intrigues by local politicians. His successor was the Quartermaster-General, Nathanael Greene, a Rhode Island anchorsmith and ex-Quaker, who had read widely in military history and theory, and was considerably influenced by Washington, to whom he was close.

With the army in too poor a state to mount a full-scale attack on Cornwallis, Greene sent Daniel Morgan to harry the British in upper South Carolina. Aware of the value of cavalry, Greene found himself obliged to rely heavily on the activities of partisan bands under such leaders as Thomas Sumter and Francis Marion. The use of partisans was an obvious response to the defeats of Charleston and Camden, the uncontrollable vastness of the South, and the need to counter Loyalist activity.

This led to a vicious and confused civil war between Patriots and Loyalists.[17] The presence of the British army led many Loyalists, now long suffering under unwisely harsh Patriot administrations, to rise in revolt. Local Patriot leaders considered them as rebels against the legitimate government, and so justified their ensuring even harsher treatment of them as that appropriate for defeated rebels or in accord with the "law of retaliation." One retaliation naturally led to another, particularly in an environment where so much of the military activity was carried out by independently operating and institutionally weak militia forces. Greene was shocked by the savagery. This conflict could not be readily assimilated into standard European patterns of warfare in this period, although there were parallels, for example in Poland in 1768–72. Elements of such conflict were also to be seen in the American Civil War, although they were relatively less important in that struggle.

The difficulty of retaining control encouraged the British to look north into North Carolina. It was tempting to feel that if only operations were extended further north, and, consequently, American supplies cut and their regular forces driven back, that this would lead to the settlement of the South.

The campaign of 1780 was indecisive in the middle colonies. The year opened with Washington's army wintering at Morristown, cold, hungry and dissatisfied, the number of soldiers and officers in actual service far fewer than those listed. Aware that money and foreign aid were required for a decisive offensive campaign, Washington felt it necessary to remain on the defensive, although that did not preclude bold steps, such as an unsuccessful raid on Staten Island in January. Throughout the year, Washington was pressed to send troops to the South, and indeed the Maryland Continentals were sent south in April 1780.

Washington's parlous situation explains why he was so needful of French support if he was to mount a major operation and why he did not seek battle without such assistance. Instead, he threatened New York without risking battle. Washington wanted the French to act against the city, not further south, and thus to ensure that the largest American force would be able to attack its British counterpart. He warned Congress that his army must disband or subsist by plunder unless its supplies were improved. American morale fell as it became clear that the French would not cooperate and that there would be no attack on New York. The French also rejected the idea of a winter expedition against Canada. Disappointed of French support, Washington still hoped for one blow against the British before winter. He decided to surprise the posts in northern Manhattan, but this was abandoned as a consequence of British naval moves on the Hudson. At least, Benedict Arnold's plan to betray West Point failed in September.

The close of 1780 saw the central themes of the 1781 campaign already clear: the need for Franco-American cooperation if a major blow was to be struck against the British; Cornwallis's problems in the South; the rising importance of the Chesapeake; and the crucial role of naval power. The contrasting results of the two campaigns indicate that these circumstances made nothing inevitable.

## THE 1781 CAMPAIGN

At the beginning of 1781, the war was still not without promise for the British. The American army was poorly supplied, and still affected by recruitment problems, and its morale was very poor. The correspondence of delegates to Congress continued to be full of the crippling financial problems that the new state faced. Joseph Reed, President of the Pennsylvania Council, wrote to Greene on 16 June: "I have often deplored your situation, to be placed in a state of responsibility with so little means of effecting anything decisive. To be at the same instant beset by the enemy and want of every species is a condition reserved for American generals."[18] As yet, little lasting benefit had been obtained from French military intervention. The French were so worried by the mutinies in Washington's army that Admiral de Grasse was given the option of evacuating the French forces from Newport if the situation continued to deteriorate.

Further south, Greene revived the American cause and showed a real strategic grasp, making effective use of detached forces. He stole the initiative from Cornwallis. At Cowpens, on 17 January 1781, Daniel Morgan, who threatened the western flank of any British advance into North Carolina, smashed a pursuing force, much of it comprised of Loyalists, commanded by Banastre Tarleton. Morgan drew up his men in three lines: skirmishing sharpshooters, a second line of South Carolina militia, and a third of Continentals and Virginia militia, with the cavalry in reserve. Aware of the propensity of the militia to break under attack, Morgan ordered the South Carolina force to fire three volleys and then withdraw to the left. Tarleton's advance, affected by the sharpshooters, was encouraged by the withdrawal of the second line in the face of British bayonet charges, but fell victim to the Continentals and to the cavalry. Enveloped from both flanks, the British infantry fled, throwing the cavalry into confusion.[19]

Cornwallis pressed north into North Carolina with his main force, while Greene was hit by inadequate local forage and supplies. The two clashed at Guilford Court House on 15 March. Greene deployed his 4,400 troops in three lines, but they were too far apart to offer support, and Greene also lacked a reserve. While some among the Continentals were many of the best and most seasoned troops in the army, Greene also had numerous newcomers who were Continentals in name only. North Carolina militia in the first line brought down many of their attackers, but most fled the British bayonet charge. The Virginia militia in the second line fired, then retreated, but the Virginia and Maryland Continentals in the third put up a good resistance before retreating. Over one-quarter of Cornwallis's force were casualties. The Americans fought well, and not all the militia justified Greene's earlier strictures on their value, while it was clear that American regulars had conquered their fear of the bayonet and that, well-led in defensive positions, they were formidable soldiers.

After the battle, Cornwallis pursued Greene but to a degree Cornwallis reacted to Greene's moves and threats throughout this campaign. Greene had far more agility and freedom of action than Cornwallis did, and even when Cornwallis went into Virginia, Greene's turn south into the Carolinas put great pressure on the British. The advance into Virginia led to demoralization and chaos among the Americans, as the British launched destructive raids in May and June. However, Cornwallis's operations in Virginia lacked a clear strategic purpose. If pacification was the British objective, wandering into Virginia, however destructive, was not going to secure it. Moreover, the flexibility that initially characterised British operations was lost when Cornwallis fortified a base at Yorktown and lost the initiative. Washington had hoped to utilize the French army and fleet in order to attack New York City. The Americans could then have turned south, reconquering what had been lost from north to south. Washington was sufficiently flexible to appreciate that such an attack might not be possible, but that, instead, it might be practical to cooperate with the French against Cornwallis. The advance of French and American forces were ably coordinated, and the British failed to respond adequately to the crisis. The Chesapeake was blocked by the French fleet, a British relief fleet was checked in the Battle of the Virginia Capes, and Yorktown was besieged and bombarded into surrender. The British troops marched out of their ruined positions on 19 October 1781.

After Guilford Court House, Greene had moved south, aiming to drive the British from their outposts in order to undermine the pacification strategy. Although a smaller British force beat Greene at Hobkirk's Hill on 19 April 1781, the outnumbered British were pushed back from their posts and retreated to the Tidewater. At Eutaw Springs on 8 September, the Maryland and Virginia Continentals fought well, using the bayonet, although the Americans' pursuit collapsed in disorder as the hungry troops looted the British camp, especially for food. This threw Greene's advance into disarray, allowing the British to rally and drive the Americans from the field. However, British losses led them to fall back on Charleston. The war in the South was essentially over. Demoralised by Yorktown, Parliament undermined the ministry of Lord North, and it was replaced by another committed to negotiations that included the acceptance of American independence. For the British, the focus of the war moved to conflict with France in the Caribbean and India.

**INEVITABLE VICTORY?**

A narrative account of the American War of Independence does not really address the issue of its exceptionalism, nor does it help locate the war in terms of the trajectory of global military history. Both issues are complicated by the nature of the scholarship on the conflict. Much of it is excellent, but there has been little attempt to offer a comparative dimension. Thus, although it is frequently suggested that the war prefigured the French Revolutionary Wars, there is a lack of detailed comparison. This is also true, at the military level, of discussion of any parallel with the Latin American Wars of Liberation.

The comparison most commonly made is with the Vietnam War; that of the 1960s, not the conflicts in Vietnam in the 1780s, 1790s, and 1800s that led to the unification of the country. This comparison tells us more about a degree of self-absorption and self-referencing in American opinion, rather than anything helpful about the two wars. The position of the British in North America was not analogous to that of the United States in Vietnam, while contrasts between the fighting techniques of the two sides in 1775–83 were less than those in the

Vietnam War were to be. The vicious guerrilla warfare in the South during the Revolution involved both Loyalists and Patriots engaging in irregular warfare. British sea-power was no equivalent to the air- and sea-power the Americans wielded during the Vietnam War, not least if the ability of helicopters to transport troops and engage in close ground-support is considered. The parallel to Vietnam can be seen as an aspect of America coming to terms with the Vietnam experience, rather than as a serious inquiry into the history of warfare.[20] The discussion of Greene's eventual strategy in the south in light of Mao Zedong's theory of revolutionary war is interesting,[21] but fails to take sufficient note of cultural and other specificities.

The struggle for independence in 1775–83 was scarcely unprecedented. Within the European world, it was possible, for example, to point to the Swiss and the Dutch, both of whom saw the successful creation of a republic and the defeat of Habsburg forces, although they were not on the same geographical scale as the American Revolution. In the case of the Swiss and Dutch revolts, there were recognisable military differences between the combatants; although, as in North America, it is unclear how far it is appropriate to stress "political" and how far "military" factors when discussing the outcome.

It is certainly too pat to claim that the British were bound to be defeated because it was impossible to prevail against the popular will, for, leaving aside the issue of how far the Patriot cause was widely popular, the comparisons with the Jacobite risings of 1715–1716 and 1745–46 in Scotland and northern England, and the Irish rising of 1798, scarcely suggest that regular troops had in some way been made redundant in such contexts. These risings are instructive because they indicate the general success of the British state and military in counter-insurgency warfare. So also for *ancien régime* states, for example, does the ability of the Habsburgs to suppress the Rákóczi rising in Hungary of 1703–11, and the rising in the Austrian Netherlands in 1790, and the Prussians to suppress the Dutch Patriot movement in 1787 and that in Liège in 1790. The Polish rising of 1794 was defeated by Russian forces with Prussian and Austrian support, although the Poles suffered from being heavily outnumbered.

Thus, maybe the American Revolution has to be reconceptualised, in eighteenth-century terms, not as a unique war (or a war paralleled only by the French Revolutionary Wars), but as a uniquely successful war in a series of unsuccessful popular risings. This would focus attention not on the political causes of the rebellion, nor on the military fact of popular warfare, but, instead, on the political and military factors that led to a successful outcome. Among these, it is possible to point to America's geopolitical exceptionalism, as the first of the European overseas colonies to rebel, and to issues that bridged both politics and military. For example, the federal nature of the revolution ensured that there was no one single centre/region of power, control over which would lead to the end of the conflict.

However, the federal structure, and the variety of ensuing political and military circumstances, also ensured that it was possible to envisage a series of possible geopolitical solutions to the conflict. Thus, it was unclear that all the Thirteen Colonies would go the same way. It was possible that British success in the South would lead to Florida,[22] Georgia,[23] and South Carolina following a distinctive path. This range of options can be underlined by pointing out that, on 30 November 1782 when American and British negotiators signed the provisional treaty, at the close of the conflict, the Americans did not control New York, Charleston, nor Florida, East and West, and Canada, while in the "Old Northwest," the area beyond the Alleghenies, the British still held Detroit and Michilimackinac, and the Natives still controlled much of the territory. Nevertheless, west of the Appalachians, the Americans were strongly present in Kentucky and Tennessee. American gains further east in the closing stages of the war were due to British withdrawals, not defeats. The British left Wilmington, North Carolina on 8 November 1781, Savannah on 11 July 1782, after an ineffectual American siege that had began that January, and Charleston on 14 December 1782. The British ceded Florida to Spain, not the United States. What the Americans would gain was therefore the consequence of British withdrawals and of negotiations, as well as warfare, and these could have followed a different course.

This illustrates the contingent nature of the shape of America, but does not tell us about the war itself. Like all conflicts, that is open to a number of interpretations. The American war was indeed the first example of a transoceanic conflict fought between a European colonial power and subjects of European descent. It was also a major example of a Revolutionary war; a struggle for independence in which the notion of the citizenry under arms played a crucial role. The new state was accompanied by a new army that was a more egalitarian and dynamic force than any in Europe; although not for the sixth of the population who were slaves. Although many of the commanders of the leading Revolutionary force, the Continental Army, were from the wealthier section of society, the social range of the American leadership was far greater than that in European armies, and discipline was different. Although the social composition of the Continental Army was similar to that of the British regulars, this was an army of citizens, not subjects.[24]

The degree to which the army represented a new political identity and social practice helped to sustain its cohesion and even the continuation of the Revolutionary cause when the war went badly, as in the winter of 1777–78, when the army camped at Valley Forge. Individual military careers indicated the growing role of American rather than state considerations. Benjamin Lincoln, in 1775 a councillor in the upper chamber of the new Massachusetts state government, and in 1776 a Major General in the Massachusetts force, was appointed to command the Massachusetts recruits levied to reinforce the Continental Army and in 1778 was chosen to command the Southern Department. Politically, this helped to tie New England to the South. In 1781–83, Lincoln served as the first Secretary at War.[25] Such careers helped to make the new state a functioning reality capable of eliciting loyalty.

The revolutionary character of the Continental Army was not unprecedented, as any overthrow of authority potentially entailed the creation of new military organizations, and these could be regarded as revolutionary in their social, political or military character. Thus, for example, the New Model Army of the English Civil War, created in 1645, had different social politics and ethos to its Royalist opponents. The successful Genoese rising against Austrian control in December 1746 was a popular rising that prefigured much that was to be associated with the Revolutionary warfare of the last quarter of the century.

## STRATEGY AND TACTICS

It would also be misleading to exaggerate the novelty of the War of American Independence in terms of battlefield operations. It was essentially fought in terms that would have been familiar to those who had been engaged in the Seven Years' War. The American response to battle was to adopt the line formations of musketeers of European warfare. This course was advocated by Washington. He was no military genius, but his character and background were very useful. A member of the Continental Congress, who had been born in America, a veteran of the French and Indian War, Washington looked like a natural leader. He did not wish to rely on militia but instead wanted a regular army that could provide America with legitimacy. Washington also stressed drill and discipline. He was a believer in position warfare (the location of units in order to protect particular positions),[26] although he had learned the value of mobility and irregular warfare in the Seven Years' War and was willing to use the militia as partisans.[27]

The alternative strategy, advocated by Major-General Charles Lee (1731–82), centred on irregular warfare, especially the avoidance of position warfare and battle. The British would have found it difficult to identify targets had such a strategy been followed, but it was not, except in 1781 after defeats in the South. Lee was a former British regular officer who had served in North America and Portugal before transferring to the Polish army, which had to confront the greater strength of Russia.

The decision to form a Continental Army was not simply a matter of military options: it was a political act. The army, a force that would not dissolve at the end of the year, even if individual terms of service came to an end, symbolized the united nature of the struggle by the Thirteen Colonies and was a vital move in the effort to win foreign recognition and support. It was not itself necessary to have such an army in order for individual colonies/states to assist each other militarily. Prior to the American Revolution, military units had been deployed outside the boundaries of individual colonies, against both Native American attacks and French and Spanish targets. During the Revolution, militia units under the control of state governments were sent to assist other states, as indeed they were sent to the Continental Army. However, by having such an army, military decisions were in large part taken out of the ambit of state government.

In theory, this made the planning of strategy easier, freeing generals in some measure from the direction of state governments and allowing them to consider clashing demands for action and assistance. In practice, the creation of the army, although essential to the dissemination of a new notion of nationhood, did not free military operations from the views of state governments, nor from the political disputes of the Continental Congress. In addition, the army did not enjoy the support of a developed system for providing reinforcements and supplies, let alone the relatively sophisticated one that enabled the British armed forces to operate so far from their bases. The provision of men and supplies created major problems, preventing or hindering American operations, and producing serious strains in the relationship between the new national government and the states. In addition, British control of the sea threw an excessive burden on the land transportation available to the Revolutionaries.[28] Furthermore, accounts of how the militia served to suppress or inhibit Loyalist activity (the importance of which is enhanced by any emphasis on the strength of Loyalism)[29] need to be complemented by an awareness of the extent to which local communities were not therefore disciplined to provide what was deemed to be necessary by Congress.

Both the Americans and the British fought in a more open order with more significant gaps than was the norm in Europe because the general absence of cavalry made the infantry less vulnerable to attack, while the enclosed nature of much of the terrain encouraged deployments that reflected the topography. Heavily-encumbered regular units, manoeuvring and fighting in their accustomed formations, were vulnerable in the face of entrenched positions and unsuited to the heavily wooded and hilly terrain of the Canadian frontier; they were also not ideal for the vast expanses of the South. Artillery and fortifications played a smaller role than in conflict in Western Europe. Compared to the armies of Frederick the Great, both the Americans and their opponents were lightly-gunned. The Americans did not inherit a significant artillery park, while, for both sides, the distances of America and the nature of communications discouraged a reliance on cannon; they were relatively slow to move. As a result, although cannon played a role in battles such as Monmouth Court House, battles were not characterised by the efficient exchanges of concentrated and sustained artillery fire seen in Europe. This benefited the Americans as the British had greater access to artillery, and had used it with considerable success in European campaigns in the Seven Years' War (French and Indian War). Thus, at Minden in 1759, the British artillery had dominated that of France.

As, more generally, with other transoceanic operations, the force-distance relationship was different to that in Europe: in America, relatively small armies operated across great distances in a war in which there were no real fronts. Although the British had extensive earlier experience of campaigning against the French in North America, American tactics were still able to pose major problems for them, especially when the Americans took advantage of the terrain. Narrow valley routes were flanked by dense woodland, deep rivers often had few crossing points, and in the north the omnipresent stone walls created ready-made defences.

Yet this did not make the Americans invulnerable, nor was there a contrast between European and American methods akin to that between, for example, European methods and those encountered in India or Egypt. The role of defensive positions can also be seen in the War of the Bavarian Succession (1778–79) in which the Austrian Field-Marshal Lacy was able to use massive concentrations of defensive forces in strong positions in the Bohemian hills to thwart Frederick the Great's bold plans for the conquest of Bohemia (the western part of the modern Czech republic). There was a parallel to the strength of the American position in New Jersey from 1777, especially in 1780, a strength that limited British options. The major difference between the two wars arose not from any exceptional character of the operations on land but from the nature of the American War of Independence as a revolution and civil war, and from British amphibious capability.

The struggle between offence and defence is a constant theme in military history, endlessly replayed and at the same time difficult to evaluate as a number of factors are involved in capability and success. This struggle played a major role in both America and Europe. In the eighteenth and nineteenth centuries, improvements in fire-power appeared to give an advantage to the defence, but, as any detailed study will reveal, the situation was in fact more complex. First there were means to counteract defensive positions, ranging from the counter fire of artillery to manoeuvre warfare, especially movements round the flanks or flank attacks. Second, frontal attacks could still be successful, as the British were to show at Guilford Court House and the French Revolutionaries repeatedly demonstrated. Finally, it is necessary not to pre-date the shift towards a defensive fire-power that encouraged more open deployments in attack such as those of the Prussians in the Franco-Prussian War of 1870–71.

In positional warfare, the Americans could be defeated, their troops outflanked, as at the battles of Long Island and Brandywine, or their strongholds captured, as at Fort Washington and Charleston; but, elsewhere, the more mobile American units could operate with deadly effect. The major role of the American militia created a serious problem for the British, both in operational terms, for example by restricting the range of the supply gatherers, and in the political context of the conflict, especially in harrying Loyalists. This helped give the Americans strategic depth. The militia could also provide at least temporary reinforcements for the Continental Army. It helped to ensure that the British were outnumbered and thus limited their effectiveness as an occupation force. At the outset of the Revolution, militia overcame royal governors and defeated supporting Loyalists. Thus, on 9 December 1775, the Earl of Dunmore, the last royal Governor of Virginia, was defeated by Virginia militia at Great Bridge, a frontal attack by regulars falling victim to front and flank fire.

It is all too easy to assume that the war's outcome was a foregone conclusion, that the British could not conquer the Thirteen Colonies, and that their defeat was inevitable because they employed an anachronistic method of warfare.[30] Instead, the British understood the need for mobility, while any reading of the correspondence of American generals underlines the difficulties of their task.

The British faced serious problems, especially with logistics and with defining an appropriate strategy. The British military command structure had serious deficiencies. However, Washington's correspondence shows that there was no major capability gap in favour of the Revolutionaries. If this was true on land, at sea America has never been weaker. The fame of privateers, such as John Paul Jones, should not distract attention from the failure of the greatly outnumbered American naval forces to cut British supply routes across the Atlantic or to threaten British positions and operations in North America. The attack on Canada, for example, could not be supported by naval operations; nor could the defence of New York. From 1778, the British had to consider the French fleet, but they never had to worry much about the American navy. Furthermore, the British managed to maintain a major war effort at a great distance, and did so for eight years without excessive problems or disruption. This was the largest military force that Britain had hitherto sent abroad. For much of the war, the British occupied the major American ports (save Boston) and controlled coastal waters, so that they could move troops and supplies along a north-south axis.

At the same time, the American cause was greatly handicapped by the problems of creating an effective war machine. This was not due to poverty, as the colonists were relatively affluent, but to the problem of mobilizing and directing resources. The anti-authoritarian character of the Revolution and the absence of national institutions made it difficult to create a viable national military system for land and, even more, sea power. Initial enlistments for one year did not amount to a standing army. Much of Washington's correspondence is an account of organization and improvisation under pressure. For example, in early 1777, when Washington had taken up a protective position at Morristown, after the British had pulled back across New Jersey after the battles of Trenton and Princeton, his army was badly affected by desertion, expiring enlistments and supply problems. These problems did not disappear. In 1780, Greene resigned as Quartermaster General because of his anger with civilian politicians and what he saw as their responsibility for his failure to meet the logistical demands of the Continental Army. Such a clash looked ahead to later disputes between the American military and their civilian overseers.

To return to the issue of modernity, in terms of the politicization of much of the American public there was an obvious contrast with most European warfare of the previous century (though Hungary in 1703–11 and Scotland in 1745–46 offered exceptions), but one that was to alter with the French Revolution. The Americans owed their independence to the willingness of some of the people to continue fighting when the struggle became more widespread, bitter and sustained than had at first seemed likely, before the British sent a major army to crush the Revolution. The Americans subsequently had to face British determination to continue the struggle on land even after French intervention. Casualties were heavy, about 0.9 percent of the population in 1780, compared to near 1.6 percent for the Civil War, 0.12 percent for World War I, and 0.28 percent for World War II.

The motivation of the troops was the major aspect of modernity. Much about the war, however, for example the weaponry, was conventional. In the American war, there was little of the emphasis on large armed forces and the mass production of munitions that was to be such an obvious aspect of the industrial warfare of the late nineteenth and early twentieth centuries. In addition, as also with the tactics of the French Revolutionary armies, it is necessary to note earlier examples. The American snipers, whether deliberately or not, could be seen as an extended development of the skirmishers and sharpshooters sent out in front of the line on the battlefield in most later eighteenth-century armies in Europe. But the new forms could not be easily adopted by their opponents, because both in part depended on enhanced commitment (initiative in the American case and élan in the French) by the individual infantryman, which derived from the fact that they were fighting for a cause they believed in: different kinds of freedom.

## COMPARISON: THE FRENCH REVOLUTIONARY WARS

If the concept of modernity should only be employed with care, it is still valuable to look for comparisons with the French Revolutionary Wars (1792–1802). Again, as with the Americans, it is necessary to note the defeats that the French suffered, for example in Germany in 1796. Alongside military factors, it is also pertinent to note political counterparts. Thus, in the War of American Independence, the British suffered from the opposition of France (from 1778), Spain (from 1779), and the Dutch (from 1780). Thus, it was not the case of a united *ancien régime* confronting the revolutionaries, but, rather, of the latter winning foreign allies. In the French Revolutionary Wars, this factor was less pronounced although French victories were to force Spain and the Dutch to side with them against Britain, while Austria, Prussia, and, in particular, Russia were also concerned with developments in Poland, and Prussia left the war against France.

As with the War of American Independence, the war created a major organisational challenge for the Revolutionaries, although this was more of an issue for the Americans as they were trying to create a new state and as they could not support the war effort by fighting on foreign soil, as the French Revolutionaries so successfully managed. There was also a difference in scale. The French Revolutionaries had to support far larger forces and also a navy. They were exposed not only to a powerful, albeit greatly fluctuating coalition, powerful on both land and sea, and also to considerable counter-revolutionary opposition within France, although there was no equivalent to Native American hostility and, in the case of America, the Loyalists constituted a considerable counter-revolutionary opposition, unlike the floundering efforts of French Royalists.

The French Revolutionary Wars also lasted longer, and this itself created a far greater strain on French resources and organisation; although the Americans faced major fiscal problems by 1781, and indeed 1778. One aspect of the strain in France, that interacted with the very different politics of the war, was the role of the military in politics within Revolutionary France, that culminated with the coup in 1799 that took Napoleon to power. Prior to that, the army had been employed to suppress both left-wing and right-wing opposition to the Revolution, and did so with considerable violence.[31]

This was very different to the situation in America. Although the Revolution there was born in violence, and involved, throughout, the overawing, if not more violent suppression, of a major group of Americans—the Loyalists—it did not see the use of force to pursue differences within the Revolutionary political structure. The ideological, particularly legalistic, background of the Revolution was important here. At the same time, this characteristic of the Revolution reduced pressure on the army, and ensured that the political consequences of differences within it were less serious than they might otherwise have been. Equally, anger with the level of civilian support did not lead generals to try to take power nationally or to overthrow local institutions. In that, as in other respects, there was a common citizenship: the soldiers came from, and were part of, civilian society. In France, the military were no longer a part of such society.

## LATIN AMERICAN COMPARISON

Alongside the contexts already discussed—of rebellions within the British world and of the revolutionary wars of the late-eighteenth century Atlantic revolution, it is also appropriate to consider that of the wars of liberation in the New World,[32] and this is a more helpful comparison than that of the Vietnam War. The Haitian revolution of 1791–1804 was very different in character. Excluding that, it is still worthwhile considering the American War of Independence alongside the Latin American Wars of Independence. From the American perspective, the most important factor in the latter was the extent to which they led to a fragmentation of the Spanish American empire. The American War of Independence did not lead to the creation of a unified state spanning what had been the British New World: Canada was not included, let alone the British West Indies. Nevertheless, the new nation was a formidable state, while all the areas that rebelled did so in order to form one state.

In Latin America, not only was Spain (the imperial power other than in Portuguese-ruled Brazil) defeated, despite major efforts on its part, but there was now no power in Latin America capable of matching the United States. It is interesting to consider how much more difficult the Texan War of Independence, or Mexican War would have been for the Americans had all the areas that had earlier rebelled against Spain formed one state. It would have had more extensive territories and stronger resources than the Mexico of the 1830s and 1840s or the Spain America fought in 1898. However, the successor states lacked the incorporating possibilities enjoyed by the United States thanks to its ideology, public culture and political structure. Instead, once independence had been won from Spain, it proved impossible to sustain wideranging confederal structures in Latin America.

Before turning to this, it is appropriate to look at the collapse of Spanish rule. As with the War of American Independence, it is impossible to separate military from political factors. Indeed, the Spaniards were weakened more by political than by military problems. The weaknesses of Spain itself were significant: alongside the disruption caused by the Peninsular War of 1808–13, there was serious post-Napoleonic disruption. Napoleon's seizure of power in Spain in 1808 had led to a breakdown of structures of authority and practices of power in the Spanish empire and to a struggle for control. There was no comparable breakdown in Britain or the British empire during the War of American Independence. There was an upsurge in political discontent in the British Isles in the early 1780s, but no comparable crisis.

Once Ferdinand VII was returned to power in Spain in 1814, his cause still faced many difficulties in Latin America. The Royalists there were badly divided, and their divisions interacted with contradictions within Spain's incoherent policies. Civil and military authorities clashed frequently, as did metropolitan and provincial administrations. Thus, in New Granada (now Colombia), the Viceroy and the Commander-in-Chief were bitter rivals. Furthermore, financial shortages forced the Royalist army to rely on the local economy, which proved a heavy burden on the population and antagonized them from Spanish rule. This was exacerbated by the use of forced loans and seizures; and this was a major contrast to the British war-effort in North America. Furthermore, the local burden was heavier in Latin America because the royalist forces sent from Spain were also hit by disease, especially yellow fever and dysentery, and they were forced to recruit locally. New Granada had largely welcomed the royal army from Spain, but, by 1819, there was widespread support for an independent Colombia.

As with the British, Spain did not possess any technological advantages, although, in addition, it lacked significant naval power. Furthermore, the insurgents in both cases had access to arms supplies: the Americans from France, the Latin Americans in part from arms dealers in the United States, but, more considerably, arms, as well as volunteers, from Britain.

Nevertheless, as with the War of American Independence, the course of the conflict was not foreordained. As in other wars of liberation, the colonial powers enjoyed more success than is frequently appreciated. This was true both of the degree of local support, seen, for example, in the pro-Spanish rising in Peru in 1824, and of conflict in the field. In both America and Latin America, the revolutionary struggle was affected by a lack of funds, and revolutionary forces lacked adequate supplies. This was less serious, however, in America where per capita wealth was higher and economic growth greater. In both cases, it is necessary to move beyond revolutionary myths to note problems in morale. Desertion underlined this in America, while in Latin America, although there was revolutionary enthusiasm among the rebel officers, the same was not true of the bulk of the peasant conscripts. Unsuccessful in Venezuela in 1817, the leading revolutionary, Simon Bolivár, was affected by low morale among the troops, which led to desertion, and by serious supply problems. The American revolutionary cause, however, was less divided; although again the area of campaigning was more coherent. It is possible to see the American War of Independence at least in part in terms of a series of struggles in the individual colonies, but in Latin America the situation was far more diverse and there was no single equivalent to the Continental Army.

The interaction of conflict in different parts of Latin America was such that success for one side in one area did not pre-empt countervailing action originating from another. This underlined the difficulty of ensuring a lasting military-political verdict and helped lead to a lengthy conflict. This both increased the burden of the warfare and put the focus on political factors. The creation and legitimization of government structures were important in providing the context for harnessing resources, and this contrasted with the situation in America where colonial government and political practice provided a structure and ethos at the level of individual colonies that could be translated into the governance of independent America.

In Latin America, the need on both sides to create new armies put a premium on overcoming problems in recruitment and in resisting desertion. Remedies were often harsh; far more so than in America where politics and public culture were not brutalised by the conflict, and certainly not to the degree in Latin America or Revolutionary France. Recruitment in Latin America was enforced with violence and the threat of violence, and desertion punished savagely, frequently with executions, and supplies were raised through force. There was much burning and destruction—of crops, haciendas and towns—in order both to deny resources and to punish. Had the American War of Independence lasted longer then it is possible that more drastic remedies would have been required, and been followed, in order to secure more resources for the conflict and to overawe those advocating compromise. Under pressure, the idealism of the revolutionary cause would have discouraged half-measures; but the idealism of the revolutionary cause incorporated a notion of virtuous (restrained) war, and that notion (both cultural and political) served to restrain the escalation of military or paramilitary violence, although it did not completely contain it.

The Latin American Wars of Independence, for which the Americans, despite their republicanism, provided little support,[33] offer an instructive comparison with the American War of Independence, not least because they suggest the difficulty both of sustaining a revolutionary struggle and of mounting effective counter-insurgency action. The problems of creating new governmental structures, including an army, that faced the Latin American revolutionaries were faced by the Americans in 1775–1783 and by the American Confederacy in 1861–65, but, in each case, the American revolutionaries were more successful in maintaining unity.

It is instructive to contrast the degree to which in Latin America and France generals seized power and played the major role in formulating political structures and conducting military operations, with the situation in America. It could have been otherwise in America. Had Washington put himself at the head of the officers at Newburgh in the winter of 1782–83, who considered intimidating Congress into granting concessions over pensions, or the troops in June 1783, who briefly held Congress hostage, then a very different legacy would have probably been offered. Military rule probably could only have been successful at the cost of civil war. Had it been unsuccessful then the legacy of hostility to any standing army, however small, would have been far stronger, as liberty would have been secured in defiance of American troops.

## NOTES

1. S. Conway, *The War of American Independence 1775–1783* (London, 1995), p. xi.

2. P. Langford, "Manners and Character in Anglo-American Perceptions, 1750–1850," in F.M. Leventhal and R. Quinault (eds.), *Anglo-American Attitudes: From Revolution to Partnership* (Aldershot, 2000), p. 85.

3. W.E. Washburn, *The Governor and the Rebel: A History of Bacon's Rebellion in Virginia* (Chapel Hill, 1957); S.S. Webb, *1676: The End of American Independence* (New York, 1984).

4. J. Shy, *Towards Lexington: The Role of the British Army in the Coming of the American Revolution* (Princeton, 1965).

5. P.D.G. Thomas, *Tea Party to Independence: The Third Phase of the American Revolution, 1773–1776* (Oxford, 1991).

6. A.J. O'Shaughnessy, *An Empire Divided. The American Revolution and the British Caribbean* (Philadelphia, 2000).

7. G.F.G. Stanley, *Canada Invaded 1775–1776* (Toronto, 1973); R.M. Hatch, *Thrust for Canada: The American Attempt on Quebec in 1775–1776* (Boston, 1979). For the earlier development of British capability, see S. Brumwell, *Redcoats: The British Soldier and the War in the Americas 1755–1763* (Cambridge, 2002).

8. I. Gruber, "America's First Battle: Long Island, August 27, 1776," in C. Heller (ed.), *America's First Battles, 1776–1965* (Lawrence, 1986), pp. 1–32.

9. S.S. Smith, *The Battle of Trenton* (Monmouth Beach, 1965).

10. *GW* vol. 10, p. 200.

11. M. Mintz, *The Generals of Saratoga. John Burgoyne and Horatio Gates* (New Haven, 1990).

12. J. Dull, *The French Navy and American Independence: A Study of Arms and Diplomacy, 1774–1787* (Princeton, 1975) and *A Diplomatic History of the American Revolution* (New Haven, 1985).

13. P. Mackesy, *The War for America 1775–1783* (London, 1964).

14. C. Royster, *A Revolutionary People at War. The Continental Army and American Character, 1775–1783* (Chapel Hill, 1996), p. 327.

15. P. Wetzler, *War and Subsistence: The Sambre and Meuse Army in 1794* (New York, 1985); H.G. Brown, *War, Revolution, and the Bureaucratic State: Politics and Army Administration in France, 1791–1799* (Oxford, 1995); T.C.W. Blanning, *The*

*French Revolution in Germany: Occupation and Resistance in the Rhineland, 1792–1802* (Oxford, 1983) and *The French Revolutionary Wars 1787–1802* (London, 1996), pp. 158–69.

16. R.A. Bowler, *Logistics and the Failure of the British Army in America 1775–1783* (Princeton, 1975).

17. T.W. Tate and P.J. Albert (eds.), *An Uncivil War. The Southern Backcountry during the American Revolution* (Charlottesville, 1985).

18. D.M. Conrad (ed.), *The Papers of General Nathanael Greene* vol. 8 (Chapel Hill, 1995), p. 396.

19. L.E. Babits, *A Devil of a Whipping: The Battle of Cowpens* (Chapel Hill, 1998).

20. See, for example, D. Higginbotham, "Reflections on the War of Independence, Modern Guerrilla Warfare, and the War in Vietnam," in R. Hoffman and P.J. Albert (eds.), *Arms and Independence* (Charlottesville, 1984), pp. 1–24; and N.L. York, "Ending the War and Winning the Peace: the British in America and the Americans in Vietnam," *Soundings* 70 (1987), pp. 445–74.

21. J.M. Dederer, *Making Bricks Without Straw* (Manhattan, Kansas, 1983).

22. M.C. Searcy, *The Georgia-Florida Contest in the American Revolution, 1776–1778* (Tuscaloosa, 1985).

23. K. Coleman, *The American Revolution in Georgia, 1763–1789* (Athens, Georgia, 1958).

24. H.M. Ward, *The War for Independence and the Transformation of American Society* (London, 1999).

25. D.B. Mattern, *Benjamin Lincoln and the American Revolution* (Columbia, South Carolina, 1994).

26. R.K. Wright, *The Continental Army* (Washington, 1983); D. Higginbotham, *George Washington and the American Military Tradition* (Athens, Georgia, 1985).

27. M.V. Kwasny, *Washington's Partisan War 1775–1783* (Kent, Ohio, 1996).

28. E. Risch, *Supplying Washington's Army* (Washington, 1981); E.W. Carp, *To Starve the Army at Pleasure: Continental Army Administration and American Political Culture, 1775–1783* (Chapel Hill, 1984); J. Hutson, *Logistics of Liberty: American Services of Supply in the Revolutionary War and After* (Newark, 1991); J. Shy, "Logistical Crisis and the American Revolution: a Hypothesis," in J. Lynn (ed.), *Feeding Mars: Logistics in Western Warfare from the Middle Ages to the Present* (Boulder, 1993), pp. 161–79.

29. For Loyalism in a state generally known for its Revolutionary sympathies, A. Hast, *Loyalism in Revolutionary Virginia: The Norfolk Area and the Eastern Shore* (Ann Arbor, 1982); A.H. Tillson, *Gentry and Common Folk: Political Culture on a Virginia Frontier, 1740–1789* (Lexington, 1991).

30. For an important evaluation of British capabilities, P. Mackesy, "British Strategy in the War of American Independence," *The Yale Review*, 52 (1963), pp. 539–57, *Could the British Have Won the War of Independence* (Worcester, Mass., 1976), and "The Redcoat Revived," in W.M. Fowler and W. Coyle (eds.), *The American Revolution: Changing Perspectives* (Boston, 1979), pp. 169–88.

31. J. Lynn, *The Bayonets of the Republic: Motivation and Tactics in the Army of Revolutionary France, 1791–1794* (2nd edn., Boulder, 1996).

32. See, most profitably, L. Langley, *The Americans in the Age of Revolution 1750–1850* (New Haven, 1996).

33. J.J. Johnson, *A Hemisphere Apart: The Foundations of United States Policy toward Latin America* (Baltimore, 1990).

# 3

# War of 1812

In November 1790, the French envoy, Louis-Guillaume Otto, reported that the Americans were unlikely to take a role in the Anglo-Spanish war that then seemed imminent over competing claims on the Pacific coast of Canada, as they needed ten years of peace in order to settle their government.[1] To foreign commentators, newly independent America seemed weak and divided, if not vulnerable, and an important recent study has argued "The new nation was at risk in every direction."[2] Fortunately for the Americans, potentially hostile powers were not in a position to do much about this. Europe was in near continuous conflict from 1792 until 1815, with Britain at war with France in 1793–1802, 1803–14, and 1815, while Spain was at war with France or Britain, culminating in a French occupation of much of the country in 1808–13 and a bitter war to drive the occupiers out. While at war with Britain, the Spanish navy had suffered serious defeats, especially at the battles of Cape St. Vincent (1797) and, alongside the French, Trafalgar (1805).

## AMERICAN EXPANSION

During this period, America overcame its early vulnerability and internal divisions without the external intervention that had such a radicalizing impact on the revolutionary French state, as later on that of Russia. This absence of external intervention greatly helped American expansion. A settlement in 1795 of the disputed frontier with Spanish West Florida brought America much of Alabama and Mississippi. Having gained Louisiana from Spain in 1800 by the Treaty of San Ildefonso, the French dictator Napoleon sold it to the Americans in 1803 for 60 million louis/$15 million.[3] This ended French options in North

America, which had, anyway, been undermined by the failure to suppress black resistance in St. Domingue (Haiti) and by the resumption of conflict with Britain. America gained all or much of the future states of Montana, North and South Dakota, Minnesota, Wyoming, Colorado, Nebraska, Iowa, Kansas, Missouri, Oklahoma, Arkansas, and Louisiana. The new nation thus reached to the Rockies, and had a far longer frontier with British-ruled Canada, while the Spanish stranglehold on the Gulf of Mexico was broken.

Americans pressed on to take advantage of these gains, which themselves involved disputes over frontiers. In particular, there was a long-standing dispute over the boundary between French and Spanish North America, between Louisiana and Texas. After the Louisiana Purchase, America claimed lands west to the Rio Grande in part on the grounds that French explorers had crossed the region, while Spain, more modestly, stated that Texas reached to Natchitoches on the Red River and south to the Gulf of Mexico along the Calcasieu River. The failure to settle this dispute through negotiation led to military moves, with the Spaniards strengthening their posts east of the Sabine River and the Americans, fearing an invasion, preparing their own forces in turn. Conflict was avoided in 1806, and a "neutral ground" east of the Sabine was defined, pending diplomacy. Based on New Orleans, American gunboats operated against French and Spanish privateers off the Mississippi Delta in 1806–10.

War in 1806 would have tested the capability of both states. Spain was then at war with Britain, and much of her navy had been sunk while joined with the French at Trafalgar in 1805. It would have been impossible to have launched amphibious attacks on America comparable to those Britain was to launch in 1814 and 1815. Conversely, the Americans were not in a position to make any major impact on Texas, let alone Mexico; not least because the Native Americans were still a powerful independent presence in southeast America. A war with Spain beginning in 1806 would probably have entailed American pressure on Florida and Spanish threats to New Orleans, but it is unlikely that either power would have been able to deliver a heavy blow. The Spanish presence in Florida and Texas was weak: both were at the margins of Spanish power. The Americans lacked the amphibious capability to strike major blows against Cuba.

In the early 1810s, the Gulf Coast and the Old Northwest offered alternative foci of American attention. When the War of 1812 broke out, the largest concentration of American regulars was at New Orleans: they were not deployed for an invasion of Canada. West Florida, which later became coastal Alabama and Mississippi, was seized from Spain in 1810–13: Americans near Baton Rouge successfully revolted in 1810 and Governor Claiborne of the Louisiana Territory occupied land as far east as the Pearl River that year. Mobile and Fort Charlotte were occupied by General James Wilkinson in April 1813, and Florida was invaded by Andrew Jackson in November 1814. He captured Pensacola on 7 November, but then, in response to British preparations, moved his troops to New Orleans, having destroyed Pensacola's fortifications. A version of Manifest Destiny has been seen in American expansion in the Gulf Region: a combination of justified national expansion and an adventurous quest for fame and destiny. Both took precedence over a pre-emptive desire to thwart the possibility of rivals consolidating their position there.[4] American expansion was registered in the admission of territories to statehood: Louisiana in 1812, Mississippi in 1817 and Alabama in 1819.

## THE QUASI WAR WITH FRANCE, 1798–1800

However, America did not seek command of the sea or trans-oceanic commercial or political dominion. The last American warship was sold in 1785, although the American navy was revived in the mid-1790s. The purpose of the naval revival was to fight the Barbary States of North Africa. Only later did the French confiscation of American commercial vessels and cargoes cause it to be used against Europeans. In 1798–1800, what was known as the Quasi War with France was waged at sea. The French sank or captured over 300 American merchantmen in response to the American role in maintaining British trade routes: France did not accept that neutral ships could carry British goods. In response, the American government pressed forward military preparations. The stress on harbor defences and on the arming and training of militia reflected anxiety about the extent to which French warships and amphibious forces could threaten American ports, although, in fact, there were to be no attacks.[5]

Such preparations did not, however, amount to any protection for trade. To achieve that, work on three frigates that had been begun in 1793 was pressed forward. American attempts to negotiate led to French demands for a loan that were in accord with the bullying methods the French were using in Europe with considerable success. In 1798, the military character of the American state was ratcheted up with the establishment of the Department of the Navy, but there was also a significant reliance on free enterprise as it was necessary to commission privateers to act against the French at sea.

The crisis also had a markedly divisive political flavour. Opposed to France, the governing Federalists linked foreign and domestic policies closely to military preparedness and built up both army and navy. "Millions for defense, but not one cent for tribute" became their slogan, and the government also passed the Alien and Sedition Acts in order to strengthen it against internal opposition. This was a divisive step. Kentucky and Virginia denounced the Acts in the name of states rights and thus in effect pressed the role of state governments in deciding the constitutional character of federal actions. War was not declared between France and the United States despite a number of clashes between warships from the summer of 1798, the majority of which were successes for the Americans. The dispute was settled in 1800 after Napoleon's rise to power led to a change in French priorities. It had underlined the differences within American political circles about the most appropriate force structure and military tasking, differences that, in part, rested on very different conceptions of the international system. Whereas Alexander Hamilton advanced a pessimistic interpretation of competing states and the need for preparedness, critics felt that a benign system was possible. Whereas Hamilton was in favor of a strong military, President John Adams was more concerned to restrict preparedness to a powerful navy.[6]

## CONFLICT IN NORTH AFRICA, 1801–5

The Barbary States of North Africa declared war in 1801 when the United States stopped the annual payments of tribute designed to prevent privateering. American trade with the Mediterranean was important; indeed in 1800 it was valued at more than $12 million annually. Barbary attacks on American trade had been a problem since independence, and one that had greatly concerned Thomas Jefferson while he had been minister to France. Indeed in 1784 he had argued that America needed six frigates to protect her trade against the North Africans. Ten years later Congress agreed that six should indeed be built or bought to use unless terms could be negotiated with Algiers, the most powerful North African state. In fact the American government settled the matter without war, agreeing to pay Dey Ali Hassan of Algiers just over $1 million in September 1795. In November 1796, Yusuf Karamanli, Bashaw of Tripoli (today, capital of Libya), was bought off for $56,000, Hamouda Pasha, Bey of Tunis, following in August 1797 for $107,000.

These were humiliating terms, but they allowed the Americans to focus on the Quasi War with France. Fortunately for America, she was able to keep her maritime foes separate in 1798–1815, just as the British benefited from their ability to defeat France at sea before fighting America.

Having settled with France, the Americans turned against the Barbary powers. Paying tribute was humiliating and expensive, it was felt that operations in the Mediterranean would help train the navy, and it was thought that it would cost little more to send it there than to keep it in home waters. In 1801, Jefferson sent Commodore Richard Dale with three frigates and a schooner to the Mediterranean, while Tripoli declared war in pursuit of tribute. In response, the Americans blockaded Tripoli. This, however, did not produce the desired result, in part because the deep-draft American ships were not suited for the blockade of shallow coastal waters. As a result, the blockade was abandoned in 1802, and Dale's successor, Commodore Richard Morris, instead, sailed in search of privateers. This unauthorised policy lacked the merit of success, and Morris was recalled and dismissed in 1803. His successor, Edward Preble renewed the blockade. Conflict focused on Tripoli, in part because Preble was able to intimidate the Sultan of Morocco into settling his dispute with America in October 1803. That month, the frigate *Philadelphia*, then on blockading duty off Tripoli, ran aground on a reef and was captured. The crew was paraded through the streets of Tripoli. The following February, Stephen Decatur led a raid on the harbour in which the *Philadelphia* was seized and burned, thus removing a powerful image of American failure. As a result, Decatur was promoted captain and given a sword of honour. Horatio Nelson called Decatur's feat "the most bold and daring act of the age."

The loss of the *Philadelphia* had lent energy to a change in the American force structure, with a decision to use shallow-draft gunboats to supplement the frigates. They were to attack jointly in 1804. Later in the year, fire attacks were made on Tripolitan ships off Tripoli. In April 1805, a joint land and sea operation, the overland force having marched from Alexandria in Egypt, captured Derna. The overland force, under William Eaton, contained only ten American marines alongside 38 Greeks and about 300 Arabs. As with many successful interventions, it was effective in part because of the ability to exploit divisions among opponents; in this case Eaton co-operated with the bashaw's exiled brother, Hamet Karamanli. Counterattacks were repulsed, and in June 1805 peace was signed with Tripoli. The prisoners from the *Philadelphia* were released in return for a ransom of $60,000, but no annual tribute was stipulated. Peace was also negotiated with Tunis.[7]

## BACKGROUND TO THE WAR OF 1812

If the War of American Independence is most helpfully compared with the French Revolutionary Wars, the War of 1812, the name given for a conflict that lasted from 1812 until 1815, can be compared to the Napoleonic Wars. These were both contemporaneous and also involved Britain. The War of Independence left a host of disputes, for example over debts owed to Loyalists. British recognition of American sovereignty was qualified by the encouragement of frontier separatists, and by continued support for Native Americans.[8] George Hammond, the first British Minister Plenipotentiary to the United States, who arrived in Philadelphia in October 1791 found that the suspicions, indeed hostility towards British policy, of Thomas Jefferson, the American Secretary of State, hindered the progress of negotiations.[9] At the same time, the Americans had to be mindful of changed relations with France and Spain. In 1790, when the Anglo-Spanish Nootka Sound Crisis opened up the possibility of Anglo-American co-operation against Spain, George Beckwith, a British agent in New York, although not an accredited envoy, explored possibilities in discussions with Alexander Hamilton, the Secretary of the Treasury, although different views about the fate of any conquests from Spain prevented these talks from being taken further.[10] Relations improved in 1794–95 with the negotiation of Jay's Treaty which settled, or at least eased, commercial and territorial disputes. It kept relations pretty calm until the Chesapeake affair of 1807 when the dispute over British warships forcibly enlisting British nationals serving as sailors on American ships led to violence.[11]

In defiance of traditional mercantilist assumptions that linked commerce to politically-controlled markets, trade with Britain had risen after independence. America was populous, still needed access to Britain's credit (often generously supplied), and lacked the range of British industrial production. This was fortunate for Britain as she faced growing problems in European markets. At the same time, the American mercantile marine grew rapidly after the War of Independence. Whaling and the China trade led the Americans into the Pacific: in 1784 the *Empress of China* made its first voyage to Canton, sailing via the Cape of Good Hope.

Relations between Britain and America deteriorated in the late 1800s and in July 1807 Jefferson and his cabinet drew up a plan for an invasion of Canada. That year, the state of New York began Castle Clinton to protect Manhattan. Disputes over trade played the key role in leading to war in 1812, although a wider range of factors contributed, including American suspicions of relations between Native Americans and the British in Canada, and the activities of British officials, officers and traders on the frontier that, in large part, justified these suspicions. Relations were complicated by disputes over the Canadian frontier and Newfoundland fishing rights.[12] The British government, which did not want war,[13] was primarily concerned with preventing the neutral Americans from trading with France, and thus circumventing the British blockade. British officials felt that the American government was pro-French.[14] Congress voted for war, in part because of bellicose over-confidence and, in part, thanks to patriotic anger with British policies. Impressment of seamen from American ships was seen as a particular outrage, as it represented an infringement of the national sovereignty of American vessels and a denial of America's ability to naturalise foreigners. This was not only a naturalisation problem: British naval officers also impressed many native-born American seamen.

The increasingly prominent West was concerned about British aid to the Native Americans and this led to pressure for the seizure of Canada: in the war, the West was to feel it was fighting an offensive-defensive war against British containment, a continuation of the struggles of the 1790s. American expansionism contributed to the crisis in Anglo-American relations. Aside from these specific issues, there was a more general sense, particularly among the Jeffersonians, that the Revolution was unfinished because Britain remained powerful and that this power threatened American interests and public morality, as Britain was a corrosive but seductive model of un-American activity.

The War of 1812, which the Americans declared on 18 June, is difficult to discuss, because it was a particularly disparate struggle, more so indeed than the other American conflicts considered in this book. There were separate campaigns on the Canadian frontier, which itself stretched from beyond Lake Michigan to Maine, in the Chesapeake, and in the Gulf of Mexico, as well as warfare on the high seas. The order in which these are discussed appears to offer a prioritisation that may be misleading. There is also the issue of "participants." The war is generally treated as a straightforward struggle between American and British forces, but that serves to underrate the independent role of the Native Americans who were allied with the British. This also serves to suggest a different geographical focus, for devoting due weight to the Native Americans leads to more consideration of the Great Lakes and the southeast.

For the Americans, this was a very divisive war, and one in which many refused to help. The Federalists, who were heavily represented in New England, were opposed to war with Britain, which they correctly saw as likely to harm trade. The Federalists saw territorial expansion as likely to benefit the rival Republicans. In addition, New England interests had only limited concern in the British relations with Native Americans that troubled frontier regions. Commentators had long detected regional sectionalism and rifts:

. . . the people of the Eastern States, I find great jealousy prevail towards their brethren of the Southern States, particularly the Virginians of whose increasing influence in the Union they seem very uneasy. The late alteration in the American constitution, which in a degree, will throw the power of electing the president to the larger states, and the purchase of Louisiana, are both viewed, by the moderate men of New England, as events that tend to loosen the Union, by giving an over preponderancy to the Southern States.

They complain likewise that as they are more commercial, they contribute more than their proportion, while Virginia enjoys the honors without the burden, having but little foreign trade.

The following year, Gilpin, the British Vice-Consul in Newport, had added: "there appears a jealousy between the Eastern and Southern states, and that seeds of contention are sown which may eventually sap the foundations of the American constitution . . . many people here speak very freely on that subject."[15]

In 1812, the Federalists were outvoted by the Republicans, but the divisions on declaring war—79 to 49 in the House of Representatives, and 19 to 3 in the Senate—reflected the depth of disquiet. It was difficult to create both a nation-state and a nationality that worked. As the constitution expressly conferred the power to declare war on Congress, and Congress alone could vote money to pay for the war and the military, the potentially unifying position of the presidency was heavily qualified. Nevertheless, in 1812, division did not lead to civil conflict and it is still appropriate to refer to American goals, albeit accepting that the depth of division not only limited the availability of resources, but also affected strategic options.

The United States was poorly prepared for war. The armed forces were weak, although, unlike in 1775, American forces at a level greater than state levies existed. Poor relations with Native Americans ensured this. On 3 June 1784, the day after decreeing that the last units of the Continental Army be disbanded, the Confederation Congress voted to establish a 700-strong regiment of one-year volunteers in order to strengthen America's presence in the Ohio Valley. In fact, fewer than 250 men reached the frontier. Henry Knox, appointed Secretary at War in March 1785 after a 17-month gap following the resignation of Benjamin Lincoln, had pressed hard for a regular army in the face of opposition to a permanent force, as well as the financial weakness of the federal government. Three-year enlistments were authorized in 1785, and became the standard term of service of what became a permanent institution: the United States Army.

Nevertheless, although more than the federalized militia that had originally been envisaged in Knox's *Plan for the General Assignment of the Militia of the United States* (1786), the army was weak, not only in manpower and political support, but also in money and matériel, and it was badly affected by desertion. The absence, until the constitution was settled and established, of a well organised government or a system of direct taxation was a fundamental limit to military capability. By the end of 1786, the regiment consisted of only 565 officers and men.

The army was subsequently expanded as relations slipped into an initially unsuccessful war with Native Americans (see chapter 4), but, after peace was negotiated, the army was cut to 3,359 men in 1796. Washington was a constitutional figure ready to leave office after eight years, not a figure like Oliver Cromwell who had used command of the army to seize power in Britain during its republican episode. Parliament had replaced the king, but Cromwell purged Parliament (1648) before finally replacing it and making himself Lord Protector (1653) and, finally, hereditary Protector (1657). In contrast, Washington, who had gone to great lengths to support the principle of civilian superiority over the army during the Revolution, now cemented it by resigning.[16]

Expanded in 1798 during the Quasi War with France, with Washington as Commander-in-Chief and Hamilton as senior-ranking Major General, the army was cut to 4,436 in 1800, and then, by Jefferson, to 3,284 only to be built up in 1808 as relations deteriorated with Britain and as an internal police force to enforce the embargo. In April 1808, Congress authorized eight more regiments, with the emphasis very much on infantry: there were to be five more infantry regiments and one each of riflemen, light dragoons and light artillery.[17]

In November 1811, in his annual address to Congress, Madison proposed increasing the army and recruiting a large number of volunteers, but in 1812, the army establishment was only 6,686 officers and men, while the navy had seven frigates, ten sloops and sixty-two gunboats. Furthermore, the American economy was better prepared for war in 1812 than it had been in 1775. The agricultural economy was more extensively developed, as was the industrial base. This had a direct impact upon the production of munitions. Thus, despite the continuing dependence on Britain for a range of supplies, there was no need to turn to foreign suppliers for arms, as there had been in the War of Independence. Instead, there was plentiful production of cannon and muskets in America.

However, whereas the French Revolution had led to a decade of war (1792–1801), a militarisation of French power and a major build-up of the French army, the American Revolution had led to nearly the same length of conflict (1775–1783), but no equivalent militarisation or build-up. Furthermore, neither was seen in subsequent years, despite lengthy and initially unsuccessful struggles with Native Americans. Constitution, political culture, politics, institutional factors, and distance from the centers of European power, combined to keep the army marginal in the new country, with a well-articulated reliance on the militia challenging its role.[18] The Constitution left little doubt of the place of the army. Aside from the principle of civilian control, there were also processes to secure the same end in the shape of appropriations and appointments.

More specifically, the army was unprepared for the conflict. Both officers and men lacked the necessary training for combat. Hamilton, appointed Inspector General of the army in 1798, when it was boosted by the Federalists at the time of the Quasi War, sought to develop the force as a powerful permanent body able to unite America against internal subversion and foreign threat, but his intentions were suspect to many, and Jefferson and the Republicans, who gained power after the election of 1800, limited the peacetime establishment to 3,284. They were not interested in a European-style military or an army of imperial size, and were suspicious of the existing army, not least because most of the senior officers were Federalists. Instead, Jefferson preferred to rely on national unity, an example of the comforting illusion that virtue would necessarily prevail. This led Jefferson in his Inaugural Address in 1801 to claim that America was the strongest country in the world.

Similarly, the Federalist plan to build up the navy was stopped when the Jeffersonians took power. Jefferson favoured coastal gunboats rather than the more expensive frigates with their oceanic range, although he failed to take steps to provide for a naval force on Lake Erie. The emphasis on gunboats conformed to the militia tradition of American republicanism. Militia could use gunboats to defend the fortifications being built. The loss of the *Philadelphia* seemed to confirm the need for gunboats in the Barbary War. Gunboats were indeed to play a valuable role in operations in the War of 1812.[19] In 1807, a new system of fortifications, the "Second System," was begun in accordance with the design of Jonathan Williams. The "First System," which dated from 1794, focused on coastal artillery positions. The overall emphasis on the defensive was not the best preparation for an invasion of Canada.

In the War of 1812, the ability of the American economy to respond to military weakness was hit by British blockade. In 1806, Gilpin had written:

I much doubt whether this country could support a war with Great Britain. I do not think any comparison will hold because America maintained the revolutionary war. Circumstances are much altered, for though this country is richer, and more populous, yet the occasion being different, the spirit could not easily be brought out. It would occasion severe strokes both to the commercial and agricultural interest of this country, which to a calculating people will always be one of their first considerations.[20]

In the war, British blockade hit trade and thus removed the fiscal basis for war. The blockade also sought to accentuate American divisions. Initially, 'licensed' neutral commerce was permitted with New England. Economic links between the two sides remained important. Indeed, Canadian deficiencies in food and other supplies were rectified by American smuggling by sea and land.

## WAR ON THE CANADIAN FRONTIER

The prime American goal was the conquest of Canada, an issue that symbolized the extent to which the American Revolution seemed unfinished, and it is appropriate that that comes first in our discussion. There is controversy as to whether the Madison government wished to retain Canada or to use it merely as a pawn in negotiations over impressment and the latter has been stressed in accounts that emphasize the defensive character of American policy; but both goals required the seizure of Canada. This also provided the British with a major objective.

However, the nature of British power was such that the defence of Canada was a task made more difficult by distance. It was easier to move troops from the British Isles to the eastern seaboard of North America than to positions along the Great Lakes. It was also easier to take advantage of Britain's maritime power by attacking this seaboard. In contrast, because warships of any size could not pass the St. Lawrence rapids from the Atlantic to the Great Lakes, the British were unable to send their ocean-going fleet there. The Americans were far weaker at sea. The effectiveness of individual American warships did not amount to a capable fleet, still less to an ability to mount amphibious attacks on the British Isles.

Although Canada provided the Americans with a clear strategic goal, the Americans were unable to devise an effective strategy to obtain this. This deficiency in planning accompanied the organisational and political limitations that affected the war effort. The absence of an effective strategy made it difficult to make use of tactical and operational successes: these comprised parts in a whole that was absent. More particularly, multi-pronged attacks were not coordinated, and did not exert simultaneous or sequential pressure on the British; although, with ten thousand regulars and 86,000 men potentially available for militia service, British North America was not an easy target. Nevertheless, the militia was untried, the regulars were few, and Britain's military attention was focused on Napoleon. Canada seemed vulnerable. One British veteran commented: "The frontier of Upper Canada is so extensive and the population so thin, that it is impracticable to guard it in every point against penetration by even a feeble enemy. Their having Lakes George and Champlain . . . within their line will also greatly facilitate by means of the river Richlieu and other routes their irruptions into Lower Canada. But if we take care to retain possession of Quebec . . ." then the Americans would be unable to consolidate their position and the British would be in a position to drive them out of Canada, as in 1776.[21] This letter indicated the extent to which the geostrategic options and constraints in the War of Independence guided thinking about the War of 1812. However, the situation was different in several important respects. In part due to the migration of Loyalists, the population of Upper Canada alone had risen from 6,000 in 1785 to 60,000 by 1811. This provided an important support for the regulars.

There were American plans for the conquest of Canada. Peter Porter, among others, pressed for an advance along the Lake Champlain corridor in order to divide Montréal from Québec, and then a siege of Québec.[22] This would prevent the British from sending troops to Upper Canada. Henry Dearborn, Secretary of War (1801–1809), who, in 1812, was appointed senior Major-General in charge of the northern border, agreed that the main thrust should be along the Champlain corridor, but pressed for ancillary assaults from Detroit and the Niagara frontier. Westerners were opposed to an emphasis on the Champlain corridor and, instead, wanted to prevent British help to the Native Americans, in particular by advancing on Fort Malden from Detroit. The common theme was an optimistic assumption that the British could be beaten. Henry Clay, the Speaker of the House (and a Kentuckian), declared in 1812 that the Kentucky militia alone could conquer Montréal and Upper Canada. Optimism culminated with Jefferson's hope to drive the British from North America: Québec was to be taken in 1812 and Halifax in 1813.[23] However, the size of Canada helped make strategic planning difficult, as did the nature of contemporary communications and command and control, and relationships between individual commanders. For these reasons, there was little prospect of coordinated campaigning that would have been the best way to take advantage of the distribution of American resources. Their massing in a single concentration of power, in order to seize and exploit a central position, in the Napoleonic fashion, was not possible for political reasons, but was also not feasible in logistical terms.

Despite the length of the border, there were few corridors in which the advance of a force of any size was viable. As a consequence, it was not readily possible to outmanoeuvre opponents. Water transport was important to both sides and control of the Great Lakes had a major impact on strategic mobility. In 1812, campaigning focused on the west where the British were able to gain the initiative and an American offensive was defeated. Brigadier-General William Hull, Governor of the Michigan Territory, and Commander of the Army of the Northwest, invaded Canada on 12 July with 2,500 men at the western end of Lake Erie. This was largely a volunteer force and it was untrained and dependent on a long and precarious supply line, that was vulnerable to Native American attack. Supply problems and a collapse of nerve led to a retreat to Detroit, and Hull then surrendered on 16 August to a smaller force under Major-General Isaac Brock. Tricked into believing he was faced by an overwhelming horde of Native warriors, Hull feared massacre by Natives if Detroit was stormed. Hull was court-martialled and thrown out of the army. Further north, the British had already captured Fort Michilimakinac on Mackinac Island near where Lakes Michigan and Huron met. Like their capture of Detroit, this both impressed the Natives and helped the British to sustain links with them.

In October 1812, the Americans struck closer to the centre of British power in Canada by advancing near Niagara. They crossed the river on the night of 12–13 October and developed a position near Queenston. A counter-attack failed when Brock was killed, but the Americans received inadequate support, in part because of the unwillingness of the militia to cross the river into Canada. By the evening of 13 October, in the face of British reinforcements, the Americans had been driven back or surrendered to Brock's replacement, Major-General Roger Sheaffe. The following month, the Americans mounted an attack under Dearborn from New England towards Montréal, the most vulnerable point in the British defence system for Canada as a whole, but it collapsed due to inadequate logistics and poor command. Furthermore, due to the offensive success of Brock's British-Native army, too many American resources had been devoted to the war further west.

Fresh American attacks were mounted in 1813. The first, under Brigadier General James Winchester, was defeated on 23 January, at Raisin River, near Detroit, and he surrendered. This blunted a winter campaign to retake Detroit. On Lake Ontario, the Americans took the initiative, and York, the capital of Upper Canada, now named Toronto, was captured by Dearborn on 27 April and burned, with an important loss of naval stores, although the Americans lost more men than the defenders. Backed by their warships, the Americans advanced on the Niagara front in May, capturing Fort George at the mouth of the Niagara River; but attempts to exploit this success were stopped at Stoney Creek (6 June) and Beaver Dams (24 June). Dearborn was relieved of command in July. The arrival in May of an effective commodore from the Royal Navy, Sir James Yeo, backed by a large number of officers and sailors challenged the American position on Lake Ontario. The failure of the Americans under Isaac Chauncey to seize naval control of the Lake in the so-called Burlington's Races of 28 September 1813 was the last change either side allowed the other to engage in a significant squadron action. Lake Ontario witnessed a shipbuilding contest for the remainder of the war.[24]

Further west, the British squadron on Lake Erie was defeated by Oliver Perry and surrendered on 10 September 1813.[25] This was a major blow, as lake travel was crucial to the infrastructure and articulation of warfare in the region. As a result of the victory, the Americans were able to recapture Detroit and then to defeat an Anglo-Native army at the Battle of the Thames (see pp. 86–87).

As in November 1812, the Americans prepared a bold step, designed to cut the St. Lawrence artery of British power. This would have weakened, if not fatally undermined, the British position further west, on the Niagara front and further west. However, the advance from Sacketts Harbor on Montréal under Wilkinson (who had been called north from the Gulf Coast) was again hit by poor leadership and logistics and by the onset of bad weather, and was stopped by firm resistance. Far larger American forces were defeated at Chateauquay (25–26 October) and Crysler's Farm (11 November).[26] Wilkinson abandoned the offensive when it became clear that there was going to be no overwhelming concentration of American strength near Montréal. This decision can be criticised, but it enabled him to avoid the fate of the 1775 invasion of Canada. Furthermore, the Americans were driven back on the Niagara Front in December, losing Fort Niagara on 19 December. Buffalo was burned down eleven days later in reprisal for the American burning of Newark, in Ottawa.

The British were greatly helped by Canadian resolve. "An Appeal to the British Public," issued in July 1814, declared:

The defenceless situation of the province of Upper Canada or the sudden and totally unexpected declaration of war against Great Britain by the United States of America, instead of dispiriting its brave inhabitants animated them with the most determined courage. Consisting chiefly of Loyalists driven from their native homes during the American rebellion, they beheld with indignation their old enemy envying them, their new habitations won from the wilderness, and again thirsting for their blood . . . they volunteered their services with acclamation. . . . Theirs was not the enthusiasm of the moment, it still burns with unabated vigour . . . enables a raw militia to suffer with patience the greatest privations [and] to face death with astonishing intrepidity . . . united with the small body of regulars . . . they have been enabled to take or destroy every enemy that has had the temerity to pass the borders.[27]

This determination extended to the French Canadians, many of whom fought in the Voltigeurs Canadiens, helping to secure Lower Canada against American invasion. In addition, recent immigrants from the United States failed to rise against the British.

Napoleon's defeat in early 1814 and his abdication on 6 April 1814 (he returned from exile in 1815 and was defeated anew at Waterloo) enabled the British to send more naval personnel and far more troops to North America than in 1812 or 1813: about 6,000 troops were sent in 1813, but close on 20,000, including many of Wellington's veterans, in 1814. This led to a much more wide-ranging campaign that year, that included a focus on the conquest of American territory, especially in the Champlain corridor and Maine; although, at first, the Americans took the initiative, benefiting from improvements in organisation and performance that reflected experience of the first two years of the war. Initially, the Americans were driven off by a smaller Canadian force at Lacoller's Mill (30 March). Later that year, however, the Americans attacked near Niagara, winning the battle of Chippawa (5 July) over the outnumbered forces of Major-General Phineas Riall, who was impressed by their tactical skill;[28] only to be held by the British counter-attack that led to the night-time battle of Lundy's Lane (25 July).[29] This is a controversial engagement in that both sides claimed victory. At the end of the battle, the Americans held the contested ground, but they had lost a higher percentage of the men engaged, and abandoned the ground after the battle. When the British then advanced, the Americans did not renew the contest. Whatever the tactical conclusion, the battle was an operational success for the British as the Americans no longer held the Chippawa River or most of the western shore of the Niagara Valley. The battles in the campaign revealed the difficulty of controlling engagements and the role of risk. Commanders took the chance of battle, but found it difficult to control, not least because of the difficulty of coordinating forces, and of creating and then using reserves.

Far from returning to the offensive, the Americans fell back to the frontier, although they retained Fort Erie against British siege, repulsing a British attack on 15 August and mounting a successful sortie on 17 September, until they evacuated it in November.[30] Britain by then had an important naval presence on Lake Ontario. The role of local naval superiority was further demonstrated when a British advance on Plattsburgh along the western shore of Lake Champlain was abandoned when the British squadron on the lake was defeated on 11 September 1814. The American squadron under Thomas Macdonough was well positioned and prepared, and it fought well. All the major British ships were sunk or captured. The caution of the British commander, Sir George Prevost, who was unwilling to move beyond Plattsburgh without command of the Lake, also played an important role. The southern bank of the Saranac River south of Plattsburgh was held by Brigadier-General Alexander Macomb. Macomb had repulsed British advances on bridges across the Saranac prior to the naval battle, but, on the day of the latter, the British mounted another assault. One column was able to cross the river, but Prevost ordered a recall once he saw that the British squadron had been lost. His angry subordinates, who felt that victory was within their grasp, complained without success. Prevost retreated into Canada. The opportunity to inflict a major defeat on the American army had been lost.[31] However, the net effect was that the Americans had failed to make gains in Canada. This was serious as only there could they hope to compensate for British conquests elsewhere.

## WAR ON THE ATLANTIC COAST

The British had also attacked on the east coast, where they were able to apply their naval power, amphibious capability, and reinforcements from the British Isles. In 1814, the British blockade was extended, greatly hitting American imports and exports. This played to British maritime strength. In August 1807, Gilpin had suggested seizing Newport in the event of war. With a garrison that he estimated as only eighty regulars, he felt it vulnerable.[32] That December, Archibald Robertson, an army engineer who had served in the War of American Independence, wrote to Viscount Melville, who had sought his advice on strategy in the event of war with America: "I deprecate the idea of making war again by land on that great continent, so distant from European support except in the defence of the British settlements should they be attacked. Our shipping alone can decidedly annoy them in every point, provided they had a safe anchorage to run to in case of a storm," which, he thought, might be provided by the islands off the New England coast. The following month, Robertson added:

In the case of an American war taking place, I do not doubt but that a flying squadron with some troops in transports, threatening either the Chesapeake or Delaware Rivers might alarm and impede any intended movement of the enemy against Canada, without (on our part) any particular attempt to land in any place, but only threatening particular points thought of consequence by the enemy and after attracting their attention to one point shift the ground and threaten some other.[33]

In the event, this strategic goal was not to be realized. Nevertheless, the British did mount an important effort against America's Atlantic coast. In an expedition that is not well known, Admiral Sir Thomas Hardy captured Eastport in Maine and by 11 September all of Maine east of the Penobscot River had been overrun. Local forces mounted no serious resistance. Governor Caleb Strong of Massachusetts focused on protecting Boston. Concern about New England was increased on 9 August when a British squadron bombarded Stonington, Connecticut.

However, the major blow came further south. The British had sent a squadron into the Chesapeake soon after the war began in order to stop it becoming a base for naval and privateering activity, to divert American forces from the Canadian frontier, and to mount raids that would emphasise American vulnerability and hit support for the war. Prior to 1814, the policy had had mixed success. American naval and privateering activity had been hit, but the attempt to drive it home by seizing Norfolk had failed both in the battle of Craney Island on 22 June 1813 and thereafter. Instead, the British fleet had had to anchor at Lynnhaven Bay and thus to depend on distant dockyards. The diversionary purpose had failed, as troops were sent north and militia were used for local defence, while the raids failed to sap support for the war and, instead, led to greater hostility to Britain.

In August 1814, the British mounted a major effort. In "compliance with . . . instructions to attract the attention of the government of the United States and to cause a diversion in favour of the army in Canada," a fleet under Vice-Admiral Sir Alexander Cochrane entered the Chesapeake. A squadron under James Gordon mounted a secondary attack, although it was delayed by shoals. Gordon forced his way up the Potomac, silenced Fort Washington, captured Alexandria on 28 August and returned with a rich haul of merchantmen. The main expedition, a force of 4,500, mostly Peninsular War veterans under Major-General Robert Ross, but also including a marine battalion, landed, without opposition, at Benedict on the Patuxent on 19 August, a move that enabled the British not to expose their main force to fire from the Potomac forts. Ross advanced on Washington, but, at Bladensburg on 24 August, he found 6,500 Americans, mostly militia, drawn up behind a branch of the Potomac under Brigadier-General William Winder. Despite being outnumbered, without cavalry and heavily outgunned, the British advanced across the river, and attacked the Americans in front and flanks, defeating them after three hours' combat. The militia did not fight well: many fled and Winder was forced to rely on his few regulars who were in turn defeated. The British had 249 casualties, the Americans 71. Ross reported that "the enemy was discovered strongly posted on very commanding heights . . . position which was carefully defended by artillery and riflemen."

However, thanks to a good attack, "this first line giving way was driven on the second which yielding to the irresistible attack of the bayonet and the well directed discharge of rockets got into confusion and fled leaving the British masters of the field," and having captured ten cannon. British tactics in the battle are a reminder that the standard impression of Wellingtonian tactics—linear defensive firepower—have to be seen more as a response to particular circumstances in the Peninsular War with France than as an overall description of tactical doctrine and practice. Indeed, in Egypt against the French, in India against the Marathas, and in America, the British attacked with alacrity. This expanded the range of tactical problems and possibilities American units could anticipate.

After the battle, Ross entered Washington that night without resistance. The public buildings were destroyed in retaliation for American destructiveness at York. Ross reported

Having rested the army for a short time I determined to march upon Washington and reached that city at 8 o'clock that night. Judging it of consequence to complete the destruction of the public buildings with the least possible delay so that the army might retire without loss of time the following buildings were set fire to and consumed—the Capital including the Senate House and House of Representatives, the Arsenal, the Dockyard, Treasury, War Office, Presidents Palace, Rope Walk, and the Great Bridge across the Potomac, in the dock yard a frigate nearly ready to be launched and a ship of war were consumed.

Ross's force then returned to the fleet, re-embarking on 30 August. Ross reported "The object of the expedition being accomplished I determined before any greater force of the enemy could be assembled to withdraw the troops and accordingly commenced retiring on the night of the 25th."[34]

Ross then struck at Baltimore, landing at North Point on 12 September. A larger force of American militia resisted in wooded terrain, but was driven back with heavy losses, although Ross himself received a mortal wound. Colonel Arthur Brooke, a veteran of operations in the Low Countries, the West Indies, Egypt and Spain, who replaced Ross, reported of the operation that the Americans had abandoned their first position on the British post, but "about two miles beyond this post our advance became engaged. The country was here closely wooded and the enemy's riflemen were enabled to conceal themselves." Brooke continued that, despite the loss of Ross, "our advance continuing to press forward, the enemy's light troops were pushed to within five miles of Baltimore," where, he reported, he found about 6,000 men drawn up. The British launched a general attack: "In less than fifteen minutes the enemy's force being utterly broken and dispersed, fled in every direction over the country, leaving on the field 2 pieces of cannon . . . this short but brilliant affair." Brooke added that, had his force included cavalry, American casualties on the retreat would have been far higher. From the American perspective, Brooke grossly overstated what happened at an outpost line.

On 13 September, Brooke advanced and occupied a position one and a half miles from Baltimore, around which city the Americans "had constructed a chain of pallisaded redoubts connected by a small breast work." Supporting warships under Cochrane moved up the Patapsco and bombarded Fort McHenry on 13 September, but were unable to destroy it. The resistance inspired the poem *The Star Spangled Banner* by Francis Scott Key. The strength of Baltimore's defences led to the abandonment of the expedition on 14 September. Brooke reported that he had planned a night attack on the 13th in order to counter American artillery superiority, but that the navy was unable to co-operate because the Americans had sunk over twenty ships and thus blocked the advance of the British warships. Brooke decided "that the capture of the town would not have been a sufficient equivalent to the loss which might probably be sustained in storming the heights." He had therefore withdrawn on the 14th. As the American forces did not follow, Brooke did not have the chance to fight again. Having re-embarked at North Point on 15 September,[35] the British troops then sailed to Jamaica.

The operations in the Chesapeake led to no permanent gains, although they influenced the peace negotiations at Ghent. The British had sent too few troops to do more than raid and there was criticism that more troops should have been sent to Canada where they might have played a major role in strengthening the British position on the Niagara front or in the Lake Champlain corridor, although this would have strained logistical capability. However, the threat of further British attacks remained. In October 1814, the Senate was told by James Monroe, Secretary at War, that New York City was at risk, and he pressed for an expansion of the regular army from 62,000 to 100,000 men, to be achieved by recruiting and by drafts from the militia. Much of this planned force was designed to protect the coast and supporting it would have been a major burden on American public finances as well as on the economy and society. The threat of British attack meant that it was not acceptable to rely solely on the militia to protect the coast. Instead, it was necessary to use some regulars for this defensive function. This affected the number of regulars who could be sent into Canada; although that did not prevent the government from planning to do so. Instead of a focus on the Niagara frontier, Monroe planned an 1815 campaign that would finally gain Montréal.[36]

## THE BATTLE OF NEW ORLEANS

The British force on Jamaica, now under Major-General Sir Edward Pakenham, Wellington's brother-in-law, was sent to attack New Orleans, only to be heavily defeated nearby on 8 January 1815. The delay in mounting the attack ensured that the Americans under Andrew Jackson had time to prepare their defences. American artillery and musket fire blunted a British attack on prepared positions, with 2,000 casualties, compared to 71 among the Americans. The British attacked in a tightly packed formation on a narrow front, providing a good target for defensive fire. Instead of pressing home the attack, they halted, losing impetus and the initiative, and increasing their vulnerability to American fire. The British withdrew on 27 January. A secondary attack on Fort St. Phillip in January near the mouth of the Mississippi also failed.[37]

## WAR AT SEA

Pakenham's defeat ensured that the war ended with a powerful impression of the proficiency of the American military methods. The expedition also, however, reflected the success of the British at sea, as it could be transported to near New Orleans. Although the Americans had an abundance of trained seamen to man their fleet, and the most powerful frigates of the age, which they were adept at handling in ship-to-ship actions, they had no ships of the line, and their total navy at the outset comprised only 17 ships. They thus lacked the capacity for fleet action. This reflected the force structure and doctrine developed under Jefferson's agrarian republicanism. It was very different in its military results to the large fleets developed by the mercantile republics of the United Provinces and Commonwealth England in the seventeenth century.

In 1812, the Americans were to capture three British frigates (*Guerrière, Macedonian* and *Java* falling victim respectively to the *Constitution, the United States,* and the *Constitution*), and this provided a valuable boost to morale. The Americans did better at sea than had been anticipated; and, conversely, did worse on land. At sea, the British suffered initially from overconfidence, inaccurate gunnery, and ships that were simply less powerful and less well prepared than those of their opponents. Most of the British navy was involved in operations against France. Napoleon had rebuilt his fleet after its heavy defeat at Trafalgar in 1805, and the British had to devote much effort to blockading French ports.

However, aside from the three frigates, the other British losses were all of smaller vessels. British gunnery improved during the war, as, more generally, did their naval effectiveness, both in Atlantic waters and on the Great Lakes. Whereas in October 1812, Decatur, in command of the *United States*, had captured the *Macedonian*, in June 1813 he was forced to surrender the *President* to superior force when he tried to run the British blockade of New York. Larger British naval forces were effective against individual privateers. David Porter, who successfully attacked British commerce in the South Atlantic and the South Pacific was forced to surrender by two British warships off Valparaiso in February 1814. Although the British suffered far more casualties when they attacked the privateer *General Armstrong* in Faial harbour in the Azores in September 1814, the Americans eventually scuttled and burned the ship. Overall, however, American privateers and small warships had an important impact on the British merchant marine.

The Americans had also shown an important ability to develop naval capability on the Great Lakes. Thus, in 1812 Isaac Chauncey, commandant of the Navy Yard at New York, built up a force that established a powerful presence on Lake Ontario, while in 1813, Oliver Perry built nine ships reversing the situation on Lake Erie. In 1814, however, the British were able to construct the *St. Lawrence*, a 112-gun ship, at Kingston on Lake Ontario. American gunboats gave a good account of themselves in several naval actions, especially on Lakes Erie and Champlain. They also resisted British warships in the Chesapeake.[38]

Naval capability gave the British major advantages. Blockade greatly harmed the American economy, and it became more effective from 1813. It was also possible to send reinforcements to Canada. Amphibious capability was retained to the end. In February 1815, Cochrane captured Mobile and, when hostilities ceased, an expedition was being planned against first Savannah and then Charleston, both of which were blockaded.[39] The American plan in May 1813 and May 1814 for a small squadron to cruise off Nova Scotia and the St. Lawrence to intercept British supply ships failed in large part due to the British blockade of American ports.

## THE COMING OF PEACE

Peace talks began at Ghent in Belgium on 8 August 1814, and a treaty was signed there on 24 December 1814, but news took a while to reach the New World, so that hostilities continued into 1815. The British initially demanded an international frontier between the United States and Native Americans, with neither the British nor the Americans able to buy land from the Natives. They also pressed for the removal of American warships and forts from the Great Lakes, although the British were to be able to keep theirs. Frontier adjustments were also demanded. Lord Bathurst, Secretary for War and the Colonies, complained in September 1814 that the leading minister, the Earl of Liverpool

proposes to be satisfied with a simple provision of peace with the Indians. I propose security for a time at least, that the lands they now occupy should not be under the pretence of sale, (which has been much abused) taken from them. [I suggest not] to begin a negotiation upon our boundaries in Canada, until we know (what must be a sine qua non) whether they will admit an article providing for peace at least with the Indians. As far as peace for the Indians goes, there can be no difference of opinion. We are bound not only in honor but in policy to include them. They would never forgive us, if we deserted them: and they would be most formidable enemies to our new settlements in Upper Canada by crossing the River St. Clair, laying waste everything, and returning back to their own country, where we must not follow them, if it be considered the territory of the United States . . . we must have an article providing for the peace and security of the Indian Nation.[40]

However, in the event, the terms essentially confirmed the pre-war *status quo*.[41] Limited goals had greatly helped the British. This was no war of reconquest. There was no attempt to regain the United States. The British would have pressed for frontier changes had their advance along Lake Champlain been more successful in 1814, and this course was pressed on them for "the future security of Canada,"[42] but the government was ready to abandon such schemes. Although the British anyway had no wish to direct their well-honed forces against a new target, Wellington emphasised the cost of any war of conquest in North America.

## THE WAR REVIEWED

The narrative can be contextualised by considering the Napoleonic wars, more specifically Britain's other transoceanic operations. It is instructive to consider British failure at New Orleans alongside the earlier failure at Buenos Aires.[43] That illustrated the extent to which, once landed, amphibious forces lost much of their operational advantage. Indeed, the same was true of the unsuccessful British expeditions to Holland in 1799, Egypt in 1807 and Flanders in 1809.[44] Thus, Jackson was far from unique in being able to stop British amphibious attacks.

In contrast, the British were more successful when they had a local base and support system, for example in their wars in India in the 1790s, 1800s, and 1810s, in Portugal during the Peninsular War (1808–14), and in defence of Canada during the War of 1812. Their other group of successful operations were those launched against the overseas bases of hostile powers, for example the attacks on Mauritius in 1810 and Batavia (Djakarta) in 1811. These attacks looked back to a long series of expeditions—for example against Havana and Manila in 1762—and testified to the vulnerability of the overseas bases of European empires when their maritime support systems were severed.

America was very different. Although the bulk of the population, industry and purchasing power was concentrated in and close to the littoral, the defence had depth as a result of "country" space. This was not required at New Orleans, but proved valuable in the Chesapeake. The British could not only take Washington without fatal effects, but, in addition, the Americans had the opportunity to withdraw without losing their capacity to maintain their forces. Furthermore, although the littoral was exposed to assault, it would be mistaken to argue that such attack was therefore easy. Instead, the processes of approach to shore and disembarkation were often slow and difficult, while, once troops were ashore, they lost the advantage of maritime mobility. Instead, they were frequently vulnerable to attack. Amphibious forces had a lopsided force structure: Ross wrote of the "serious disadvantage being experienced from the want of cavalry."[45]

The War of 1812 directs attention to the deficiencies and limitations of the American military, and thus of the state. Important in itself, this issue also invites some comparison with the more successful impression created by the War of American Independence. In essence, both conflicts showed that the American system was more appropriate for defence than for conquest, and, to that extent, the failure to conquer Canada in both conflicts is the most appropriate point of comparison. The failure in 1812–14 was more important as America already had gained independence and, due again to British naval power, Canada was the sole sphere in which the Americans could take the initiative and strike directly at the British. Because the attacks on Canada played a far greater role in the War of 1812, it is easy to imply that American military capability had declined since the War of Independence, but that is misleading, for the 1775–76 failure showed the difficulty of the task.

In the War of 1812, American advances were poorly co-ordinated, although it was difficult to be otherwise, given the distances involved, the nature of communications, and the logistical and transport problems that any attacking force faced. Many military goods and other supplies had to be transported from the eastern seaboard. It was not possible to obtain sufficient supplies in the relatively unpopulated frontier areas and it was not possible to transfer the burden to the Canadians by invading, for the border areas of Canada had insufficient supplies. The Americans also suffered from a lack of specie and from limited confidence in the financial system.[46] The very assembly of a larger force ensured greater difficulties in moving and supplying it. Although there was no comparison with France, where Napoleon raised 1.3 million conscripts in 1800–11 and 1 million in 1812–13 alone, the major expansion of the American army, and the heavy reliance on the militia all entailed coping with the difficulty of dealing with men with little experience of military service, let alone campaigning. Gilpin described the Rhode Island militia in 1807 as "little more than an undisciplined rabble."[47] The training of American soldiers in the war was frequently poor or non-existent and their performance was accordingly poor. Political culture, partisan divisions, resource issues, and over-confidence combined to ensure that there was scant preparation.

Institutionally, America was not a war state. The absence of a commanding general, let alone a general staff, drew command functions on land onto the Secretary of War, who had a myriad of responsibilities and little power. This was compounded in 1812 by the deficiencies of William Eustis, the Secretary of War, who was not up to the job of providing or supporting leadership. He was not a shadow of Marshals Berthier and Clarke, French Ministers of War in 1799–1807 and 1807–14 respectively. Rather than preparing before the War, Congress in 1812 sought to remedy the institutional crisis by establishing Quartermaster, Ordnance, Hospital, Pay, Adjutant and Inspector General, and Commissary Departments. However, they were poorly prepared for their tasks, and this contributed to serious logistical failures, especially once forces advanced into Canada. These failures help to explain the lack of operational movement that characterised much of American campaigning. They exacerbated, and were exacerbated by, the poor state of internal transport, both in terms of routes and of other aspects of infrastructure. The structural problems that face any military that rapidly expands under the pressure of war were compounded by administrative weaknesses, for example a failure to provide a clear ranking of officers, not least to define relations between regular and militia commanders. These institutional weaknesses were then played out in a situation made bitter by a shortage of money, matériel, and supplies and with issues provided by problems such as the lack of any comprehensive set of general regulations or uniform system of tactics. Supply shortages hit morale and health and encouraged desertion.[48]

The British were helped by American hostility to a large standing army and by the degree to which American naval power did not match their maritime commercial strength. As so often in military history, resources were less important than the ability to utilize and direct them. As a consequence, despite her strenuous military efforts against Napoleon, the British were able to hold off the Americans in 1812–13, and then in 1814 to carry the war to them.

The militia character of the American military, in terms both of organisation and of assumptions, helps to minimise the appropriateness of comparisons with the Napoleonic Wars. There, long-service regulars, under firm discipline and with coherent supply systems, dominated warfare. Yet, as a reminder of the theme of military diversity, there were also other forms of organisation. The irregulars that resisted Napoleon's forces were not always successful. The rising in the Tyrol was crushed and that in Calabria was suppressed, although the latter took six years. In Spain, however, the irregular forces were not destroyed, although the successful defeat of the French there also owed much to regular troops. Further east, Serbian irregulars had considerable success against their Turkish rulers.

Within this context, it is again less appropriate to think of American exceptionalism, other than in terms of being an ocean away. Yet in the 1810s this was no longer unique. In the Latin American Wars of Liberation, the difficulty of sustaining offensives parallels the problems the Americans encountered against Canada.

Ultimately, the War of 1812 lacks attention because it is not seen as glorious. The attempts by both sides at power projection had failed, with the Americans using land-based operations and the British sea-based ones. Failure alone does not explain neglect, as the attention devoted to the Confederacy shows, but a lack of glory is the problem. This is unfortunate. The war was important, and not only in the negative sense that it kept Canada out of American power, and therefore underlined the extent to which, up to the present day, it is possible to point to two very different trajectories in the development of what had been British North America. Britain's goal was essentially defensive: she intended to retain Canada, not to reconquer America. However, defeat at New Orleans ensured that the British ended the war having created the impression of failure.

## ANGLO-AMERICAN RELATIONS AFTER THE WAR

More positively for the Americans, this was matched by a definite failure on the part of Britain's Native American allies. This combination of failures cemented not only independence but also expansion for the United States. In 1814, British negotiators had demanded a major Native American buffer state in the

Old Northwest, as well as the exclusion of American warships from the Great Lakes, and the British free to navigate the Mississippi. None of these demands were to be met, but they are a reminder of the unpredictability of the struggle and help explain the depth of Native anger with the settlement. Subsequent American control was registered in the creation of new states: Indiana in 1816, Illinois in 1818 and Maine in 1820, while, in the late 1810s, troops were deployed to protect America's frontier in the further reaches of the Northwest.

The British defensive success in Canada (combined with the setbacks, or worse, to their attacks on America) also encouraged post-war conciliation of the United States, seen, for example, in the willingness to accept, or at least not challenge, the Monroe Doctrine for Latin America, and in the settlement of frontier disputes. The Treaty of Ghent had provided for adjustments of boundary disputes and, in 1818, a Convention extended the boundary along the 49th parallel from the Lake of the Woods to the Rockies, with the Oregon Territory to the west to be jointly administered by Britain and America for ten years, an administration extended indefinitely in 1827; and in practice until the Oregon Boundary Treaty of 1846. This division excluded the two other powers that bordered the region, Mexico and Russian-ruled Alaska. The Russians had established a base in California—at Fort Ross—in 1812. The Pomos, who lived nearby, reacted violently, but disease and Russian firepower cut their numbers. However, California was too far for the Russians effectively to deploy their power. Fort Ross did not serve as the basis for fresh expansion and it was abandoned in 1841. The American-Spanish treaty of 1819 (which came into effect when ratifications were accepted in February 1821) had accepted American interests in Oregon, and Mexico did not try to overturn this.[49]

The American presence in the Oregon Territory reflected the value of good relations with Britain as, in the War of 1812, Fort Astoria, the American base on the south bank of the Columbia River established in 1811 by John Jacob Astor's Pacific Fur Company, was successfully besieged by HMS *Raccoon*. Other Pacific Fur Company bases were taken, including Forts Okanagan and Spokane in 1813. The British-owned Hudson's Bay Company, which, in 1821, united with the North West Company, established many bases below the 49th parallel, including Forts Boise, Colville, Flathead, George, Nez Percés, Nisqually, Okanagan, Umpqua and Vancouver. Several were on or south of the Columbia, including Fort Nez Percés, established in 1818 and Fort Vancouver in 1825. This major presence did not ebb prior to 1846. Instead, the Company dominated international trade from the region with direct sailings from London. James Polk campaigned for the presidency in 1844 on the platform "54–40 or fight," but, in the event, was willing to settle without British Columbia and Vancouver Island. Manifest Destiny could only provide so much.[50]

However, it would be misleading to suggest that Anglo-American difficulties were restricted to Oregon. It was true that the American army showed little concern about the Canadian border, and American fortifications along it were not maintained or replaced. Nevertheless, there were concerns and these became more acute in the 1830s, with even the possibility of conflict over the disputed Maine frontier leading in 1838 to the bloodless "Aroostook War" between Maine and New Brunswick, and in 1839 to American strategic planning for war. In 1838, Alexander Macomb, the Commanding General, toured the Vermont border, as well as going to Florida to try to negotiate a truce with the Seminole, the first time he had taken such an active role since gaining the rank in 1828. Political concern was greater, with Democratic expansionists seeing Britain as a threat.

Such a conflict is one of the major counterfactuals that is worth considering as it affects issues of capability and potential effectiveness. The American army was not up to the task of conquering Canada as, aside from the permanent British garrison, it was possible to reinforce British forces from across the North Atlantic: indeed the insurrection of 1837 in Canada and the American Civil War led to significant increases in the garrison. Despite the politico-economic problems of the Panic of 1837 in America, the American and British commanders considered the logistical situation in 1837–38 much better for the Americans than in 1812: with the Erie Canal and new roads, there was much more infrastructure available. However, a combined regular-volunteer invasion would have faced problems similar to those in the War of 1812, and, as then, the British would have benefited from Loyalist support—the Loyalists played a major role in suppressing insurrection in 1837–38. Britain's success in the War of 1812 had ensured an increase in the population of Canada. In 1815–30, the majority of emigrants from the British Isles went to Canada and, partly as a result, the population of Upper Canada rose from 60,000 in 1811 to 150,000 by 1824. Furthermore, the American army in the late 1830s was also involved in the Second Seminole War.

There is plentiful correspondence in the British archives about defence planning for Canada. The eventual location of the capital at Ottawa was a defensive measure to overcome the vulnerability of Toronto, Kingston and Montréal. Rumours of American invasion preparations, for example in Tennessee and New York in late 1845,[51] were followed carefully. There was concern about the British position on the Great Lakes, not least in response to the number of steamships that the Americans had available.[52] A report in the winter of 1845–1846 on the forts of the Hudson's Bay Company categorized them as "capable of making a good defence against irregular or Indian forces," "incapable of making any defence," or "capable of resisting a sudden attack from Indians or an irregular force without field guns."[53] A report by Wellington, then Commander-in-Chief of the Army, on the defence of Canada led to a government response acknowledging deficiencies:

concur with your Grace in attaching the greatest importance to a well organised and well disciplined militia, in support of any force which this country may employ in the event of a war in Canada; and I have not failed to press this subject earnestly on the consideration of the Governor General. In the last session I regret to say that he failed in inducing the legislature to make provision by law for this important object.[54]

Despite these problems, the British were in a stronger position than at the start of the War of 1812. Their navy remained the most powerful in the world, and their attention was not diverted by conflict in Europe. Concern about the British led to the programme of coastal fortification. Thus, New York harbour was strengthened with Fort Hamilton from 1825 and Fort Wadsworth from 1847. The programme also served to give the Corps of Engineers, the Ordnance Department and the artillery particular roles. As a result, they actively lobbied for the programme, especially in the early 1850s when it was threatened by political opposition and concern about its military value in the face of developments in naval artillery.[55] Concern about the possibility of a British invasion led Brigadier-General Edmund Gaines, in the 1830s and 1840s, to press for a rail system, built by the federal government and able rapidly to move militia from the interior.[56] No such system was created by the government (although its equivalent developed privately, at least in the northern states); had it been, it might have prefigured the military purpose and economic and social consequences of the interstate highways authorised under Eisenhower.

Two conflicts at once were beyond American military capability, which was a reason why it was helpful to settle the Oregon dispute peaceably while fighting Mexico. Earlier, expansion into Florida had benefited by the settlement of Anglo-American differences. The Spaniards could not turn to Britain to resist American territorial demands in 1818–19.[57] The Americans were assisted by the peripheral character of the Canadian frontier to British decision makers. Jefferson suggested in July 1816 that war was in the interest of neither power:

Both ought to wish for Peace and cordial friendship; we, because you can do us more harm than any other nation; and you, because we can do you more good than any other. Our growth is now so well established by regular enumerations thro' a course of 40 years, and the same grounds of continuance so likely to endure for a much longer period, that, speaking in round numbers, we may safely call ourselves 20 millions in 20 years, and 40 millions in 40 years . . . Of what importance then to you must such a nation be, whether as friends or foes . . . the different degrees in which the war has acted on us. To your people it has been a matter of distant history only, a mere war in the Carnatic, with us it has reached the bosom of every man, woman and child. The maritime parts have felt it in the conflagration of their houses and towns, and desolation of their farms; the borderers in the massacres, and scalping of their husbands, wives and children, and the middle parts in their personal labours and losses in defence of both frontiers, and the revolting scenes they have there witnessed.[58]

To take the longer view, "while the British were consistently viewed as the principal competitor by the Americans, the United States always ranked much lower in the British rivalry schedule."[59] The British were willing to make concessions rather than be dragged into war with a crucial trading partner. Again, in the long-term, the development of canals, steamships and railways, enabled the Americans to exploit their interior without having to gain control of the St. Lawrence,[60] and thus altered the geopolitics of North America. Nevertheless, concern about the British helped to dictate the tasking of the American military.

American willingness to act against the Canadian Patriots when they rebelled against the British crown in 1837–38 played a major role in reassuring the British, and was an aspect of a more general lack of enthusiasm for republican internationalism, whether in policy or in public culture, and a more general willingness to accept the principles and notions of international law, not least the recognition of state sovereignty. The Ashburton-Webster Treaty of 1842 settled disputes over the Maine, New Hampshire and Minnesota boundaries,[61] although anglophobia remained important and included anxiety about British political and commercial plans, not least unfounded concern about British meddling in Texas.[62]

## AMERICAN POWER PROJECTION

Earlier, peace with Britain had enabled the Americans to intimidate each of the Barbary States in turn, and to fight Algiers in the Algerine War of May-June 1815. Decatur was sent to the Mediterranean with ten warships. The Algerian flagship, *Mashouda*, was captured on 17 June, and another Algerian warship ran aground two days later, in each case a result achieved by larger American forces. Peace, "at the mouths of the cannon," obliged the Algerians to release American prisoners and to accept the end of American tribute. This was followed by successful demonstrations by the squadron off Tunis and Tripoli, which obtained recompense for attacks during the War of 1812, and then by a regular naval presence in the Mediterranean which helped America's commercial and diplomatic presence. In 1826, the United States signed its first treaty with Turkey. The following year, landing parties were sent against pirate bases in the Cyclades Islands.

Very different power projection was reflected in the state of Liberia, originally established in West Africa by an antislavery group, the American Colonization Society (founded in 1816), as a home for freed American slaves. The first settlers landed in 1821. The new state reflected American power, with the capital, founded in 1822, Monrovia, named after President Monroe. Colonists were transported by American warships.

Monroe himself was responsible for a statement of American intentions that threatened greatly to extend national commitments. In December 1823, in his annual message to Congress, Monroe announced that attempts by European powers to establish or re-establish colonies in the New World would be seen "as dangerous to our peace and safety."[63] It did not prove necessary to give effect to this policy. Spanish weakness and the intimidatory strength of the British navy deterred Spain from persisting in attempts to regain its colonies, while California was too far from the centre of Russian power to encourage further expansion. The Russians in this period were far more interested in expanding at the expense of Turkey and Persia. Aside from political reasons, these conflicts enabled them to use their army. The Pacific was far more peripheral to Russian policy-makers and, for logistical reasons, it was anyway difficult to project power there. In particular, Russia did not have a significant long-range naval capability. Instead, her navy focused on the Baltic and Black Seas.

The Americans were not declaring policy in a vacuum: they wanted to speak independently of the British, but the British had already offered to speak with the Americans against the Holy Alliance of European conservative regimes. The Americans could put forward their new policy with confidence that the British would enforce it. American policymakers knew that they could not do everything implied in it themselves, but they knew that British would do much the same, with some of the same effect.

Nevertheless, although it was a manifesto not a planning document, what became known as the Monroe Doctrine represented a major expansion in geo-political aspirations for America. Again, counterfactualism is appropriate. There was concern that Spain would be backed by the conservative regimes of Europe: Austria, Russia, and, in particular, France. French forces were sent into Spain to suppress liberalism in 1823 (as Austrian troops had earlier moved into Naples and Piedmont), and there was little reason to assume that they would not try to extend this policy. Although Britain was the leading naval power, there was a major expansion in the French navy after 1815, in particular in frigates; although the Spanish fleet did not recover from its decline during the Napoleonic wars. France had the second largest navy in the world. Although many new ships were left in dock or on the stocks, the French launched warships with a displacement tonnage of 73,000 in 1816–25.[64] A major attempt to support a restoration of Bourbon authority in Latin America would have created considerable embarrassment for the American government unless the British had chosen to try to prevent it. There was little doubt that Latin America was within the reach of France, which had earlier sent an expeditionary force in an unsuccessful attempt to suppress the Haitian revolution.

Thus, the Monroe Doctrine was in many respects foolish. It was to have meaning after the Civil War, when America was a powerful state, but far less so earlier. Spanish forces seeking to regain Mexico were defeated by the Mexican general Santa Anna at Tampico in 1829: the Americans were in no position to determine the struggle. Equally, a Spanish or French attack on the United States might have fared no better than the Spaniards at Tampico. The British were probably the only state that was economically strong enough and had a fleet big enough to sustain power projection against the United States.

In 1831–32, the USS *Lexington* sought to protect American interests in the Falkland Islands, where American sealers had been captured, but the British thwarted both Argentina and the United States and established control in 1833. They were concerned about the potential threat that the Falklands in other hands might pose to British seaborne and political interests in South America and the southern oceans. Viscount Palmerston, Secretary of State for Foreign Affairs in 1830–34, 1835–41, and 1846–51, was influenced by the views of William Gore Ouseley, envoy in Rio de Janeiro, who argued that if the Falklands were developed as a headquarters of trade, ship repair and shipbuilding, they would assist the steady ascendancy of British seaborne activities along the coasts of South America. The American government was reluctant to co-operate with Argentina against Britain.[65]

However, the Monroe Doctrine reflected more than a bombastic inability to understand the limits of power. It was also a product of a confidence born of success. This success was heavily based on a partial reading of the last year of struggle, and "the selective nature of public memory,"[66] with the focus on the defence of Fort McHenry, the naval victory on Lake Champlain, and the triumph at New Orleans, but it is not usual for states to dwell on their failures. When they did so, the Americans were, correctly, struck by their rapid recovery from the blows that the British had aimed in 1814.

Independence had been reasserted and interests defended. This encouraged a potent patriotism that was also partisan. The war left the Democratic-Republicans in a secure position. Federalist opposition to the war had led to a convention at Hartford in late 1814 that proposed changes to the constitution, but this was coloured in the public eye by extremist talk of secession by New England. This compromised the Federalists, helping James Monroe to win the 1816 and 1820 presidential elections, and thus ensuring not only a continuity in Democratic-Republican government but also in control by the group that had waged the recent war.

American society grew rapidly in the early nineteenth century. As its population rose from 9.6 million in 1820 to 17.1 million in 1840, so its economy expanded and its wealth grew. It was scarcely surprising that this encouraged a marked degree of assertiveness. In 1824, David Porter, commander of the West Indies Squadron, threatened bombardment when one of his officers, who was pursuing a suspected pirate, was, himself, imprisoned as a pirate by the Spaniards in Puerto Rico. This led to the release of the officer and an apology, but a subsequent protest caused Porter's recall, court martial and suspension. Angry, he resigned and became commander of the Mexican navy. Marines were landed at Buenos Aires in 1833 and 1852–53, and at Callao and Lima in 1835–36 to protect American interests during insurrections, while attacks on Americans led to the landing of forces on Fiji (1840), Drummond Island (1841), Samoa (1841), and Canton (1843).

A different form of power projection was that of exploration. In 1838, Lieutenant Charles Wilkes was placed in charge of the Depot of Charts and Instruments and also given command of a six-ship expedition to explore the Pacific. This led to the first human sightings of the Antarctic continent. Wilkes also explored the Pacific coastline of North America, a means of asserting American interests. Also in the Pacific, in 1826, the USS *Peacock*, under Thomas Catesby

Jones, commander of the Pacific Squadron, became the first American warship to call on Tahiti before sailing to Hawaii, where he drew up a treaty with King Kamehameha III, the first treaty signed by the Hawaiians.

The aftermath of the War of 1812 was not such as to encourage a critical debate about American military capability. The acquisition of Florida in 1819, the replacement of imperial Spain by a weaker Mexico, and the ability to settle differences with Britain had transformed the situation, greatly easing geopolitical concerns,[67] and this was rapidly registered in relations with the Natives, not least in bitter complaints by disillusioned leaders, such as the Sauk chief, Black Hawk, in 1817.[68]

## POLITICAL AND MILITARY WEAKNESSES

As a consequence, there was little popular emphasis on the political and military problems revealed by the War, although there was much debate and pressure for reform in governmental circles. The failure of the Federalists led to an underplaying of the fissiparous tendencies integral to state authority. During what they termed "Mr. Madison's War," New Englanders, especially in Connecticut, Massachusetts and Rhode Island, were opposed to the conflict, unhelpful to the war effort, and keen to retain links with Britain.[69] Thus, in those three states, and especially in Rhode Island, there was opposition to the use of the militia in the war. This made it harder to raise the manpower and logistical support for striking at the St. Lawrence artery of British power in North America. Thus, American strategic options were directly related to the domestic political situation. There was an emphasis on invading Canada further west than was militarily most wise.

This emphasis on a regional perspective looked back to the plans associated with Vice-President Aaron Burr in 1804–6 that included the secession of New York and New England (1804) and, subsequently, the "Spanish Conspiracy" that appears to have included plans for a western secession.[70] These schemes nearly put paid to the career of the best American general prior to the Civil War, for, in 1810, Winfield Scott was court martialled and suspended for a year for criticising his commander, Brigadier-General James Wilkinson, for involvement with Burr's schemes; Wilkinson had indeed been heavily involved, although his self-serving treason was not dependent on Burr, nor restricted to his schemes.

Despite a measure of integration through economic growth and better communications (although far less than was to follow the conflict), the state/regional focus of loyalties and identities had been shown to be a challenge for American political coherence and military effectiveness, and nothing was done to alter the situation. In that respect, the War of 1812 was too brief and limited to lead to the sweeping political and governmental changes that the protracted character of the French Revolutionary and Napoleonic Wars led to in Europe. Phrased differently, there was a protracted crisis due to American vulnerability in the face of a hostile international situation during the period, and an agenda for governmental change to tackle the crisis was offered by the Federalists, but the crisis never became sufficiently severe to lead to a major reconfiguration of government. Furthermore, although the Jeffersonian Democratic-Republicans adopted a number of Federalist views and programs once in power—the Bank, a standing army, and, after 1812, a oceanic navy and a general staff, their inclinations, attitudes, and ambitions were different to those of Hamilton.

Although the War of 1812 led to increased reliance on the regulars, seen most clearly in Monroe's call for an army of 100,000, and led to reform of the military system, it did not extend to a sweeping reform either in terms of the organisation of large-scale power projection or with regard to the militia. This left America in a weak position in the event of any great power war, but, fortunately, none arose until 1917, and, then, the Americans only played an auxiliary role, important as that was.

This weakness has in part been concealed by the nature of America's opponents in the nineteenth century: heavily outnumbered and divided Native Americans, poorly supported Mexicans, and her own citizens in 1861–65, few of whom were prepared for a conflict, let alone a major one. Thus, the pattern was set. America became the world's leading economy with a military that was poorly prepared for trans-oceanic power projection (although it was very successful against Natives and Mexicans). Again, this was partly hidden by the legacy of the nineteenth-century conflicts. They all occurred in "near America": along the Canadian and Mexican borders and in war with Native Americans or civil conflict. None entailed the distant projection that, for example, took British troops to Batavia (Djarkata) in 1811 or British and French forces to Beijing in 1860. Success against the Barbary states was no real exception. The American military thus lacked the capability for distant force capability. Winfield Scott was to show in invading Mexico at Veracruz in 1847 that an amphibious operation could be safely mounted, but this was scarcely conquest on the opposite side of the world.

## CONCLUSIONS

This can be directly related to tasking. The conquest of African or Asian territories was not part of American policy and, unlike Britain, America was not involved in a war with another power that involved strikes at her territory on the other side of the world. Although operations against California (then part of Mexico) in 1846 indicated the long-range capability of the American navy, it was not in a position to mount a comparable lift of a significant amphibious force. Large-enough forces were absent, but so also was relevant doctrine and a network of colonial bases.

If the War of 1812 is to be related to Napoleonic warfare, this is most pertinent at tactical level, in terms of similarities in engagements, rather than at operational and strategic levels where contrasts between circumstances in North America and Europe readily emerge. At the same time, it is important to note the diversity of European warfare in this period, both in terms of conflict and of scale.

Nevertheless, at the tactical level, there were important differences in scale between the War of 1812 and the mainstream of Napoleonic campaigning, and both sides in North America also lacked the quantity of artillery that was increasingly apparent on the European battlefield and that posed particular challenges in terms of combined arms operations. Thus command and control requirements were different in North America. The role of the militia and of Native Americans also contributed heavily to distinctive characteristics of the war. It was not surprising that subsequent American interest in Napoleonic warfare led to no comparable searching of the War of 1812 for examples of Napoleonic-style campaigning.

In the War of 1812, as in the War of Independence and later in the Civil War, there were important improvements in American performance during the conflict. This reflected the natural trajectory of a force much of which comprised a large number of civilian officers and men rapidly thrown into war. More specifically, the Americans learned to respond both to their opponents and to the nature of their own military system, while officers and men also gained combat and manoeuvre experience. The net result was that the Americans fought better in 1814–15 than they had done in 1812–13. This helps to explain why the terms of the peace were the *status quo ante bellum*, and indeed why the Americans under Jackson were able to get away with violating the Treaty of Ghent by retaining Creek lands and then forcing the Natives still farther south and west. This cannot be explained by victory at New Orleans alone. Instead, British tactical and, sometimes, operational success did not translate into strategic triumph. This owed something to the grand strategic situation, including the difficulty of "defeating" the United States in the normal sense, the extent to which British public opinion and government finances were affected by the Napoleonic Wars, and the desire to resume trade, but also to capable American tactical and operational performance, at least on the defensive. Failure at Washington was unrepresentative. As a result, American deficiencies at every level of war led not to disaster, but to stalemate, an impressive result against the world's leading military power.

Looking toward the next chapter, the war played a decisive role in destroying the southeastern and northwestern Native confederacies. In the southeast, the scene of struggle shifted from Florida to Alabama during the war, but the Creek War suggests some of the continuities in American expansionism from the efforts under Madison to seize the Floridas to operations after 1815 along that frontier. This helps situate the War of 1812 firmly in the course of American territorial expansionism.

## NOTES

1. Paris, Ministère des Affaires Etrangères, Correspondance Politique Etats Unis 35 fols. 136, 188.

2. P.S. Onuf and L.J. Sadosky, *Jeffersonian America* (Malden, Mass., 2002), p. 186.

3. A.P. Whitaker, *The Spanish American Frontier, 1783–1795: The Westward Movement and the Spanish Retreat in the Mississippi Valley* (Boston, 1927) and *The Mississippi Question, 1795–1803: A Study in Trade, Politics, and Diplomacy* (New York, 1934); A. DeConde, *This Affair of Louisiana* (New York, 1976); T.D. Clark and J.D.W. Guice, *Frontiers in Conflict: The Old Southwest, 1795–1830* (Albuquerque, 1989).

4. R.W. Patrick, *Florida Fiasco: Rampant Rebels on the Georgia-Florida Border, 1810–1815* (Athens, 1954); F.L. Owsley Jr., "Jackson's capture of Pensacola," *Alabama Review*, 19 (1996), pp. 175–85; W.S. Brown, *The Amphibious Campaign for West Florida and Louisiana, 1814–1815* (Tuscaloosa, 1969); W. Waciuma, *Intervention in Spanish Florida, 1801–1813: A Study in Jeffersonian Foreign Policy* (Boston, 1976); J.T. Heidler, *Old Hickory's War: Andrew Jackson and the Quest for Empire* (Mechanicsburg, 1996); Owsley and G.A.Smith, *Filibusters and Expansionists: Jeffersonian Manifest Destiny, 1800–1821* (Tuscaloosa, 1997); R.E. May, "Young American Males and Filibustering in the Age of Manifest Destiny: The United States Army as a Cultural Mirror," *Journal of American History*, 78 (1991), pp. 857–886, but, as a counter to May, S.J. Watson, "Army Officers Fight the "Patriot War": Responses to Filibustering on the Canadian Border, 1837–1839," *Journal of the Early Republic*, 18 (1998), pp. 485–519.

5. A. DeConde, *The Quasi-War: The Politics and Diplomacy of the Undeclared War with France, 1797–1801* (New York, 1966).

6. S. Elkins and E. McKitrick, *The Age of Federalism* (New York, 1993); D.S. Ben-Atar and B. Oberg (eds.), *Federalists Reconsidered* (Charlottesville, 1998).

7. J.B. Hattendorf, "The American Navy in the World of Franklin and Jefferson, 1775–1826," *War and Society*, 2 (1990), pp. 10, 17; M.L.S. Kitzen, *Tripoli and the United States at War: A History of American Relations with the Barbary States, 1785–1805* (Jefferson, North Carolina, 1993); R.J. Allison, *The Cresent Obscured: The United States and the Muslim World, 1776–1815* (New York, 1995); G.A. Smith, " 'To Effect a Peace through the Medium of War": Jefferson and the Circumstances of Force in the Mediterranean," *Consortium on Revolutionary Europe 1750–1850. Selected Papers, 1996* (Tallahassee, 1996), pp. 155–60.

8. J.L. Cross, *London Mission: The First Critical Years* (East Lansing, 1968); C.R. Ritcheson, *Aftermath of Revolution: British Policy toward the United States, 1783–1795* (Dallas, 1969).

9. Hammond to Grenville, 1 Nov. 1791, BL. Add. 58939.

10. Beckwith's reports, PRO. FO. 4/12; H.C. Syrett (ed.), *The Papers of Alexander Hamilton* Vol. 7 (New York, 1963), pp. 70–74; J.P. Boyd, *Number 7, Alexander Hamilton's Secret Attempts to Control American Foreign Policy* (Princeton, 1964), pp. 4–13.

11. For American foreign policy, earlier work can be followed through R. Horsman, *The Diplomacy of the New Republic, 1776–1815* (Arlington Heights, 1985) and B. Perkins, *The Creation of a Republican Empire, 1776–1865* (New York, 1993), pp. 118–40. On relations with Britain see, in particular, Perkins, *The First Rapprochement: England and the United States, 1795–1805* (Philadelphia, 1955) and *Prologue to War: England and the United States, 1805–1812* (Berkeley, 1961) and B. Spivak, *Jefferson's English Crisis: Commerce, Embargo, and the Republican Revolution* (Charlottesville, 1979).

12. J.L. Wright, *Britain and the American Frontier, 1783–1815* (1975); R.C. Stuart, *United States Expansionism and British North America, 1775–1871* (Chapel Hill, 1998); F.M. Carroll, *A Good and Wise Measure. The Struggle for the Canadian-American Border, 1783–1842* (Toronto, 2001) focuses on the period from 1816.

13. BL. Add. 49990 fol. 25.

14. For an interesting view from the eastern seaboard, J. Gilpin, Vice-Consul in Newport, to Viscount Sidmouth, former Prime Minister and still a leading cabinet minister, e.g. 10 Jan., 27 March, 27 May 1806, 22 Aug. 1807, DRO. 152M/C1806/OF1,2,4, C1807/OF1.

15. Gilpin to Sidmouth, DRO. 152M/C1804/OF5, C1805/OF3.

16. P. Longmore, *The Invention of George Washington* (Berkeley, 1988).

17. J.R. Jacobs, *The Beginning of the U.S. Army, 1783–1812* (Princeton, 1947); F.P. Prucha, *The Sword of the Republic: The United States Army on the Frontier, 1783–1846* (New York, 1969); W.H. Guthman, *March to Massacre: A History of the First Seven Years of the United States Army, 1784–1791* (New York, 1970); R.H. Kohn, *Eagle and Sword: The Federalists and the Creation of the Military Establishment in America, 1783–1802* (New York, 1975); T.J. Crackel, *Mr. Jefferson's Army: Political and Social Reform of the Military Establishment, 1801–1809* (New York, 1989); W.B. Skelton, "Social Roots of the American Military Profession: The Officer Corps of America's First Peacetime Army, 1784–1789," *Journal of Military History*, 54 (1990), pp. 435–52.

18. L.D. Cress, "Radical Whiggery on the Role of the Military: Ideological Roots of the American Revolutionary Militia," *Journal of the History of Ideas*, 40 (1979), pp. 43–60 and *Citizens in Arms: The Army and Militia in American Society to the War of 1812* (Chapel Hill, 1982); E.W. Carp, "The Problem of National Defence in the Early American Republic," in J.P. Greene (ed.), *The American Revolution: Its Character and Limits* (New York, 1987), pp. 14–50.

19. S.C. Tucker, *The Jeffersonian Gunboat Navy* (Columbia, South Carolina, 1993); J. Seiken, " 'To Obtain Command of the Lakes': The United States and the Contest for Lakes Erie and Ontario, 1812–1815" in D.C. Skaggs and L.L. Nelson (eds.), *The Sixty Years' War for the Great Lakes, 1754–1814* (East Lansing, 2001), p. 355. For another aspect of naval development, C. McKee, *A Gentlemanly and Honorable Profession: The Creation of the U.S. Naval Officer Corps, 1794–1815* (Annapolis, 1991).

20. Gilpin to Sidmouth, 27 Aug. 1806, DRO. 152M/C1806/OF6.

21. James Glennie to Sidmouth, 18 Aug. 1812, DRO. 152/M/C1812/OF1A.

22. J.C.A. Stagg, "Between Black Rock and a Hard Place: Peter B. Porter's Plan for an American Invasion of Canada in 1812," *Journal of the Early Republic*, 19 (1999), pp. 385–422.

23. R. Horsman, "On to Canada: Manifest Destiny and the United States Strategy in the War of 1812," *Michigan Historical Review*, 13 (1987), pp. 1–24.

24. R. Malcolmson, *Lords of the Lake: The Naval War on Lake Ontario, 1812–1814* (Toronto, 1998).

25. D.C. Skaggs and W.J. Welsh (eds.), *War on the Great Lakes: Essays Commemorating the 175th Anniversary of the Battle of Lake Erie* (Kent, Ohio, 1991); G.T. Altoff and Skaggs, *A Signal Victory: The Lake Erie Campaign, 1812–1813* (Annapolis, 1997).

26. D.E. Graves, *Field of Glory: The Battle of Crysler's Farm, 1813* (Toronto, 1999).

27. DRO. 152M/C1814/OC6.

28. J.P. Kimball, "The Battle of Chippawa: Infantry Tactics in the War of 1812," *Military Affairs*, 31 (1967–68), pp. 169–86; Graves, *Red Coats and Grey Jackets: The Battle of Chippawa, 5 July 1814* (Toronto, 1994).

29. Graves, *Where Right and Glory Lead! The Battle of Lundy's Lane, 1814* (2nd edn., Toronto, 1997).

30. J. Whitehorne, *While Washington Burned: The Battle for Fort Erie, 1814* (Baltimore, 1992).

31. A.S. Everest, *The War of 1812 in the Champlain Valley* (Syracuse, 1981).

32. DRO. 152M/C1807/OF1.

33. H. Lydenberg (ed.), *Archibald Robertson. His Diaries and Sketches in America* (New York, 1930), pp. 36, 38.

34. PRO. WO. 1/141, pp. 31–35.

35. PRO. WO. 1/141, pp. 75–84; J. Whitehorne, *The Battle for Baltimore, 1814* (Baltimore, 1997); A.S. Pitch, *The Burning of Washington: The British Invasion of 1814* (Annapolis, 1998).

36. Valuable recent work on the war includes J.M. Hitsman, *The Incredible War of 1812: A Military History* (2nd edn., Toronto, 1999) and R.V. Barbuto, *Niagara 1814: America Invades Canada* (Lawrence, Kansas, 2000).

37. R.V. Remini, *The Battle of New Orleans. Andrew Jackson and America's First Military Victory* (London, 2001).

38. L.A. Norton, *Joshua Barney: Hero of the Revolution and 1812* (Annapolis, 2000).

39. A.T. Mahan, *Sea Power in its Relations to the War of 1812* (Boston, 1905); L. Maloney, "The War of 1812: What Role for Sea Power?" in K.J. Hagan (ed.), *The People's Navy: The Making of American Sea Power* (New York, 1991), pp. 46–62; R. Morriss, *Cockburn and the British Navy in Transition: Admiral Sir George Cockburn 1772–1853* (Exeter, 1997), pp. 83–120.

40. Bathurst to Sidmouth, 15 Sept. 1814, DRO. 152M/C1814/OF15.

41. F.L. Engleman, *The Peace of Christmas Eve* (New York, 1962).

42. DRO. 152M/C1814/OF11.

43. I. Fletcher, *The Waters of Oblivion. The British Invasion of the Rio de la Plata, 1806–1807* (Tunbridge Wells, 1991).

44. P. Mackesy, *Statesmen at War: The Strategy of Overthrow, 1798–99* (1974); G.C. Bond, *The Grand Expedition. The British Invasion of Holland in 1809* (Athens, Georgia, 1979).

45. PRO. WO. 1/141, p. 36.

46. J. Kimball, "The fog and friction of frontier war: the role of logistics in American offensive failure during the War of 1812," *Old Northwest*, 5 (1979–80), pp. 323–43.

47. DRO. 152M/C1807/OF1.

48. J.C.A. Stagg, *Mr. Madison's War: Politics, Diplomacy, and Warfare in the Early American Republic, 1783–1830* (Princeton, 1983); R.S. Quimby, *The U.S. Army in the War of 1812: An Operational and Command Study* (East Lansing, 1997); C.E. Skeen, *Citizen Soldiers in the War of 1812* (Lexington, 1999).

49. W.E. Weeks, *John Quincy Adams and American Global Empire* (Lexington, 1992).

50. F. Merk, *Albert Gallatin and the Oregon Problem: A Study in Anglo-American Diplomacy* (Cambridge, Mass., 1950); B. Gough, *The Royal Navy and the Northwest Coast of America, 1810–1914* (Vancouver, 1971), and *The Northwest Coast. British Navigation, Trade and Discoveries to 1812* (Vancouver, 1992); J.E. Dykstra, *The Shifting Balance of Power: American-British Diplomacy in North America, 1842–1848* (Lanham, 1999).

51. PRO. WO. 1/555, pp. 331–33.

52. PRO. WO. 1/555, pp. 17, 29, WO. 6/86, p. 287.

53. PRO. FO. 5/457 fols. 122–25.

54. PRO. WO. 6/86, pp. 300–301.

55. W.B. Skelton, "Officers and Politicians: The Origins of Army Politics in the United States before the Civil War," *Armed Forces and Society* 6 (Fall, 1979), pp. 34–35; W. Robinson, *American Forts: Architectural Form and Function* (Urbana, 1977); E.R. Lewis, *Seacoast Fortifications of the United States* (Annapolis, 1979); J.W. Moore, *The Fortifications Board 1816–1828 and the Definition of National Security* (Charleston, 1980); R.S. Browning, *Two If by Sea: The Development of American Coastal Defense Policy* (Westport, 1980); R.S. Gilmore, *Guarding America's Front Door. Harbor Forts in the Defense of New York City* (Brooklyn, 1983).

56. J.W. Silver, *Edmund Pendleton Gaines: Frontier General* (Baton Rouge, 1949), pp. 223–57.

57. J.E. Lewis, *American Union and the Problem of Neighbourhood: The United States and the Collapse of the Spanish Empire* (Chapel Hill, 1998).

58. Jefferson to Sir John Sinclair, 31 July 1816, DRO. 152M/C1816/OF30.

59. W.R. Thompson, "The Evolution of a Great Power Rivalry: The Anglo-American Case," in Thompson (ed.), *Great Power Rivalries* (Columbia, South Carolina, 1999), p. 218. See, more generally, K. Bourne, *Britain and the Balance of Power in North America, 1815–1908* (Berkeley, 1967).

60. D.C. Skaggs, "The Sixty Years' War for the Great Lakes: An Overview," in Skaggs and Nelson (eds.), *Sixty Years' War*, p. 18.

61. R.C. Stuart, *War and American Thought, from the Revolution to the Monroe Doctrine* (Kent, 1982) and *United States Expansionism and British North America, 1775–1871* (Chapel Hill, 1988); B. Perkins, *Castlereagh and Adams: England and the United States, 1812–1823* (Berkeley, 1964); J.M. Belohlavek, *'Let the Eagle Soar!': The Foreign Policy of Andrew Jackson* (Lincoln, 1985); D.M. Astolfi, *Foundations of Destiny: The Foreign Policy of the Jacksonians, 1824–1837* (New York, 1989); A.B. Corey, *The Crisis of 1830–1842 in Canadian-American Relations* (New Haven, 1941); H. Jones, *To the Webster-Ashburton Treaty: A Study in Anglo-American Relations, 1783–1843* (Chapel Hill, 1977); K.R. Stevens, *Border Diplomacy: The Carolina and McLeod Affairs in Anglo-American-Canadian Relations, 1837–1842* (Tuscaloosa, 1989); H. Jones and D. Rakestraw, *Prologue to Manifest Destiny: Anglo-American Relations in the 1840s* (Wilmington, Delaware, 1997).

62. S.W. Haynes, "Anglophobia and the Annexation of Texas. The Quest for National Security," in Haynes and C. Morris (eds.), *Manifest Destiny and Empire. American Antebellum Expansionism* (College Station, 1997), pp. 115–45; E.D. Adams, *British Interests and Activities in Texas* (Gloucester, 1963).

63. E.R. May, *The Making of the Monroe Doctrine* (Cambridge, Mass., 1975).

64. J. Glete, *Navies and Nations. Warships, Navies and State Building in Europe and America, 1500–1860* (Stockholm, 1993), p. 422.

65. B. Gough, *The Falkland Islands/Malvinas: The Contest for Empire in the South Atlantic* (1992).

66. G.K. Piehler, *Remembering War the American Way* (Washington, 1996), p. 36.

67. L. Langley, *Struggle for the American Mediterranean: United States-European Rivalry in the Gulf-Caribbean, 1776–1904* (Athens, 1969).

68. C.G. Calloway, "The End of an Era: British-Indian Relations in the Great Lakes Region after the War of 1812," *Michigan Historical Review*, 12 (1986), pp. 1–20. For Black Hawk, pp. 16–17.

69. R.C. Stuart, "Special Interests and National Authority in Foreign Policy:

American-British Provincial Links during the Embargo and the War of 1812," *Diplomatic History*, 8 (1984), pp. 311–28; J.M. Banner, *To the Hartford Convention: The Federalists and the Origins of Party Politics in Massachusetts* (New York, 1970).

70. T.P. Abernethy, *The Burr Conspiracy* (New York, 1954); J.J. Ripley, *Tarnished Warrior: Major-General James Wilkinson* (New York, 1933).

# 4

# American-Native Warfare

Disputes and conflict between Native and European Americans can be found throughout the period although their context varied, not least in terms of their relationship to tension between European Americans and European powers, particularly Britain. This chapter will offer a narrative of major episodes as well as considering the conflicts in the light of Western expansion elsewhere in the period. Similar factors affected this expansion for example in Argentina, Brazil and Russia. In one respect, expansion was less difficult in America as the environment was less hostile for Western activity and expansion. This may appear surprising in light of the difficulties that were present, including, to Americans, the unprecedented aridity of the southwest, and the height and extent of the Rockies, let alone the extent of the area of America to be controlled. However, compared to the cold of northeast Siberia or the forests of central Africa and Amazonia, or the hostile (to Westerners) disease environment in the Tropics, America was a relatively benign sphere for expansion, as was recognised in much of the narrative about exploration.

Furthermore, once American expansion had moved from preponderantly wooded terrain to lands covered with grass or sparse vegetation then it became easier to wage warfare with Native Americans. There was of course the problem of becoming familiar with a new environment, but the forested east of the country had provided more opportunities for Native ambush and had made it more difficult to use the superior numbers of the Americans. Operations frequently had to be mounted along tracks that could be blocked or ambushed. In contrast, further west it was easier to attempt coordinated advances, although these risked ambush in detail.

Initially the Native Americans had held their own during the War of Independence. Most had supported the British, who had tried, under the North America Act of 1763, to protect their lands from American expansion. This offered a parallel to the French Canadians in Québec most of whom also preferred British rule to American expansion. It is worth pointing out the extent to which the incorporating character of American society and ideology did not work for other inhabitants of North America. Instead, they experienced America as an imperial power and one that was not necessarily a particularly attractive one. Thus, the British in Canada and, subsequently, the government there had better, and certainly less violent, relations with their Native Americans than was the case in the United States. In the nineteenth century, although the British encountered problems with regional separatism in Canada, they did not lead to violence comparable to the American Civil War. This highlights the extent to which the success of political systems creates the context within which military tasks are set.

In the American War of Independence, the Natives were an important force who had already proved their mettle against the British in the widespread series of risings usually collectively referred to as Pontiac's War (1763–64). The Natives were well suited to fighting in the backcountry, an area in which the British military presence was sparse, and were trained in the use of arms and in operating in units. Native military potential was considerable given their hunter-warrior training and their not inconsiderable numbers, particularly in the South, especially in comparison to the backcountry whites. Native forces were militarily sophisticated. Their battlefield manoeuvring made expert use of flanking movements proceeding from the half-moon formation into which they flowed from files upon contact. These movements could be used for advance or retreat. Natives were adept at ambushes, feints and ruses.

Native Americans had adapted well to the weapons introduced by the Europeans, both the rifle, with its capacity for accurate, long-range fire, and the horse, which brought both operational and tactical mobility. The arrival of the horse had brought a far greater mobility, allowing the Natives in the Plains to follow herds of bison or deer for hundreds of miles, and the resulting improvement in diet led to a larger and healthier population. Bison drives required much organization and planning, and served as preparation for human conflict. As far as firepower was concerned, accurately-aimed fire and an astute use of cover were more important than the weapon which was used, whether bow and arrow or musket, although musket shot was less likely to be deflected by vegetation. Ammunition was generally obtained from Europeans. Although some Native peoples were able to repair muskets and even rifles, and, in the heyday of the musket, to mould musket balls as well, there was a continuing struggle with the problem of repair. This was an important aspect of the increasing dependence of Natives on Europeans for the tools of war. Much of their diplomacy revolved around this need, and the loss of the French and then the British as an imperial competitor was an essential factor undermining their resistance, not the shift in geography from the wooded eastlands to the Great Plains.

## THE AMERICAN WAR OF INDEPENDENCE

The independence that made the Natives the formidable warriors that they were, also made it difficult to control them in conjunction with regular forces. In addition, the Natives were divided and their politics often factionalized. There were numerous rivalries both between and within traditional groups, and this led to the splintering of war bands. Natives were also vulnerable to smallpox, which affected the Creek in 1779, uninterested in a defensive strategy involving garrison duty, and disinclined to abandon the winter hunt for campaigning. However, although the Natives were not always reliable allies, they were allies, and, allowing for different cultures and styles of fighting and so on, no more unreliable than most other allies.

The British were unsure about how best to use the Natives. In 1775, Gage ordered Guy Johnson and John Stuart, the Superintendents of the Northern and Southern Indian Departments, to obtain Native help, but Stuart saw the Natives as auxiliaries who should fight in conjunction with regular or Loyalist forces. A savage frontier war that included attacks on women and children might antagonize Loyalists. Indeed, the American Patriots made extensive propaganda use of the scalping of Jane McCrea by one of Burgoyne's Native scouts in 1777. The use of Natives was also criticized in Parliament, and British soldiers could think them cruel. Similar factors discouraged attempts to arm African Americans. It was argued that this would enrage white opinion in the South and the West Indies. Certainly the experience in Virginia, where the Earl of Dunmore did arm some blacks and this helped greatly to increase Revolutionary sentiment, was not encouraging.

Sensitivity to the use of non-white auxiliaries was a limitation in British capability that reflected the effects of operating in settlement colonies, as opposed to South Asia or West Africa where the European presence was substantially restricted to trading posts and, anyway, lacked any appreciable European presence unattached to imperial agencies. In the Americas, the colonial powers primarily supplemented regular troops with militia or volunteers raised among the settler population, and the latter was ambivalent about any extension of arms or military responsibilities to others. These attitudes were to be translated to independent America. There was a distinct ambivalence about, if not widespread hostility to, the recruitment of free blacks or Native Americans to regular or militia forces, and to the use of slaves and Natives in ancillary forces.

In the mid-1770s, the Cherokee were under pressure from illegal settlements, and, in 1776, rejecting Stuart's request to await the arrival of British troops, they attacked the Virginia and Carolina frontier. However, the isolated Cherokee were attacked by large militia forces and obliged to cede much of their territory.

Inexperienced Americans were given operational experience which would later prove to be beneficial. The Cherokee barely resisted the approaching columns. They, instead, largely abandoned their towns to be burned by the militia, disappeared into the mountains, and repeatedly returned once the militia had departed to cause sufficient trouble to provoke repeated militia incursions. This style of war had become a standard pattern, as Natives had come to appreciate that defending any given point against a large force was dangerous, and, instead, developed alternative strategies reliant on the likelihood that the militia would not remain for long. In turn, their opponents focused on destroying crops and shelter, which made life difficult for the Natives in the long run, and made them more likely to negotiate.

In 1777, British forces invading from Canada were assisted by Natives who were seen as important in controlling the backcountry. John Hayes wrote of the American garrison at Ticonderoga: "our savages will hem them in, in such a manner that they all must be taken."[1] They were, however, to prove a disappointment, although that owed much to their being poorly supplied and supervised. A force of Seneca and Mohawk warriors played the major role in ambushing American militia under General Herkimer sent to relieve Fort Stanwix, but their subsequent decision to decamp obliged the British to abandon the siege, and the warriors plundered and attacked British and Loyalist soldiers. The Natives at Bennington scattered when attacked by New England militia.

Most of the Natives fought on the British side and their attacks put a lot of pressure on the American backcountry, on, for example, the Pennsylvania-New York frontier in 1778. The defeat of the militia there by an Iroquois-Loyalist force under John Butler, in the "Wyoming Massacre," was followed by the devastation of the Wyoming valley, with some of the population scalped. American counter-attacks, by George Rogers Clark into the Illinois country in 1778 and 1779 against the Ohio country tribes, and by John Sullivan into western New York against the Iroquois in 1779, brought successes, such as Clark's capture of Vincennes in February 1779 and Sullivan's victory at Newtown in August 1779, but they were indecisive. Sullivan was affected by the logistical problems facing expeditions into the interior, especially a lack of transport. Nevertheless, thanks to careful reconnaissance, Sullivan's army was able to avoid ambush. There was no comparison to the failures of British advances at Saratoga and, in India, against the Marathas, at Wadgaon (1779), although the Natives were weaker.

The Natives maintained the pressure in New York, on the upper Ohio and in Kentucky until the end of the war. In December 1780, John Rutledge, the refugee Governor of South Carolina, wrote, "I am afraid the mischief lately committed by the Cherokee, in Rutherford County, will prevent our receiving aid from the backcountry, and lessen what we should have from the neighbouring [counties]."[2] The same month, Cornwallis noted that such action was being actively encouraged in order to prevent the frontiersmen from attacking the British.[3] In 1782, the Natives defeated the Americans in Kentucky.[4]

However, Natives were better at ambushes than at attacking fortified posts, and were vulnerable to attacks on their settlements, which presented targets for their opponents and could be battered by cannon. The Natives had very few cannon to use either for counter-battery fire in defence of their own positions, or to use against American fortified positions. The vulnerability of native positions can be seen in warfare with Western powers around the world, but it was not invariable. In New Zealand, the Maoris used well sited trench and *pā* (fort) systems that were difficult to bombard or storm. Attacks on them led to heavy British casualties, as in 1860, 1863 and 1864. Native Americans lacked an equivalent, although some, such as the Foxes, created fortifications with timber palisades and trenches. The Natives lacked the numbers to man any fortification system, and individual positions could, justifiably, be seen as traps. As a consequence, when American units approached Native positions, the Natives generally tried to attack them, rather than simply waiting on the defensive. This reflected cultural norms about conflict as well as a response to the balance of military capabilities. The Natives had abandoned their traditional fortification systems in the face of European siegecraft capabilities.

Frontier warfare posed particular logistical problems for both sides, as it was difficult to transport supplies and to obtain sufficient food locally. A projected American expedition to take Detroit, in order to blunt the Native threat, was agreed to in June 1778, but abandoned the following month as impracticable, Patrick Henry, Governor of Virginia, referring to "a scarcity of workmen and materials, the want of wagons, the exhausted state of this country, as to several articles called for, and the distressed situation of our people, resources and supplies." He also suggested that, whereas an attack on the hostile tribes near the frontiers would be useful, Detroit was too far: "a post will be difficult to maintain while the great intermediate country is occupied by hostile Indians, and from which it seems easy for the enemy to retreat with all their stores while they are superior upon the adjacent waters."[5]

Had the British been more successful in uniting and supporting the Natives, they could probably have put more pressure on the American frontiers and this might well have affected the operations of Washington's army, if not from strictly military necessity, then for political reasons. As it was, Native advances to German Flats and Cherry Valley in New York and Forty Fort in Pennsylvania, all in 1778, took them within striking distance of centres of American power, and, that year, two Continental regiments were sent to join the Western Department, which had been created in 1777. In 1779, Sullivan's army included three brigades of regulars. Had Native pressure been greater, it is probable that even more units would have been diverted. State governments kept up a continual pressure for assistance against Native attacks, and this acted as a counterweight to requests for help to the Continental army. Nevertheless, the Natives were distant from the principal theatres of operation; and not in a position to advance towards them. Furthermore, the cumulative pressure of sustained conflict damaged Native society and disrupted their economies. In 1779, Sullivan destroyed many villages and 160,000 bushels of corn, causing much suffering.[6] Such damage caused a great strain on the Native war-effort, in the short term, distracting warriors from operations, and in the longer term, making it difficult to sustain these operations.

## 1783–95

The Natives were not consulted in the peace settlement that closed the conflict, but it affected both important areas of settlement and the power context within which they operated. Instead of a territorial settlement restricting the Americans to what they had conquered, or a boundary line west from the northern boundary of New York, or another expedient, the British accepted a line-of-lakes boundary dividing all the Lakes (bar Michigan) down their centre. The cession of the "Old Northwest" (modern Illinois, Indiana, Michigan, Ohio, and Wisconsin), abandoned large numbers of Natives to American suzerainty, although the Natives did not accept the American view that they now ruled these lands by right of conquest and international treaty. Six thousand Natives, from the "Six Nations," who had been allies of the British, were dispossessed from their lands in western New York, and were provided with land along the Grand River, north of Lake Erie. Although the British were unwilling to hand over Detroit, Michilimackinac and Niagara to the Americans, the lessening of British support after American independence left Natives more vulnerable when the pace and pressure of American settlement accelerated. In 1783, treaties between Georgia and both the Cherokee and the Creek had defined boundary lines, but these could not restrain American expansionism.

The importance of foreign support was shown in 1786 when the Creek of Alabama and Mississippi used arms supplied by Spanish governors to check the Americans' westward advance from Georgia, and a new treaty was signed that November. The challenge this posed was noted by Beckwith in a report from New York on 7 April 1790:

The Creek Indians under the direction of [Alexander] Macgilivray have for some time attracted the attention of this government. They are both numerous and warlike, they derive advantages from their vicinity to the Spanish provinces, and their leader is a man of talent and ambition; irritated at the confiscation of his property, and influenced by the effects of an education in Great Britain, he looks forward to objects very unusual for Indians, and amongst others to the establishment of a port for European commerce . . . the Indians have been too powerful for Georgia, and the general [federal] government has been resorted to for assistance.

Beckwith added that this had led to unsuccessful negotiations with the Creek, followed by the decision to send troops, which he thought had three objectives:

The first is an Indian War; the second, the strengthening the general government of the Union, by an increase in the military establishment; and the last leads to the idea of possessing hereafter in the Western Territory, a force not only equal to overawe the neighbouring Indian tribes, but with such assistance as may be derived from the growing population and resources of that New World, the being in a condition to undertake offensive war.[7]

In fact, in 1790, the Americans had to concentrate on the Northwest and were in no position to mount a major expedition against the Creek, with whom they negotiated the Treaty of New York.[8] However, in 1795 (the treaty was implemented in 1796), Spain accepted the thirty-first parallel as the northern border of West Florida, opening the way for American penetration into the lands of the south-eastern tribes.[9]

The American War of Independence was followed by a major upsurge of American settlement, especially in Kentucky and Ohio, and by American political pressure, particularly in Ohio: in 1784–86, three treaties ceded much of southern and eastern Ohio to American settlement. This settlement was seen by most Americans as a rightful response to the God-given opportunities for expansion, and this expansion as a recompense for their struggle for independence. In July 1787, Congress passed the Northwest Ordinance. This not only reasserted American sovereignty over the region, but also made it clear that this sovereignty was to be the prelude to settlement. The Ordinance provided for the establishment of new states there and thus for an advancing frontier of settlement combined with a dynamic political structure. The Ordinance declared that Native rights would only be infringed "in just and lawful wars authorized by Congress," and that Native lands would only be acquired with their consent; a policy that was to be widely honored in the breach.

Henry Knox, Secretary at War 1785–89 and Secretary of War 1789–94, wanted to avoid a war, for which he, correctly, believed the tiny army to be unprepared. General Arthur St. Clair, a veteran of the Seven Years' War and the War of Independence, who in 1779 had served on Sullivan's expedition, was made Governor of the Northwest Territory (1787–1802), and was instructed to settle differences peacefully. However, his harsh and tactless approach to negotiating with Natives had the opposite effect.

Once the Natives had recovered from their demoralisation at British abandonment, they responded to the American pressure from 1786 with resistance. They were determined to protect their lands, lifestyle and fur trade from the Americans. Settler raids, in response, further exacerbated the situation, and discouraged the development of better relations with the Natives; relations which would have cut across the drift of two centuries of rivalry. Neutralist Natives, and federal governmental hopes of avoiding a full-scale war were undermined by the ambition and pace of the settlers. Violence flared in Kentucky and along the Ohio River. Relations deteriorated and, in 1790, full-scale war broke out. There was a similar problem in Brazil, with settlers exacerbating relations with natives, but, across much of the Western world, frontier policies were more under the control of the military and thus responsive to state direction.

Meanwhile, the few regular troops in the area (and indeed anywhere) had been unable to preserve order. Thus, in 1788, at Vincennes on the Wabash River, where a regular garrison had been established after fighting between Whites and Natives in 1786, Major Patrick Brown, a Kentucky Indian fighter arrived and began attacking Natives. The garrison commander, Major John Hamtramck, whose supply route had been attacked by Natives, ordered Brown to leave, but could not enforce the order as Brown had sixty men to Hamtramck's nine. In 1789, there were only 672 men in service, and only about 400 were to be available for the 1790 offensive. Congress voted to increase the regular army to 1,216 in 1790, but also cut pay in half to contain costs. This was not the best way to maintain effectiveness, and, specifically, to prevent desertion. Thus, reliance had to be placed on non-regular forces, which was, indeed, the intention of politicians unhappy about building up the regulars. In September 1789, Congress gave the President authority to call out the state militias to defend the frontiers. Their numbers were also required for any attack on the Natives.

The limited number of regulars also had implications for any policy of expansion by fortification: there were insufficient troops for any widespread garrison policy. Furthermore, garrisons could only work as part of an expansionist policy if they were accompanied by "pacification" of areas brought under control. If not, expansion simply brought the need for far more garrisons. Pacification, however, tended to be construed in terms of subjugation followed by re-settlement. This was a result of American ideology, as well as the drive to create space for settlement. As a consequence, there was no chance that the large sections of America still occupied by Natives would be conquered rapidly by a tiny number of Americans. The ratio of conquerors to conquered was far less favourable to the former in Latin America in the sixteenth century or India in 1750–1850, but in the latter two cases there was no policy of clearing natives from the land, and both areas were subjugated more rapidly. In Latin America, natives were required as the labour force, and in India, as with most European colonies in the Tropics, there was no social revolution at the level of the cultivator of the soil. In contrast, in the United States, although initially lacking the troops necessary for the conquest of the Natives, civilian settlement nevertheless continued, and assumed the form of scattered fortified settlements, or stations, until, eventually, either the white population overwhelmed the Natives, or a crisis sufficiently motivated the federal government to increase its own forces and conduct a regular campaign.

In 1790, the American attack on the Shawnee and Miami relied largely on Kentucky and Pennsylvania militia, neither of which matched the fighting quality of the Natives, who proved much better in both gaining surprise and in combat. Greater American activity was only partially matched by more signs of unity among the Natives. For long their disunity had provided opportunities for European powers and American settlers, or, looked at differently, the latter had contributed, especially through the supply of arms and ammunition, to rival Native interests. However, from the mid-eighteenth century, there was, if not initially much sign of unity, a growing disinclination to allow disunity to expose Natives to kill each other in the cause of European quarrels. Pontiac's War in 1763–64 had seen more wider-ranging Native unity than hitherto, and during the War of Independence there was again important signs of unity.

This offers a most tenuous connection with recent suggestions about conflict between Europeans (in this case the British) and natives in India. There, it has been argued, that, in place of an earlier teleological view predicated on the inevitability of British success due to better technology, it is, instead, possible to stress the growing Indian responsiveness to Western military techniques and thus the absence of any marked capability gap enjoyed by the British. To look back to North America, it can be suggested that the growing unity of the Native Americans lessened the capability gap enjoyed by the Americans, while the continued rivalry among the Western powers further created opportunities for native powers opposed to the United States, just as the possibility of French *revanche* after 1763 created opportunities for native powers opposed to Britain in India. Whereas, for 1760 until 1775 there had been no effective rivalry among the European powers in North America, the situation changed thereafter because the Americans failed to expel the British from Canada. Instead, Britain remained as an unpredictable presence that Natives could try to recruit.

In October 1790, Miami under Little Turtle twice successfully ambushed advancing American forces under Colonel Josiah Harmar. In each case, the militia fled while the regulars stood and fought hand-to-hand, only to be overwhelmed, with the loss of 183 men. That was the end of the campaign. The success of the Shawnee, Miami and other tribes marked most of Ohio off as impenetrable until American victory in 1794.

In 1790, Harmar was able to fall back on Fort Washington (now Cincinnati), which he had established in the spring of 1789. The combination of forts and the lack of Native capability for major offensives was a major advantage for the Americans. The Americans had suffered from underrating their opponents, and exaggerating their own capability, but were to get an opportunity to remedy these problems. Washington replaced Harmar as commander by St. Clair, and Harmar resigned from the army in 1792.

More than American command faults and Native skill were at issue. In addition, the Americans did not fight well. The absence of trained regulars was particularly serious. The regulars were not prepared for frontier warfare. Their preference for muskets which could bear bayonets, over the slower-firing rifles which could not, was inappropriate, as, in wooded terrain, it was accuracy not rate of fire that was important. Seeking to maximise their opportunity to deliver aimed fire and to minimise the target they offered, the Natives fought in open, not close, order; but the Americans lacked the confidence and training to do so, although when their troops held their order they did well. The problem was when they broke and ran. The militia also tended to lack relevant experience.

The militia's lack of enthusiasm for discipline made it difficult to compensate for a lack of experience with training.

Harmar's failure encouraged Native militants, and made it impossible to negotiate a settlement. This led the Americans to resolve on a greater effort, and also to plan a new policy, that of establishing a fort on the Maumee River in the centre of the opposing confederacy. Believing it necessary to outnumber the Natives, Knox planned to send 3,000 men. As a consequence the regular army's establishment was increased to 2,128. Although in percentage terms this was a major increase on the figure of effectives for 1789, it did not match that for any other major Western power, nor, indeed, for most minor ones. This was a powerful instance of American exceptionalism, as was the stress on militia that flowed from it. Furthermore, the decision to increase army size in response to conflict with a non-Western people/power was very different to the experience of other Western militaries.

Aside from the greater number of regulars, Knox also recruited 2,000 men for six months. This was a hybrid with the temporary soldiers of the militia, as these men were under regular command and discipline. However, as with the newly-raised regulars, they lacked relevant training and experience. As in 1790, the invasion force was to be supplemented by the Kentucky and Pennsylvania militia. Other militia forces were too distant and insufficiently committed. Beckwith reported in July, "The system adopted for the present Western campaign seems to have been to strengthen and increase the frontier posts, with regular infantry, and to make rapid incursions into the Indian country with bodies of horsemen: this plan appears to me to be every way judicious and perfectly conformable to the soundest military principles, as applying to a warfare of that nature."[10] In fact, St. Clair's army was poorly supplied, trained and led, and, fatally, over-confident. On 4 November 1791, at the side of the Wabash River, the Natives under Little Turtle surprised the poorly-prepared American camp. Unable to offer an effective response, with musketry, cannon or bayonet charges, to elusive Natives firing from cover, the Americans were badly shot up before abandoning their position, breaking out and fleeing in disorder with over 600 dead to the Native 21. As in 1790, Native tactical superiority was well demonstrated. Such a result, was a salutary reminder of the folly of assuming that Western formations and tactics were necessarily superior.

Victory boosted Native morale, militancy and unity. It also made the Natives more attractive allies for the British. The Americans tried negotiations with the Natives in 1793, but found an understandable lack of trust in their promises, and a determination among militant Natives to insist on the Ohio River as the boundary of American land purchases and settlement. This was unacceptable to the Americans, as it would have represented a reversal of land gains and settlement since the mid-1780s.

The failure of negotiation encouraged a pressing on in the revitalisation of the American military. In 1792, the government created the Legion of the United

States, which was intended to contain 5,190 men. It was placed under the command of Anthony Wayne, an experienced commander from the War of Independence, who had also had success in an expedition against the Creek and Cherokee in 1782. In March 1792, Wayne became both a Major-General and Commander-in-Chief of the army in the Northwest. Wayne was an effective trainer and for Wayne training meant preparation for combat, not the parade ground. He also was helped by the flexibility of the Legion's structure. It was divided into four sub-legions, each a self-contained unit containing dragoons, artillery, infantry and riflemen. As a microcosm, this offered the operational and tactical flexibility, specifically the combination of firepower and mobility, that the French were to use so effectively with their division and corp structures in the 1790s and 1800s.

Wayne was ready to attack in 1793, but was delayed by the government's determination to try to settle disputes with the Natives through a special commission. Its failure enabled Wayne to take the offensive in 1794. The Americans' advance benefited from serious divisions among their opponents, and from Wayne's determination to win the Intelligence conflict. This lessened the danger of surprise and provided valuable information about the Natives. Having advanced successfully, Wayne defeated the Natives at the battle of Fallen Timbers on 20 August 1794. Native fire defeated Wayne's vanguard, but the subsequent Native advance exposed them to attack. An American bayonet charge played a crucial role in this victory. The Natives, who had fasted before the battle, were malnourished, and, in part, taken by surprise. They were also affected by a withdrawal of British support. The Natives lost several leading chiefs, as well as confidence both in the British and in the struggle. As a result, peace became more attractive, and, by the Treaty of Greeneville of 3 August 1795, the Natives confirmed earlier cessions and made new ones.[11] In Jay's Treaty, the British agreed to evacuate Detroit, Michilimackinac and Niagara.

## 1795–1815

Victory helped encourage the forward drive of American expansion, demographic, economic and political.[12] Tennessee became a state in 1796, following Kentucky in 1792. Together, they represented a major westward expansion, and one that hampered links between the Natives of the northwest and those, such as the Creek, in the southeast. Ohio became a state in 1803, the year in which the Louisiana Purchase of lands from France led to an unprecedented westward extension of American sovereignty. The Greeneville boundary on White settlement rapidly became redundant as Native lands in Ohio, Indiana, Illinois and Michigan were purchased, particularly by the Treaty of Fort Wayne of 1809 which led to the acquisition of much of eastern and southern Indiana. The Natives were unable to mount a coherent response for several years, but, from 1805, Native ideas of resistance received new direction from a stress on spiritual revival and a widespread rejection of accommodation with the Americans. This was to lead to new conflict with the Americans, although many prominent Natives chose to remain neutral or to seek to maintain good relations.[13]

The American advance was consolidated by their victories in the 1810s over tribes with close ties to the British: the Shawnee at Tippecanoe, on 7 November 1811, and at the battle of the Thames, near London, Ontario, on 5 October 1813. Prior to the War of 1812, the British government denied instigating Native attacks on the Americans.[14] In so far as such encouragement occurred, it was a case of policy being set by officials on the ground, especially military commanders, rather than by the Foreign Secretary and the diplomatic system. The role of frontier disputes in relations with the United States provided the best example of the potential clash between formal diplomacy and other agencies of the British state. From the American perspective, the reality on the ground was a degree of co-operation between Britain and Natives that was a threat. As a consequence, defeating the Natives was, in part, to the Americans a way of hitting Britain, whether or not the two powers were at war.

At Tippecanoe, a force of 910 Indiana militia under Major-General William Henry Harrison, fought off an early morning attack by about 450 Natives under Tenskwatawa, the "Prophet," who had inspired the Shawnee to resist the Americans. He misled the Natives by promising them immunity to American musket fire. Harrison's robust defence exposed that claim, and, their morale falling and ammunition running out, the outnumbered Natives withdrew, allowing Harrison to claim a victory.

A very brief mention of Native-American conflict during the War of 1812 would focus on Tecumseh's defeat, but it is necessary to devote more space and to note the extent to which, prior to this defeat, the Natives had shown during the war both considerable military prowess and their value to the British, a value that was not always fully appreciated, although it both diverted American attention from the Lake Champlain corridor and gave the British important strategic possibilities. Natives played the major role in the capture of Fort Michilimackinac on 17 July 1812, and in inducing General William Hull to order the evacuation of the garrison of Fort Dearborn at Chicago. Fear of the impact of Native hostility destroyed the American position west of the Great Lakes. Aside from a collapse of confidence, there was a threat to supply routes. The American column retreating from Fort Dearborn was ambushed and destroyed. Increasingly anxious about ambush and massacre, especially after a supply column was ambushed at Brownstown, Hull lost mobility and then surrendered Detroit.

His successor, Harrison, was more robust, relieving Fort Wayne and attacking Native villages, but, in January 1813, another advance, by General James Winchester to the River Raisin, ended in disaster due to a surprise Anglo-Native attack exposing a lack of defensive preparations. On 5 May, an Anglo-Native force inflicted heavy casualties on Kentucky militia who attempted to relieve Fort Meigs (Maumee, Ohio). However, at the battle of the Thames, Tenskwatawa's brother, Tecumseh, the leading Shawnee warrior, who had tried to unite the Natives against the Americans, was killed. The Anglo-Native force was outnumbered by their militia opponents. The British troops under General Henry Procter were routed by Kentucky mounted riflemen, and the Natives were then surrounded and defeated: only 33 were killed, but there was no replacement for Tecumseh.[15] Like other battles of the period, American victory reflected an improvement in fighting quality. This was due to better training and tactical skill, and to a clearer understanding of Native techniques and their limitations.[16]

Nevertheless, further west, the balance of force was still against the Americans. Thus, Zachary Taylor's advance down the Mississippi in 1814 to assert government authority was blocked by a Native attack at Credit Island in September. William Clark, Governor of the Missouri Territory, had pressed the establishment of blockhouses and the construction of gunboats in the Mississippi and Missouri valleys, and led an expedition to Prairie du Chien, Wisconsin, where he constructed Fort Shelby in 1814; but he was subsequently obliged to withdraw.

The building of forts was important to the advance of American power. Thus, in 1813, Harrison built Forts Meigs and Stephenson (Fremont, Ohio) to stabilise the situation after Winchester was defeated at the River Raisin; in 1811, he had built Fort Harrison (Terre Haute) when he advanced against Tecumseh. Natives were unwilling to mount frontal assaults, and there were generally too few British regulars for the task; the British and, especially, the Natives also lacked heavy guns. Thus, in 1813, Forts Meigs and Stephenson successfully resisted attack.

Further south, the Creek were defeated at Tallasahatchee and Talladega on 3 and 9 November 1813 by Tennessee militia under John Coffee and Andrew Jackson respectively However, as the militia enlistments then expired, while the supply system had broken down, operations came to an end, and, in the winter, Jackson had to reorganise and resupply his force. This might sound like an indictment of the military system, but there were numerous instances during the Napoleonic Wars in which European supply systems broke down. Furthermore, there was always a problem with expiring enlistments when employing non-regulars. There were simply too few regulars to spare for defeating the Creek, and, therefore, it was necessary to rely on militia. Regulars were to be deployed in the southeast in greater numbers during the mid- and late 1830s, in order to fight the Seminole and to enforce resettlements, but, by that stage, the northwest was quiet.

In 1814, Jackson and a total force of 3,000 attacked the centres of Creek power and stormed their fortified camp at Horseshoe Bend on the Tallapoosa River (27 March). Far from relying solely on militia, Jackson benefited from the support of about 500 Cherokee and Creek. Cherokee and cavalry under Coffee attacked the Creek base from the rear, while Jackson mounted a frontal attack. He was astute not only in his tactics, especially his envelopment of Native forces, but also in his response to the topography and possibilities of particular battlefields. Eight hundred Natives, out of a force of 1,000 died, at

Horseshoe Bend, the largest Native number of fatalities in any battle with American forces. The war ended that August when Jackson imposed the Treaty of Fort Jackson. He had benefited from the debilitating Creek divisions into Lower/ White and Upper/Red towns, with the former siding for the most part with the American invaders. The Creeks were also greatly dependent on trade with the Americans. The relationship of military and civilian control in frontier areas was shown in 1821 when, after his successful invasion of Florida, Jackson resigned his commission as Major General in the regular army and, instead, became governor of Florida.

American victories in the early 1810s greatly weakened the Natives east of the Mississippi, especially in the Gulf Coast region, and helped ensure that the Americans encountered only localised resistance over the following decades. The Peace of Ghent reinstated the Natives of the "Old Northwest" to their position in 1811, but the intervening American victories had decisively altered the situation. Furthermore, the British settlement with the United States ended the prospect of foreign support. The British expedition sent to the Gulf of Mexico in 1814–15 had carried "a number of rifles, carbines, and an adequate quantity of ammunition for the purpose of arming the friendly Indians."[17] Vice Admiral Sir Alexander Cochrane had counted on support in the New Orleans expedition from "some thousand Indians and by their assistance after the fall of the city to drive the Americans out of Louisiana beyond the Spanish boundary."[18] There were to be no more such expeditions. This again exposed the fundamental Native weakness (once depopulation through disease is accounted for): although tactically adept, the Natives depended on European weaponry, and also on the rivalry between the non-Native powers that had been the case since the mid-sixteenth century.

It is too easy to assume that the narrative of expansion was restricted to that of America. Instead, in what was to become the modern United States, there was also activity by a number of European powers. North of Mexico, the Spaniards faced pressure from tribes on the Great Plains moving south, especially the Comanche and the Ute. Well mounted and armed with Western firearms, tribes such as the Apache were able to thwart the Spanish expedition sent against them in 1775. The following year, there were only 1,900 Spanish troops to defend an 1,800-mile frontier of Spanish North America. A successful Spanish attack on the Comanche in 1779 was followed by treaties with them in 1785–86. Peace was now the Spanish goal, and they used goods and trade to lure the Natives into their way of thinking. Once they were allied with the Comanche, the Spaniards pressed the Apache hard. In the 1790s, they persuaded many of them to settle on "peace establishments," the precursors of later reservations.[19] Further west, however, the successful Yuma rebellion in 1781 thwarted Spanish plans for expansion through the Colorado Valley and into central America.

Pressure on Natives was less intense on the Pacific littoral. As yet, the Americans, like the Europeans, focused on trade and were present in only limited numbers. The Pacific coast was remote from centres of power. Spanish advances in coastal California from 1769, Russian pressure in Alaska, and the American and British presence on the intervening coast, were completely or heavily dependent on sea links. As so often across the world in this period, these links could not be challenged effectively by non-Westerners. Western powers were able to apply direct military pressure from the sea; and, more significantly, to support their presence and to integrate it into global trading networks. This made the process of advance both possible and profitable, which was crucial to the Russian quest for furs in the Aleutian Isles, southern Alaska, and down the coast towards California. The Americans, however, were eventually to be far more effective.

## THE SEMINOLE WARS

American expansion came from landward rather than seaward frontiers. The process of rapid aggrandisement seen against the Creek in the south was then directed against the Seminole in Florida. They were not an ethnically coherent "tribe" but rather a group of Creek who had fled to Florida over the previous century as a result of feuding within the multi-ethnic Creek confederacy or to escape white encroachment, combined with escaped African-American slaves incorporated into the population. The Seminole were seen as a threat to the Georgia frontier, and, more generally, as a focus for chaos alongside America. Thus, escaped slaves fled south to Florida and their ability to remain with the Seminole greatly frustrated slaveholders.[20]

There was also a strong aggressive drive in American policy that can be seen more generally in this period and that in part reflected the strengthening of anti-Native attitudes as a consequence of the War of 1812 and the rise of politicians who had played a prominent role in the conflict.[21] In their operations against the Seminole, the Americans were hindered by the terrain, but helped by divisions among the Natives. In the First Seminole War (1817–18), Andrew Jackson was helped in his 1818 invasion by a force of Lower Creek. Jackson destroyed Seminole villages west of the Suwannee River and exposed the weakness of Spanish rule in Florida, capturing Pensacola on 24 May 1818, and St. Marks.

This led to the Spanish cession of the colony by the Adams-Onís or Transcontinental Treaty, agreed in 1819, approved by the King of Spain in 1820, and the ratifications finally exchanged in 1821. In return for East Florida, the American government had to surrender its claims to Texas and to satisfy American financial claims against the Spanish government up to $5 million. The treaty also settled the western boundaries of the Louisiana Purchase, and all this was accomplished without any reference to the Native American population. The Sabine, Red and Arkansas rivers became the agreed border as far as the 42nd parallel which was then to be the border until the Pacific. Combined with Spain dropping her claims to Oregon in favour of the USA, this treaty carried American sovereign pretensions to the Pacific in 1819–21.

The Seminole were the first Native group to be affected. The Moultrie Creek

Treaty of 1823 left the Seminole four million acres of poor land, but the reservation policy was unacceptable to them. They were not assimilationist like the Cherokee. In the early 1830s, the Seminole rejected the government's removal policy: the Removal Bill of 1830 and the Treaty of Paynes Landing.[22]

The Second Seminole War (1835–42) began when a number of Seminole chiefs agreed in 1835 to resist removal to Oklahoma. Although not a chief, Osceola, the son of an English father and a Creek mother, took a prominent role. He had been arrested by Wiley Thompson, a government Indian agent, for his refusal to sign the agreement to move. Released when he signed, he then renounced the agreement. On 28 December 1835, Osceola killed Thompson at Fort King, while, in the Wahoo swamp on the Whitlacoochie River, his war band began the Second Seminole War with a dramatic display of the vulnerability of regulars in unfamiliar terrain—108 regulars under Major Francis Dade were ambushed and all but three were killed.[23] This led to a panic among the settlers in which many fled to the towns or left Florida.

The Seminole war band was pursued by a larger force of regulars and volunteers, and, on 31 December at the Withlacochee River, this force clashed with Osceola. The battle was poorly handled by the American force, and it was defeated. Four soldiers were killed and fifty-nine wounded, as was Osceola. He was able to retreat into the swamp.

In the Second War, over 40,000 American troops were eventually deployed, especially after the Seminole, about 5,000 men at the strongest, won several battles in the initial stages. The numerical ratio of the two sides was different to that which generally prevailed in conflict between Western and non-Western forces and more favourable to the Americans. The ratio was different, for example, in West Africa, where the British had a force destroyed in Sierra Leone in 1824 or in Afghanistan where another was destroyed in 1842.

In Florida, a three-pronged encirclement planned by Winfield Scott in 1836 miscarried: it was not easy to apply the grand strategy of symmetrical warfare (conflict with those with similar arms and doctrine) in Florida. The Americans were affected by the great difficulties of fighting in the waterlogged and humid terrain, and were hampered by disease, a lack of supplies, poorly-trained troops, and the rivalries of officers, for example Gaines versus Scott. In addition, many officers were unhappy with the war's goals, and this led to a high rate of resignations. The Seminole generally avoided fighting in the open, and preferred guerrilla tactics. Scott thought that this would make the war perpetual. A system of forts provided an infrastructure for the American forces, but these forts could not prevent the Seminole from moving between them. The labour that led to forts and to the roads that linked them was symptomatic of a major characteristic of the Western military presence, its eagerness to build.

Losses led the Seminole chiefs Micanopy, Jumper and Alligator to agree an armistice in January 1837, and Osceola surrendered to the authorities in May. However, when the Americans allowed slavers to enter Florida and seize Seminole and Blacks, Osceola returned to the swamps, as did Micanopy's and

Jumper's followers. Osceola was captured in October 1837 during negotiations under a flag of truce. The Americans considered themselves justified in seizing Native leaders by this means. Imprisoned, he died of malaria in 1838. Osceola's loss was a major blow to Seminole resistance, as no other leader was able to get the Seminole bands to co-operate. The ability of Colonel Zachary Taylor to lure the Seminole to battle and defeat near Lake Okeechobee on 25 December 1837 was an encouraging sign for the army, although the Americans took 138 casualties out of their 800-strong force, a warning that was not adequately digested about the consequences of a frontal attack on well-prepared positions.

The Seminole speedily reverted to guerrilla conflict, forcing on the Americans a warfare of pursuit. They transformed the struggle in March 1838, when Major-General Thomas Jesup announced that Negroes who abandoned the Seminole and joined the Americans would become free. This cost the Seminole the co-operation of 400 Negro fighters. They, and captured Seminole, helped guide the small detachments increasingly used by the Americans to Seminole bases. The Americans were also increasingly effective in gaining operational mobility and in using the extensive waterways of the region. In the 1841 campaign, the Americans, under Brigadier-General William Worth, for the first time campaigned in the summer, a harsher environment (and one that modern readers, accustomed to air conditioning and motorised transport, find difficult to grasp), but one that stopped the Seminole from raising their crops, hitting their numbers. They eventually took shelter in the more inaccessible parts of the Everglades.

Worth saw little point in pursuing them. Having driven the small number of surviving Seminole to these refuges, where they were short of ammunition and food, the government wound down the war in June 1842, in part because the army commanders entrusted with the negotiations sought an end to the struggle. In September 1842, Lieutenant-Colonel Josiah Vose refused to resume operations against the Seminole, despite orders from the War Department. Indeed, Vose blamed local settlers, not the Seminole, for disturbances, by now an old refrain of the regular army officers operating in Florida. The Second War cost the Americans over 1,500 men (although only 383 died in action) and $20 million. Yet, it also showed that Natives could only preserve their independence in exceptional circumstances.[24]

The war can be paralleled elsewhere, for example in the Java War of 1825–30 in which the Dutch were initially thwarted by the mobility and guerrilla tactics of their opponents, but developed a network of fortified bases from which they sent out mobile columns.[25]

Although the government had removed most of the Seminole to Oklahoma, there had been no complete removal, and the surviving Seminole (about 350 strong) were involved in the Third Seminole War of 1855–58. This was touched off by settler pressure on the remaining Native preserve. The Seminole attacked an army camp on 20 December 1855 and fighting continued until 5 March 1857, with the U.S. government declaring the war officially over in May 1858. There were too few Seminole to prevail against the Americans, who relied on volunteers rather than regulars: the latter were largely deployed in the West, not least on the Mormon expedition. It was not possible to track down the Seminole, but, instead, money helped. In 1857, one of the leaders, Billy Bowlegs, agreed to leave with 165 followers in return for cash: the cause seemed lost to him. Only 120 Seminole were left.

## 1815–48

Elsewhere east of the Mississippi, the Native presence was dramatically lessened by the removal policy pursued from 1815,[26] and, more explicitly, from 1830, when the Indian Removal Act was passed. Natives lost their homelands in return for land west of the Mississippi, which, from 1834, meant the Louisiana Purchase minus Louisiana, Arkansas and Missouri. The Chickasaw, for example, signed a removal treaty in 1832.[27] This policy of separate development provided land for American settlers and also removed what was seen as an unwelcome alternative presence. The latter was important, as land itself was not the sole issue: much land remained unsettled, although it was now allocated to American owners.

The army was responsible for supervising the removal policy, and, if necessary, enforcing it. Force was employed against the Creek in 1836.[28] The Cherokee were moved in 1838–39, with about 4,000 out of 14,000 dying as a result of the hardship and disruption, now infamously known as the Trail of Tears. The Americans deployed 2,200 federal troops under Scott and close to 5,000 volunteers to achieve this. They did not need to suppress Cherokee resistance, but, instead, used force to overawe what was a fairly well-assimilated Native population. A number of senior officers complained bitterly about the harshness of the policy.[29] The Winnebago of Wisconsin, who had been "pacified"— brought under control—in 1827, in a military deployment known as the Winnebago War (there was no fighting), were moved by the army to Iowa in 1840, a key part of the process by which most of Wisconsin had been cleared of Natives by 1848 without any large-scale resistance. The policy of removal was typical of the way in which military tasks did not reflect a united public culture. Removal enjoyed less support in New England than in frontier regions and the South. It completed the total disruption of Native society, destroying any sense of identity with place.

The frontier of American control and settlement also moved west of the Mississippi. The War of 1812 had been followed in 1815–18 by a series of treaties that in effect curtailed Native independence and led to the American government as seeing itself as akin to a trustee. In military terms, this could be seen in occasional expeditions, and, more insistently, in the building of forts, such as Fort Jesup near Natchitoches in 1822, built by Zachary Taylor, and in the construction of roads. The posts evacuated by Britain after the War of 1812 were occupied, American forts lost in the conflict were rebuilt, and new forts were constructed to provide a chain from Lake Michigan to the Upper Mississippi

River. The government encouraged John Jacob Astor's fur-trading in order to reduce the British economic role in the region.

The Americans were not always successful. In 1819, Colonel Henry Atkinson's expedition up the Missouri towards the Yellowstone was cut short by supply problems, ill-health and Native hostility. However, in 1824–25, Atkinson did lead an expedition to the Yellowstone. The focus of American military activity moved west. There was more continuous military service along the Oregon and Santa Fé trails and in border areas, especially Kansas and Oklahoma. To take an individual career, Stephen Kearny, "the Pathfinder," in 1826 built Jefferson Barracks in St. Louis as a major military installation for the Great Plains (Atkinson chose the site), negotiated the Treaty of Prairie du Chien of 1830, which strengthened the American position in Wisconsin, and did the same in Oklahoma where he commanded at Fort Touson in 1831–32, constructed a road from Fort Leavenworth to the Arkansas River in 1837, intervened in Native rivalries in 1838–40, and led an expedition to Wyoming and Colorado in 1845. Most of such activity, for example the expedition in 1834 into Comanche and Pawnee country, was peaceful, but it also reflected the American willingness to deploy and use force. Missouri became a state in 1821, followed by Arkansas (1836), Michigan (1837), Florida (1845), Iowa (1846), and Wisconsin (1848).[30]

From the Native perspective, there was no doubt of the pressure of American advance and aggression, which included the campaign of 1823 against the Arikaras and that of 1827 against the Winnebagos, but the Americans had a capacity to fear Natives, or at least to employ such fears in order to justify action. In December 1830, the British envoy reported: "It appears that the Indians upon the Southwestern and Northwestern borders of the United States, excited the fears of the government during the last year, which required detachments of troops to be sent to those points."[31]

There was scant need for American concern. The defeat of Black Hawk and his band of 1,000–2,000 Sauk and Fox in the Black Hawk War by regulars and Illinois militia under Atkinson, now a Brigadier-General, in Illinois and Wisconsin in 1832 reflected the vulnerability of tribes east of the Mississippi especially when they received no assistance. After the War of 1812, in which many had fought the Americans, the tribes had returned to peace although increasingly troubled by American settlers. A treaty of 1804 in which lands in Illinois had been yielded for settlement was a particular cause of dispute, as the federal government regarded it as valid, while the Sauk who had signed it had not been authorised to do so: this was a typical problem in the treaty process. Like the British earlier, the Americans required leaders in order to validate treaties and thus agree land transfer, but the resulting moulding of native politics was frequently divisive.

The Sauk divided, with one leader, Keokuk, ready to migrate west of the Mississippi, while the older Black Hawk, who had fought in the War of 1812, was keen to retain traditional lands. This division, which was a common one in tribes confronted with American expansion, interacted with the wider context within which the Sauk had to operate. The tribe had moved to Iowa in 1831, but about 1,000–2,000, under Black Hawk, recrossed the Mississippi on 5 April 1832 in the face of the hostility of the Sioux there and after a harsh winter. In an echo of earlier rivalries, those who looked to Black Hawk (not all of whom were Sauk) were known as the British Band: Black Hawk had seen himself as linked to Britain as much as America and visited Fort Simcoe in Canada on a number of occasions after the War of 1812.

Once in Illinois, the Natives moved up the Rock River Valley, hoping to live in peace and be able to cultivate crops. However, although Atkinson accurately reported Black Hawk's peaceful intentions, the Governor of Illinois, John Reynolds, saw the episode as an invasion and called out over 1,200 mounted militia. Bereft of support from the local Natives and aware of the hostile governmental response, Black Hawk decided to return to Ohio. However, when, on 14 May, his band tried to parley with militia, they were attacked by the fearful militia who did not understand Sauk. This began the conflict, which was reported within America in terms of Native aggression, the British envoy noting on 20 June, "several tribes of hostile Indians have lately committed great atrocities upon the inhabitants of the Western part of the state of Illinois."[32] In the "battle" of Stillman's Run, the pursuing militia were then ambushed in the Sauk encampment. Black Hawk's band fled into Wisconsin where they were eventually tracked down. The pursuers were delayed at the battle of Wisconsin Heights (21 July), but, when they reached the Mississippi on 1 August, their passage was blocked by a steamship. Next day, Black Hawk was crushingly defeated at the mouth of the Bad Axe River: women and children were killed as well as men.

Andrew Jackson's impatience with Atkinson led him to send Winfield Scott to lead up American reinforcements and assume command, but Scott was delayed because his force was affected by cholera. Scott, nevertheless was able to help negotiate the Treaty of Fort Armstrong with the tribes: the Sauk and Fox ceded six million acres of their best land for a small sum. Once captured, Black Hawk was imprisoned and then sent to the eastern seaboard to see American power, before being returned to Iowa where he died in 1838. Captain Abraham Lincoln and Lieutenant Jefferson Davis both took part in the campaign.[33]

After the war, the army's force structure was changed with the introduction of mounted regiments in 1833 and 1836. There had been none since the War of 1812, and this change reflected the experience of the Black Hawk War, and, more generally, the need to adapt both to greater distances and to the advance beyond wooded terrain into the Plains. Mounted forces were both a response to the Natives and permitted a lower density in fortifications than would otherwise have been necessary, although cavalry was more expensive. Another infantry regiment was added in 1838 when tense relations with Britain accentuated the manpower implications of the Second Seminole War. However, in the 1830s, strategy focused on the idea of an essentially stable frontier rather than on supporting farflung expansion.

Newly-independent Texas was more exposed to Native raids than other frontier areas, and, in turn, sought to enforce its control over the Natives. This led to campaigns against the Plains Natives. In August 1840, the Great Comanche Raid was ended at the battle of Plum Creek. Further east, the Texans faced opposition from rebellious Natives and Mexicans near Nacogdoches in 1838.

## 1848–61

The situation changed greatly in scale in 1848 when success in the Mexican War left the American state in control of very extensive new territories in which about 150,000 Natives dominated, while the pace of overland emigration to the West, not least to California (where gold was discovered in 1849), increased greatly. The transfer of control was initially ignored by much of the Native population, but it was not unwelcome to all who were aware of it. At Santa Rita del Cobre in 1846, Mangas Coloradas and other Apache leaders met Kearny, swore allegiance to the United States, and offered to help against Mexico. Kearny met no Native opposition on his march to the Pacific. Others were less content and saw no reason why their profitable raiding of settlements should cease just because Mexico was no longer the sovereign power. This attitude threatened the stability of American rule in its new conquests. It had been suggested by the British envoy in Mexico, in 1846, that the Mexican population of New Mexico would back American rule, as the Americans could provide a protection against Native attack that the Mexican government had failed to do.[34] This led, in 1849, to a punitive expedition against the Navajo by Lieutenant-Colonel John M. Washington in which artillery was used with considerable effect against Navajo villages in the Canyon de Chelly. In 1851, Colonel Edwin W. Vose Sumner, commander of the Department of New Mexico 1851–53, had to campaign against the Navajo, although Sumner doubted the value of controlling the barren territory. In 1854, the Jicarilla Apache were defeated; in 1854–55, the homelands of the Mescalero Apache were invaded; and, in 1855, the Ute were quelled.[35] Treaties signed at Fort Thorn in 1855 helped reduce tension in the region. A Mojave rebellion was ended in 1857.

The government tried to lessen disputes by moving the Indian Bureau with its responsibility for relations with the Natives from the War to the Home Department in 1849. However, after the Mexican War, white settlers began to enter the territories in substantial numbers. As a result, the army found itself forced to take up armed constabulary duties in the 1850s on an hitherto unprecedented scale. By the Treaty of Fort Laramie in 1851, Arapaho, Cheyenne, Crow and Sioux chiefs agreed to restrict their hunting grounds to designated lands, and also not to hinder the Oregon Trail, and the government provided annuities. This attempt to keep the peace was, however, not an adequate response to the pace of American migration and the nature of American activity. In particular, the migrant depredations on the bisons that the Natives relied upon for food was a real threat to the livelihood of the latter. The Natives had no real alternative to the bisons. In Oregon, there was pressure from settlers to move the Natives from the valleys of the western Cascades to eastern Oregon and to that end the Williamette Valley Treaties were negotiated in 1851.

There was conflict on the Plains, and in both the Northwest and Southwest, for example conflict with the Cheyenne, Comanche and Kiowa in west Texas, and, further west, against the Apache in 1859. The Comanche were also defeated that year, but conflict continued. Some operations were brutal. The Plains Indian Wars were touched off by American aggression in the Grattan Massacre near Fort Laramie on 19 August 1854, in which Conquering Bear, the Sioux leader, was killed.[36] General William Harney refused to take male Brulé Sioux as prisoners in 1855 and permitted the killing of their women and children. Harney killed Chief Little Thunder at the battle of Blue Water Creek on 3 September 1855. The Sioux submitted the following spring.[37] In response both to more difficult opponents, and to a sense that Manifest Destiny required that the Natives be driven from the land, far more violence was used against women and children after 1848 than in earlier conflict, and there was also a greater willingness to massacre Natives.

The fame of opponents, especially the Apache, Cheyenne, Comanche and Sioux, ensures that some wars are well known. Others, such as the Rogue River uprising in southwestern Oregon in 1855–56, and the Spokane war in 1858, are far less well known. They were touched off by the pressures of American settlement and the policy of forcing tribes into reservations in Oregon and Washington. Native hopes of British assistance were ended when the Hudson Bay Company sent arms and ammunition to the Americans. The Natives in the region benefited from their skill in fighting from cover and from their knowledge of the terrain, but they were disunited. Converging columns of regulars and expeditions of volunteers led to the Native surrender that ended the Rogue River uprising, while in 1858 the tactical skill of Colonel George Wright and the superior capabilities of the new 1855 Springfield .58 calibre rifled muskets brought victory in the Battles of Four Lakes and Spokane River.[38]

Further south, the Native population of California was brutally reduced in the 1850s by conflict as well as disease. The federal army did not control the situation there: instead, local volunteer forces inflicted great damage.[39] They were in a position to do so there, as the American population in California rose greatly in the 1850s, while the Natives lacked unity or a strong military tradition.

The net effect for the army of the gains in 1848 was a policy of dispersal, as the new territories, which were further enlarged by the Gadsden Purchase of 1853 from Mexico, were secured by forts. There was no equivalent enlargement of the army to reflect the lands gained, but, instead, a transfer of forces from east of the Mississippi. New commands, such as the Departments of the Pacific and of Texas, reflected this new military reach.[40]

Throughout the course of American expansion, the Natives suffered from a lack of unity. The Plains Natives were not tribes but bands, although various groups could be fitted under a general designation, such as Sioux or Comanche, which was linguistic rather than organizational. From mid-century, the Natives also suffered from the replacement of the weak presence of Mexican control (and the accommodating views of the British in the Oregon Territory), by the more insistent territorial demands and military activity of the burgeoning American state. Lack of unity was fairly typical of Native resistance to Western expansion, as seen, for example, with the response to the British in India and to the Russians in Central Asia. In Australia, Aborigine resistance was affected by the very fragmented nature of the Aboriginal "nation," which greatly lessened the prospect of co-operation. When Tecumseh travelled to the southeast in 1811, he won support from Creek militants, the Red Sticks, but found scant backing among other Creek, or among Cherokee, Chickasaw or Choctaw. Old rivalries played a role in preventing unity, but so also did different strategies in coping with American pressure: the Cherokee were particularly keen on accommodation. Indeed, in 1831, they appealed unsuccessfully to the Supreme Court for support against oppressive acts by agents of the state of Georgia.[41] Earlier, the Shawnee had been divided between support for Tecumseh and an accommodationist party led by Black Hoof and William Anderson that sought to adapt to American interests and values. This led to tension among the Shawnee (and other tribes) and, at the battle of the Thames, there were more Shawnee with the American army than with Tecumseh.

There was more, however, at stake than lack of unity; instead, there was active and long-standing rivalry between Natives.[42] In the Black Hawk War, Black Hawk did not receive help from most of the Sauk and Fox, nor from the Pótawatomi and Winnebago, and, once the survivors of his band had recrossed the Mississippi, they were attacked by their Sioux enemy. On the northern and central plains, the Lakota Sioux, allied to the Cheyenne and Arapaho, used the mobility given by their embracing of a nomadic horse culture to dominate, and, at times, brutalise sedentary, agricultural tribes such as the Pawnee and Arikara, who had the horse but had not become nomadic. This encouraged many of the latter to look to the Americans. Their willingness to do so emphasises the degree to which any discussion of relations in terms of conflict alone would be incomplete. Military, political, economic, cultural and religious ties crossed American/ Native divides, turning them into zones of interaction in which symbiosis, synergy and exchange occurred alongside and, often, instead of conflict and war.

Much of the violence also involved an important measure of collaboration between Americans and Natives. In the Plains Indians Wars, which began in 1854, Crow, and Pawnee cooperated with the Americans against the Lakota Sioux. The Ute, Crow and Pawnee provided the army with scouts. After the Civil War, Nelson Miles used Crow assistance when he attacked the Sioux and northern Cheyenne after Custer's defeat at Little Bighorn. Such cooperation was a major element in Western expansion as a whole, and was particularly important when the Western population was sparse.

Nevertheless, it was the demographic weight of the European-Americans that was crucial, combined with their willingness to migrate and force their way into regions already settled by Native Americans. Rapid American population growth led to significant levels of migration within America. The railway played a major role, not only in speeding American troops, but also in developing economic links between coastal and hinterland America and integrating the frontiers of settlement with the exigencies of the world economy. This was important both in the spread of ranching, with the cattle being driven to railheads, and of mining. Steamships also aided integration. They were important on the great rivers, in the Gulf of Mexico and, especially, on the Pacific coast.

As elsewhere with expansion by Western powers, their advances were in part expressed through the building of forts. These could be bypassed by Native raiders, but they were difficult to take. The forts helped to control communication routes and were a solid sign of American power. Thus, the annexation of Texas and the Mexican War were followed by a major extension of the federal fortification imprint. This was not just a matter of random building. Instead, the forts reflected a series of politico-strategic objectives. Thus, the peace treaty with Mexico included an obligation on the Americans to prevent Native Americans raiding Mexico from the newly-annexed lands. This encouraged a series of border fortifications that also served to define the border and to mark a federal presence there, including Camp Ringgold at Rio Grande City (1848), Fort Bliss at El Paso (1848), Fort Duncan near Eagle Pass (1849), and Fort Drum at Zapata (1852).

Forts were also built along the edge of settlement in order to protect it from Native attack. Thus, the war was followed in Texas by the establishment under General George Brooke of Fort Worth (1849), Fort Graham (1849), Fort Gates (1849), Fort Croghan (1849), Fort Martin Scott (1848), Fort Lincoln (1849) and Fort Inge (1849). Westward moves of the line of settlement led to new forts, and to the closure of many earlier ones. Thus, in Texas in the early 1850s, new forts included Merrill (1850), Belknap (1851), Chadbourne (1852), McKavett (1852), Terrett (1852), Ewell (1852) and Clark (1852). There were also camps such as Joseph E. Johnston (1852) and Elizabeth (1853). A double line of forts was seen as the best way to deter Native raids. However, strategic thinking developed in favour of using forts as a base for offensive campaigns against Native homelands.[43] The general desire to control the Native Americans led to the construction of forts in west Texas, for example Davis (1854), Lancaster (1855), Quitman (1858) and Stockton (1859).

Forts were also built further north. The Santa Fé Trail was guarded by Forts Atkinson (1850) and Union (1851). In Minnesota, Fort Snelling, the first American fort, built in 1819, was followed in 1848 by Fort Marcy (renamed Fort Ripley in 1850), which was designed to establish government authority and, in particular, to keep the Winnebago peaceful. In the 1850s, the American presence in Minnesota was consolidated by a network of roads which were surveyed and built through the War Department. The onward movement of the frontier of concern led to the foundation in 1853 of Fort Ridgely on the Sioux reservation on the upper Minnesota River, and in 1856 to an expedition to the Red River

Valley in Minnesota and the establishment of Fort Abercrombie. Fort Ripley was evacuated in 1857, although that led the Chippewa to an outbreak of violence, which caused the reoccupation of the post. The Chippewa lands in northern Minnesota had been opened to settlement in 1855 and the Winnebago had again been moved that year. The fort was not finally abandoned until 1877.[44]

The establishment of garrisons in forts met the needs of settlers for reassurance, but the War Department preferred to see troops concentrated in large forces, which was seen as the best way to maintain discipline and training, and also to intimidate opponents. There was a tension between military and political interests.[45] A comparison of the distribution of regulars in 1843, 1850, and 1860 showed a movement of troops into garrisons beyond the Mississippi and, by 1860, the end of most garrisons on the Canadian border, on the Atlantic coast, in Florida and in the Mississippi valley. This process was accentuated in the 1850s as more garrisons were established in the West.[46] The cost of supplying these distant posts were heavy. Fortification was always a preferred option for dealing with frontier instability and conflict, but only the increasing wealth of the United States in the nineteenth century permitted it. In contrast, in the eighteenth and early nineteenth century, such extensive fortifications had not been possible.

## THE COMPARATIVE DIMENSION

As elsewhere with Western expansion, for example the British in New Zealand in the 1860s and early 1870s, forts had to be complemented with mobile units. Thus, in the Algerian War, the French had to break with their established methods, those of Napoleonic conflict, namely mass manoeuvre and the holding of territory by posts creating a front, and, instead, in the 1840s, emphasise a more fluid strategy, in order to deal with an elusive opponent who only risked battle in the harsh terrain when it suited them. Many posts were abandoned in order to free troops for a more aggressive strategy in which rapidly moving columns and cavalry units attacked the Algerians, threatening their agricultural base. The *razzia* (raid) became a devastating instrument designed to terrorize the population. It depended on fast-moving columns and threw much responsibility onto unit commanders. Jefferson Davis, the Secretary of War, looked to French strategy in Algeria in his annual report for 1856.[47]

Unlike the Americans, however, the French were present in overwhelming force. By 1846, they had 108,000 effectives, in Algeria, a number that was possible because of the large size of their regular army. Western forces elsewhere in Africa were far smaller. As in North America, an ability to adapt to local conditions and to devise specialized tactics was important.

A sense of mission was important in the spread of American power. Expansion was normative. This drew on triumphalism, racialism and cultural arrogance. All supported a belief, especially seen from the 1840s, that America was unbeatable and was bringing civilization to the Natives and to the West. Divine purpose, natural right, geographical predestination, the appropriate use of natural resources, and the extension of the area of freedom and culture all apparently combined. These cultural politics encouraged commitment, as well as persistence in the face of adversity, while success appeared to vindicate the policy of expansion.[48] Demographic advantage, a sense of mission, and divisions among opponents interacted to ensure an American advantage both in the contact zone and more generally.

Unlike in much of the world, however, the American advance was within areas whose sovereignty had already been ceded to America. There was not the need to advance and fight in order to gain sovereignty that can be seen for example in European expansion in Africa in this period. This made it easier for the Americans to achieve their goals of conquest at their own pace and without a major mobilisation of strength. At this stage, the Americans did not need to go overseas in order to fulfil their conception of their national purpose and make conquests. Instead, America's national and imperial boundaries coincided, helping encourage Americans to believe that their empire building was different to that of Europeans. This was further encouraged by the thinly settled nature of the West. In addition, once the Natives were exposed to diseases endemic in "white" society many of them died. Thus, the Americans faced no resistance from a large and resilient population comparable to that encountered by the French in Algeria or the Russians in Central Asia.

Furthermore, unlike in Africa and South Asia, where rivalry acted as a prompt for expansion, there was little danger from competing Western powers and no need to pre-empt them. The British were not seeking to press south from Oregon into California, let alone trying to reverse American sovereignty in areas gained in 1803. The allocation of the future territory of the United States between powers that recognised each other's sovereignty was complete by 1820. The cartographic and other knowledge that permitted such allocation greatly helped American power.

The situation worked both ways. Success against Native Americans transformed the wider geo-strategic situation. There was no longer need to fear the Anglo-Native axis, and therefore it was possible to take a different attitude to Britain's position in Canada, one that more closely moved to the rhythm of Anglo-American relations. Similarly, there was far less danger that Mexico would be able to undermine America's position. Once the two nations got over the hostility stemming from the Mexican War, Mexico rendered the United States considerable assistance in overcoming the Apache. Had Britain remained an ally of important Native tribes and been willing to provide them with support, then it is likely that there would have been far more pressure within America to annex Canada. A failure to settle differences with the Natives would have encouraged a search for scapegoats and solutions, and Canada would have provided both.

There are examples of Western assistance helping non-Western powers resist expansionism by Western rivals. The Ethiopians used French and Russian weaponry to help defeat the Italians at Adowa in 1896, the Japanese drew on British naval expertise to shatter the Russian fleet in 1905, and German advisers helped the Turks defeat the British, Australians, New Zealanders and French at Gallipoli in 1915. However, all these instances were of non-Western states with considerable forces at their disposal. The Native Americans were not in the same position. As a consequence, foreign assistance could not have achieved much. The Natives did not need foreign advisors but rather more manpower and a greater degree of co-operation. Neither was on offer from Canada.

## DURING AND AFTER THE CIVIL WAR

Most regular troops were withdrawn from the West during the American Civil War. They were replaced by local volunteers who reacted very violently to Native American actions, and continued their tradition of being far less able to keep the peace than regulars. The situation was particularly tense in Colorado. Pressure on Native lands had risen in 1858–59 as gold finds west of Denver led to a surge in immigration. Pressure on Native lands led to the Treaty of Fort Wise in 1861 by which the Arapaho and the Cheyenne gave up much of their land. However, many members of the tribe did not accept the treaty and violence between them and settlers led to an increasingly tense situation. In June 1864, the Governor of the Colorado Territory, John Evans, instructed "friendly Indians" to present themselves at military posts, but also prepared a military response. In August, Evans was given governmental permission to raise the Third Colorado Cavalry, a regiment of hundred-day volunteers that was to be commanded by Colonel John Civington, the head of the Army military district in Colorado. Native chiefs sought to negotiate a settlement and thought they had done so with Evans and Chivington at Camp Weld on 28 September. As a consequence, Arapaho and Cheyenne moved to Fort Lyon in accordance with Evans' proclamation of June and what they believed to be the Camp Weld agreement. However, Evans was preparing to destroy the tribes. At dawn on 29 November, Chivington's men attacked the Native encampment killing many both there and a mile further on where the fleeing Natives adopted a defensive position only to be bombarded by twelve-pounder mountain howitzer guns. In the Sand Creek Massacre, at least 150 and maybe about 200 Natives, mainly women, children and the elderly, were slaughtered. Ten soldiers were killed. Chivington's men were applauded in Denver, but the episode was swiftly condemned in Washington. This massacre helped to touch off a major bout of fighting across the Plains.[49]

There had already been serious fighting further north. The Minnesota rising of 1862 also affected the Dakota Territory, and again was a response to the pace of settlement. Eastern Sioux attacked American settlements in Minnesota, although they failed to capture the forts, while other Sioux attacked Americans crossing their lands on the Bozeman Trail en route to gold workings in Montana. The American army responded by driving the Eastern Sioux back from Minnesota, and then, during the summers of 1863, 1864 and 1865, launching columns under Brigadier Generals Henry Sibley and Alfred Sully against the Sioux in Dakota and Montana. Sully beat Sioux opponents at Whitestone Hill on 3 September 1863 and defeated Sitting Bull at Killdeer Mountain, North Dakota, on 28 July 1864.

Further south, plans for a winter campaign against the Navajo in 1860–61 had been abandoned due to the gathering political crisis. However, federal columns forced the Navajo to agree to move to reservations in 1864. That is a bland description of the use of scorched earth policies and of the subsequent forced march of the Navajo, and their confinement in the bleak reservation of Bosque Redondo. In Texas, the Confederates were not able to protect their Western settlements, and an outnumbered ranger force was routed by Kickapoo at Dove Creek in January 1865. In contrast, California troops defeated Shoshone in Idaho and Ute in Utah in 1863. That year, treaties were negotiated with Native tribes in California and Oregon. It is possible that attacks on Natives during the war were in part inspired by rumours of Native support for the Confederacy. There was indeed some support, and a number of treaties were signed, although in each of the Five Civilized Tribes loyalists also rallied to the Union and fought for it.[50]

The pace of expansion at the expense of Natives was to resume after the disruption of the Civil War, not because the war-engorged regular army sought a new challenge, but, instead, because of the demographic, economic, cultural and political pressures driving expansion. The war had badly disrupted the continuity in army experience of fighting Natives. Many commanders from the 1850s were dead or had lost their commissions by serving the Confederacy, although it is important not to exaggerate the Civil War hiatus. The notion that it was the Civil War veterans, for example Sherman and Sheridan, who inaugurated an exterminationist approach to Plains warfare has been hard hit. General Harney before the war and General Carleton during the war both advocated and practised to the best of their ability wiping out their Native enemies. This was also when the useful tactic of winter campaigning got its start.

Trained in, and from, the Civil War, with its emphasis on commanding and fighting large numbers of regulars, their replacements were not adept at dealing with the very mobile Native Americans, although Custer did defeat the Plains tribes at the Washita River in 1868, Crook forced some of the Arizona Apache to surrender in 1871–73, and Ranald Mackenzie won successive victories, against the Comanche at Palo Duro Canyon (1874) and over Dull Knife's Cheyenne at Crazy Woman Creek (1876).

The sharp reduction of the army in the aftermath of the Civil War, ensured that there were few troops available for frontier warfare. When Philip Sheridan took command of the Department of the Missouri, which covered much of the frontier, in 1867 he had only 6,000 troops. It proved difficult to force the mobile Native Americans to battle: they knew the terrain and were adept at surprise. The Sioux showed this in 1866 in their successful campaigning against the army in Montana and Wyoming in the Bozeman Trail War (also known as Red Cloud's War).

As a consequence, the army developed techniques that focused on winter campaigning, and the coordination of independently-operating columns advancing from different directions. The former were used in late 1868 in attacks in north Texas, the latter, successfully, in the Red River War of 1874–75 with the Southern Cheyenne. Native American villages were attacked, their crops and food stores destroyed, and their horses seized, which crippled their mobility. Settlements were particularly vulnerable in the winter as those who escaped risked starvation and death by exposure. The killing of bison was seen as a way to weaken the Natives. Mackenzie destroyed Native camps at both Palo Duro Canyon and at Crazy Woman Creek. Similarly, in 1876, Crook destroyed the Sioux village at Slim Buttes, while, the following year, Miles destroyed Crazy Horse's village at Wolf Mountains.

The totality of such methods can be compared to the devastation of parts of the Confederacy in 1864–65, but the wholesale destruction and persecution of the Native Americans was further justified by depicting them as pagan savages. The shortage of troops and the precedent of the assault on enemy civilian life in the Civil War, encouraged a preference for quick and brutal campaigns, directed at crippling resources and maintaining the tempo of attack. In the Nez Percé War of 1877, pursuing federal cavalry were defeated at White Bird Canyon (17 June), Clearwater (11–12 July), Big Hole River (9–10 August) and Canyon Creek (13 September), but ultimately a far larger force under Miles forced the surrounded Nez Percé to surrender at Eagle Rock (5 October).[51]

The American focus on mounted troops was not shared by all Western powers, but it was necessary in order to track down the mobile Natives of the West. In contrast, most imperial forces pursued mobility through light infantry with only light artillery support. This was seen with French campaigns in West Africa in the 1850s and 1860s, and also in rapidly-moving British columns. Subsavanna Africa was not suitable for cavalry. In battle, Western forces tended to rely on massed formations that provided controlled fire-power. Volley firing, hollow squares and close-packed lines were all employed. These were far less appropriate in North America.

From the 1840s, the Americans were no longer interested in pushing the Native Americans back. They now sought total control of the whole of America, a situation that matched the trend throughout the West. Thus, in Argentina, native peoples were brutally subjugated in the "Conquest of the Desert" and then of Patagonia. In America, after 1877, there were still problems with Native Americans, especially the Apache, but Native American resistance had been largely broken and a successful military methodology had been evolved. Its focus on wrecking civil society, or rather on the notion that there was no civil sphere separate to the military, had been seen in the latter stages of the American Civil War. In the West, this system was made especially effective thanks to the mobility of the regulars and their ability, through a good logistical service, to stage winter campaigns. This showed the potential of the American army to adapt its military style and methods and to develop an appropriate action-reaction routine, an ability already shown for example by Wayne and Jackson, and in the latter stages of the Second Seminole War.

## NOTES

1. Nottingham, University Library, Mellish papers, 172–111/4.

2. Rutledge to Sumter, 16 Dec. 1780, Library of Congress, Manuscript Division, Sumter papers.

3. PRO. 30/11/72 fol. 71.

4. Valuable accounts include J.R. Alden, *John Stuart and the Southern Colonial Frontier* (Ann Arbor, 1944); B. Graymont, *The Iroquois and the American Revolution* (Syracuse, 1972); J.H. O'Donnell, *Southern Indians in the American Revolution* (Knoxville, 1973); J.M. Sosin, *The Revolutionary Frontier, 1763–1783* (New York, 1974); M.D. Green, "The Creek Confederacy in the American Revolution: Cautious Participants," in W.S. Coker and R.R. Rea (eds.), *Anglo-Spanish Confrontation on the Gulf Coast during the American Revolution* (Pensacola, 1982); I. Kelsay, *Joseph Brant, 1743–1807: Man of Two Worlds* (Syracuse, 1984).

5. *Madison Papers* I, 249–50.

6. J.R. Fischer, *A Well-Executed Failure: The Sullivan Campaign against the Iroquois, July-September 1779* (Columbia, South Carolina, 1997); M. Mintz, *Seeds of Empire: The American Revolutionary Conquest of the Iroquois* (New York, 1999).

7. PRO. FO. 4/12 fols. 1–2.

8. J.L. Wright, "Creek-American Treaty of 1790: Alexander McGillivray and the Diplomacy of the Old Southwest," *Georgia Historical Quarterly*, 51 (1967), pp. 379–400. See, more generally, C. Saunt, *A New Order of Things: Property, Power, and the Transformation of the Creek Indians, 1733–1816* (New York, 1999).

9. A.P. Whitaker, *The Spanish-American Frontier, 1783–1795: the Westward Movement and the Spanish retreat in the Mississippi River Valley* (Lincoln, 1969).

10. PRO. FO. 4/12 fol. 150.

11. W. Sword, *President Washington's Indian War: The Struggle for the Old Northwest, 1790–1795* (Norman, Oklahoma, 1985); P.D. Nelson, *Anthony Wayne: Soldier of the Early Republic* (Bloomington, 1985); H.L. Carter, *The Life and Times of Little Turtle: First Sagamore of the Wabash* (Urbana, 1987); R.S. Allen, *His Majesty's Indian Allies: British Indian Policy in the Defence of Canada, 1774–1815* (Toronto, 1992); R.D. Hurt, *The Ohio Frontier: Crucible of the Old Northwest, 1720–1830* (Bloomington, 1996); L.L. Nelson, *A Man of Distinction Among Them: Alexander McKee and British-Indian Affairs along the Ohio County Frontier, 1754–1799* (Kent, Ohio, 1999).

12. M.J. Rohrbough, *The Trans-Appalachian Frontier: People, Societies, and Institutions, 1775–1850* (New York, 1978).

13. R. White, *The Middle Ground: Indians, Empires, and Republics in the Great Lakes Region, 1650–1815* (New York, 1991); G.E. Dowd, *A Spirited Resistance: The North American Indian Struggle for Unity, 1745–1815* (Baltimore, 1992); J. Sugden, *Tecumseh: A Life* (New York, 1997).

14. BL. Add. 49990 fols. 59–60.

15. S. Antal, *A Wampum Denied: Procter's War of 1812* (Lansing, 1997).

16. A. Starkey, *European and Native American Warfare 1675–1815* (1998), pp. 159–63.

17. PRO. WO. 1/141, p. 21.

18. PRO. WO. 1/141, p. 67.

19. E.A.H. John, "Nurturing the Peace: Spanish-Comanche cooperation in the early nineteenth century," *New Mexico Historical Review*, 59 (1984), pp. 345–69; W. Griffen, *Apaches at War and Peace: The Janos Presidio, 1750–1858* (Albuquerque, 1988).

20. J.D. Milligan, "Slave rebelliousness and the Florida Maroon," *Prologue*, 6 (Spring 1974), pp. 4–18.

21. D.S. Heidler, "The Politics of National Aggression: Congress and the First Seminole War," *Journal of the Early Republic*, 13 (1993), pp. 501–30; D.C. Skaggs, "The Sixty Years' War for the Great Lakes: An Overview," in Skaggs and L.L. Nelson (eds.), *The Sixty Years' War for the Great Lakes, 1754–1814* (East Lansing, 2001), p. 17.

22. J.K. Mahon, "The Treaty of Moultrie Creek, 1823," *Florida Historical Quarterly*, 40 (1962), pp. 350–72.

23. M.F. Boyd, "Florida aflame: background and onset of the Seminole War, 1835," *Florida Historical Quarterly*, 30 (July 1951), pp. 1–115; F. Laumer, *Dade's Last Command* (Gainesville, 1995).

24. J.K. Mahon, *History of the Second Seminole War* (Gainesville, 1967); G.E. Buker, *Swamp Sailors: Riverine Warfare in the Everglades, 1835–1842* (Gainesville, 1975); S. Watson, " 'This Thankless . . . Unholy War." Army Officers and Civil-Military Relations in the Second Seminole War in P.D. Dillard and R.L. Hall (eds.), *The Southern Albatross. Race and Ethnicity in the American South* (Macon, Georgia, 1999), pp. 9–49.

25. M.C. Ricklefs, *A History of Modern Indonesia since c. 1300* (2nd edn., 1993), p. 117.

26. R. Horsman, *The Origins of Indian Removal, 1815–1824* (East Lansing, 1970).

27. R.N. Satz, *American Indian Policy in the Jacksonian Era* (Lincoln, 1975); M.P. Rogin, *Fathers and Children: Andrew Jackson and the Subjugation of the American Indian* (New York, 1975); R.V. Remini, "Indian Removal," in Remini, *The Legacy of Andrew Jackson: Essays on Democracy, Indian Removal, and Slavery* (Baton Rouge, 1988), pp. 45–82.

28. J.A. Campbell, "The Creek War of 1836," *Transactions of the Alabama Historical Society*, 3 (1899), pp. 162–66.

29. W.G. McLoughlin, *Cherokee Renascence in the New Republic* (Princeton, 1968); J.L. Wright Jr., *Creek and Seminoles: Destruction and Regeneration of the Muscogulge People* (Lincoln, 1986).

30. G. Foreman, *Advancing the Frontier, 1830–1860* (Norman, 1933).

31. BL. Add. 49964 fol. 11.

32. BL. Add. 49964 fol. 49.

33. J. Lambert, "The Black Hawk War: a military analysis," *Journal of the Illinois State Historical Society*, 32 (1939), pp. 442–473; R.L. Nichols, "The Battle of Bad Axe: General Atkinson's Report," and "The Black Hawk War in Retrospect," A.F.C. Wallace, "Prelude to Disaster: the Course of Indian-White Relations which Led to the Black Hawk War of 1832," *Wisconsin Magazine of History*, 50 (1966), pp. 54–58, and 65 (1982), pp. 239–288; J.W. Silver, *Edmund Pendleton Gaines: Frontier General* (Baton Rouge, 1949); Nichols, *Black Hawk and the Warrior's Path* (Arlington Heights, 1992); P.J. Jung, "The Black Hawk War Reconsidered: A New Interpretation of its Causes and Consequences," *Journal of the Indian Wars*, 1, 2 (1999), pp. 31–69.

34. BL. Add. 49968 fol. 177.

35. L.R. Bailey, *The Long Walk: A History of the Navajo Wars, 1846–68* (Los Angeles, 1964); F. McNitt, *Navajo Wars: Military Campaigns; Slave Raids and Reprisals* (Albuquerque, 1992); F.D. Reeve, "The Government and the Navaho, 1846–1858," *New Mexico Historical Review*, 14 (1939), pp. 92–114.

36. P. Hedren, *The Massacre of Lieutenant Grattan and his Command by Indians* (Glendale, 1983).

37. R.L. Clow, "Mad Bear: William S. Harney and the Sioux Expedition of 1855–56," *Nebraska History*, 61 (summer 1980), pp. 133–51; R. Mattison, "The Harney Expedition against the Sioux: The Journal of Capt. John B.S. Todd," *Nebraska History*, 43 (1962), pp. 89–130; G.R. Adams, *General William S. Harney: Prince of Dragoons* (Lincoln, 2001).

38. R.C. Clark, "Military History of Oregon, 1849–1859", *Oregon Historical Quarterly*, 36 (1935), pp. 14–59; W.N. Bischoff, "Yakima campaign of 1856," *Mid-America*, 31 (1949), pp. 162–208, and "Yakima Indian War, 1855–1856: a problem in research," *Pacific Northwest Quarterly*, 41 (1950), pp. 162–69; R.I. Burns, "Pere Joset's account of the Indian War of 1858," *Pacific Northwest Quarterly*, 38 (1947), pp. 285–314; F.P. Prucha, *Broadax and Bayonet: The Role of the United States Army in the Development of the Northwest, 1815–1860* (Madison, Wisconsin, 1953).

39. W.H. Ellison, "The Federal Indian policy in California, 1849–1860," *Mississippi Valley Historical Review*, 9 (1922), pp. 37–67.

40. R.M. Utley, *Frontiersmen in Blue: The United States Army and the Indian, 1848–1865* (New York, 1967).

41. BL. Add. 49964 fol. 17.

42. A. McGinnis, *Counting Coup and Cutting Horses: Intertribal Warfare on the Great Plains, 1738–1889* (Evergreen, Colorado, 1990).

43. See also, G.D. Harmon, "The United States Indian policy in Texas, 1846–60," *Mississippi Valley Historical Review*, 17 (1930), pp. 377–403, and R. Wooster, "Military Strategy in the Southwest, 1848–1860," *Military History of Texas and the Southwest*, 15, 2 (1979), pp. 5–15.

44. F.P. Prucha, "Fort Ripley: The Post and the Military Reservation," *Minnesota History*, 28 (1947), pp. 205–24.

45. Prucha, "The Settler and the Army in Frontier Minnesota," *Minnesota History*, 29 (1948), p. 233.

46. See the maps in Prucha, "Distribution of Regular Army Troops before the Civil War," *Military Affairs*, 16 (1952), pp. 172–73.

47. Wooster, "Strategy," p. 10.

48. F. Merk, *Manifest Destiny and Mission in American History* (New York, 1963); A. Stephanson, *Manifest Destiny: American Expansionism and the Empire of Right* (New York, 1995); S.W. Haynes and C. Morris (eds.), *Manifest Destiny and Empire. American Antebellum Expansionism* (College Station, 1997).

49. S. Hoig, *The Sand Creek Massacre* (Norman, 1961); E. West, *The Contested Plains: Indians, Goldseekers, and the Rush to Colorado* (Lawrence, 1998); C. Whitacre, "The Search for the Site of the Sand Creek Massacre," *Prologue*, 33 (2001), 96–107.

50. V. Deloria and R.J. DeMallie, *Documents of American Indian Diplomacy. Treaties, Agreements, and Conventions, 1775–1979* (2 vols., Norman, 1999), I, 587.

51. W.H. Leckie, *The Military Conquest of the South Plains* (Norman, Oklahoma, 1963); S.L.A. Marshall, *Crimsoned Prairie: the Wars Between the United States and the*

*Plains Indians during the Winning of the West* (New York, 1972); R.M. Utley, *Frontier Regulars: The United States Army and the Indian, 1866–1891* (New York, 1973); P.A. Hutton, *Phil Sheridan and His Army* (Lincoln, Nebraska, 1985); J.A. Greene, *Yellowstone Command: Colonel Nelson A. Miles and the Great Sioux War, 1876–1877* (Lincoln, Nebraska, 1991); R. Wooster, *Nelson A. Miles and the Twilight of the Frontier Army* (Lincoln, Nebraska, 1993) and "Expansion and the Plains Indian Wars" in *Encyclopedia of the American Military*; P.R. DeMontravel, *A Hero to His Fighting Men: Nelson A. Miles, 1839–1925* (Kent, Ohio, 1998).

# 5

# Mexican-American Wars

It is a frequent maxim that armies prepare for the last war. Such an assessment indicates the perennial attraction for commentators of being wise in hindsight, but also captures not so much the military shortsightedness that is its apparent target, but rather the difficulties of predicting tasks and the problems of preparing for multiple tasking. In 1815, it would have been very surprising to plan for the next major war to be with Mexico, a state that was not even then independent; while the Spanish empire from which it was to gain independence was still recovering from French occupation.

## DEVELOPMENTS, 1815–45

The 1812 war was followed by post-war demobilisation, with the army cut from its official authorised size of 62,674 men (troop strength was actually lower),[1] but there was a determination not to return to the pre-war situation. The core of the wartime staff system was retained, with a new reform leadership instigating new procedures for efficiency and accountability, and there was a *de facto* acceptance of the regular army as the true first line of land defence.

The 1812 war had left a conviction that America required a stronger military, but no clear target for this force other than the Native Americans. The major challenges of 1814 and 1815 had been defensive ones and the pressure for an improved military from 1815 focused on defensive forces—on land and sea, with the former to include a stronger peacetime army and a programme of fortification. This was not simply a matter of greater funds to support a larger military, although, on 3 March 1815, Congress voted to reduce the army from its wartime level to a new establishment of 12,383 officers and men (as opposed to the 3,284 in 1807), and in 1816 voted $1 million per annum for eight years to construct a navy including nine 74-gun ships of the line.

There were also attempts at administrative improvement in order to enhance America's military capability, including the creation in 1813 of an administrative General Staff, although, initially, it was too decentralised and disunited to provide coherent administrative oversight. The staff was further enhanced in 1816 and 1818. Structures were created, and systems improved. The net result was a network of permanent administrative bureaus in Washington.[2] This was a powerful advance in federal administrative control, and an important aspect of the degree to which the War of 1812 had led to the professionalisation of the army. A centralized command system followed in 1821. John C. Calhoun, who became Secretary of War in 1817, was determined to reform the army in order to make both its administration and its command structure more effective. Military leaders wished to avoid any repetition of the failures of 1812–13 and to create an effective peacetime force that could serve as the kernel for a successful wartime army.

These promising moves approximated to the developments in European armies that had been defeated by Napoleon, especially Prussia, as they prepared for the warfare that overthrew him in 1813–15; although there is also the important context of postwar American nationalism and a more general attempt at state-supported improvement.[3] The Bonus Act of 1817, backed by Calhoun and Henry Clay, provided for federal money for canals and roads, which would help economic and military capability.

However, just as the European military developments proved difficult to sustain, and indeed less appropriate to the peacetime period that began in 1815, so the American military reforms ran into difficulties. In part these reflected the difficulties of creating an effective organisational structure, not least because of tensions between the position of Secretary of War and that of Commanding General, a post designated in 1821, and because of tensions within the staff and between it and line officers.[4]

During the early national period, effective means emerged for maintaining civil control—not only in the Constitution, but also in the ongoing arrangements of military administration. There was a parallel (much commented on throughout the nineteenth century) between the American and British methods of civil control: the division of control under the President between the Secretary of War and the Commanding General was similar to the situation in Britain, although the President had more effective power than the British monarch. In the United States, the command system produced constant friction until the adoption of the General Staff in 1903.

Aside from problems within the military after the War of 1812, there was also a less benign public attitude as the impact of war wore off, and a severe financial crisis in 1819. These led to pressure for retrenchment, a move opposed by all the generals. Calhoun faced this in December 1820 by suggesting an

Expandable Army Plan designed to cut the number of privates while retaining officers and non-commissioned officers in order to keep an experienced cadre that could serve as the basis for rapid wartime expansion. Determined to save money, the House rejected the scheme, although its impact can be seen in the approval of a somewhat diluted version of it in the eventual Senate compromise, which became law in March 1821. Congress cut the size of the army to 6,126 and also halved the naval construction budget.[5]

There was no apparent need for a large army. Whereas the Austrians crushed liberal uprisings in Naples and Piedmont in 1821 and in central Italy in 1830, the French did likewise in Spain in 1823, and the Russians in Poland in 1831, and the Dutch failed to do the same in Belgium in 1830 and 1831, the American military lacked any comparable task. At the same time, European governments, like the American, preferred long-service regulars rather than large numbers of conscripts in this period. Rather than seeking large numbers of untrained conscripts, the cannon-fodder of big formations, European commanders preferred experienced men. They were of value for formalized battlefields, and for more irregular operations. Furthermore, in Europe, long-service regulars were seen as more politically reliable.

It would be mistaken to consider the 1820s simply in terms of missed opportunities, for there were also important post-war attempts to improve military effectiveness that were sustained in this period. The most significant was that of enhanced military education, again a tendency that the United States shared with Europe. West Point was revived and flourished from 1817 when Sylvanus Thayer became superintendent. Although West Point overwhelmingly remained an academy that focused on engineering, Thayer made an effort to introduce French military learning, and benefited from the energy and ability of one of his professors, Dennis Hart Mahan. Mahan's work explicitly looked to Napoleon, rather than searching for a uniquely American theory of war, although there was very little what is now termed doctrine taught or discussed. Mahan's biweekly meetings to discuss strategic issues were only open to a small portion of the West Point class. Again this, and the role of Napoleon, were similar to the situation throughout the West. Winfield Scott's drill regulations of 1834 drew heavily on their French counterparts of 1831.

None of this was of any help to those campaigning against Native Americans, but that goal enjoyed little backing among the officer corps. They tended to think of their role in terms of battle. There were also attempts to create institutions to take military education further. The Artillery School of Practice was founded at Fortress Monroe in 1824 and the Infantry School of Practice at Jefferson Barracks in 1827. However, in part due to the extent of commitments in the 1830s, this thrust was not sustained and the schools were cut short, the Artillery one closing in 1835.[6] Furthermore, no staff college was created.

This might suggest a limited professionalisation, but it is more pertinent to argue that its institutional basis was precarious. This was true throughout the West, but in America there was the added factor of a strong emphasis on the citizen-soldier and a concern about the possible elitist consequences of professionalisation. This led to criticism of West Point, but, in part, this was a product of its success as a focus of professional education and military coherence. The officer corps was increasingly peopled by West Point graduates. The percentage in the officer corps rose from 14.8 in 1817 to 63.8 in 1830 and 75.8 in 1860.[7]

As a consequence, the impact of national politics, which had been so important in the first three decades of the army, slackened. In its place came a measure of institutional cohesion bred of shared education, long-service, professionalisation, and institutional development. This did not end the influence of national political alignments, but it ensured that factions within the military became more important. So also did an image of the military as a distinct culture with values that were different to those of civilian society. In military terms, this accentuated hostility towards citizen-soldiers.[8]

The latter continued to play a role in political rhetoric and public culture; but in practice both the War of 1812 and the social consequences of a developing economy much of which was removed from the advancing frontier led to a decline in the militia.

In its place came a volunteer militia movement in which volunteer units enabled citizen-soldiers to affirm solidarity and sociability through soldiering. This, however, was not the basis of American military strength. Regulars had clearly replaced militia in this function as a consequence of the War of 1812, and the volunteer units were recognisably secondary to the regulars. They were also particularly strong in New England and New York, which were far distant from the frontier of conflict. Nevertheless, the numbers offered by the volunteer militia was such that any major conflict would oblige their use alongside regulars. Thus, in the Second Seminole War, 30,000 volunteer militia served alongside 10,000 regulars.

Such a remark provides no clue to the animosity that could characterise relations between regulars and volunteer militia, nor to the extent to which this animosity in part reflected differences about American society. In Florida, regulars complained about the military value and cost of the volunteer militia, who represented and symbolised a more general lack of control by the regulars seen for example in the difficulty they found in implementing War Department instructions to protect the Seminole during truces. The progress of the war was accompanied by mutual complaints about conduct in the face of the enemy. Thus, in 1838, after the battle of Okeechobee, there was angry controversy about the respective conduct of the regulars and volunteers in the engagement. The regulars, not least Colonel Zachary Taylor, bitterly criticized the courage of the volunteers, especially those from Missouri, and claimed that it was the regulars who had done the actual fighting. More generally, regulars were critical of the volunteers for a lack of discipline, subordination, and cohesion. This criticism can be located in a wider context with a stress on regulars seen as a sign of military modernisation after 1815. The French shifted to an emphasis on a smaller, professional army, a focus that also matched that of the British army.

Hostility to the regulars was especially pronounced among Democrats who saw the army, more specifically the officer corps, as redolent of class values and of a professionalism that was self-seeking and incompatible with democratic citizenship, and also as inappropriate for conflict with the Natives who stood in the way of a populist conception of America's Manifest Destiny. In 1828, there was an attempt to abolish the post of Commanding General that, in part, reflected hostility to the standing army, but the Bill died in the Senate. Economic problems in the early 1840s led to renewed political pressure for cuts in the army.[9]

To a certain extent, attacks by Democrats said far more about the critics than the officers, but the criticism also captured an important tension within the protean force that was American society. The army, a federal body, was seen as metropolitan and European-looking, rather than really American, with the latter understood in populist terms. To a certain extent, this was ironic, as many officers and soldiers had more experience of the frontier than their critics; although some older commanders, such as Brigadier-General Edmund Gaines in 1839, were unhappy about officers who had gained a patina of professionalism through studying French works, rather than the true knowledge of combat.[10]

In a wider context, tension over the role of the military was symptomatic of the difficulty of defining a non-political identity for the army in a republican society: to dispense with monarchy and create a citizen army did not solve problems of goals and images. The regulars pressed for a larger army in order to be able to have the operational coherence that the volunteers and militia challenged. Such an army would also bring promotion, and that in a force whose career options had been very badly affected by the demobilisation that followed the War of 1812. The number of commissioned officers under the reduction of the army voted by Congress in March 1815 fell from 3,495 to 674, and this included only eight generals and thirty-eight field officers in the line branches.[11] Many officers had been reduced in rank and the reduction of the army in 1821 brought further demotions. Thereafter, career prospects, in both army and navy, had been limited, a situation exacerbated by the absence of a retirement system in the army until 1861: officers stayed in their posts until they resigned or died. Thus, Farragut (1801–70) was appointed a naval midshipman in December 1810 but did not become a commander until 1841, and did not gain a squadron command until 1861. Such a situation increased tension.[12] In functional terms, a reliance on volunteers thus ensured that the regular army could not develop as a large force capable of handling substantial bodies of men. Senior officers lacked the relevant command experience, and this was to have a major impact in strategic, operational and tactical terms during the Civil War.

However, valuable experience was provided by the War of 1812 and the Mexican War. They were each obviously very different to the Civil War, not least in scale, but they did provide experience of the problems of command. Many leading commanders of the 1820s and 1830s had served in the War of 1812, most obviously Jacob Jennings Brown, who in 1821 became the first Commanding General of the Army, a post he held, despite his interest in land speculation and politics and although he was sickly, until his death in 1828, as well as Alexander Macomb, Brown's successor, and, after his death in 1841, Winfield Scott, who held the post until 1861. Service in 1813–14, first in the winter encampment at French Mills and then in the Niagara campaign was important in the formation of the leadership of the postwar army and in the postwar drive for administrative improvement.[13] At a more junior level, the army also benefited from the presence of many veterans. Similarly, in other Western armies, veterans of the Napoleonic Wars held command positions into mid-century. Wellington was Commander-in-Chief in 1827 and from 1842 until his death in 1852, when he was succeeded by a former aide-de-camp, Lord Raglan, who had lost an arm at the battle of Waterloo.

In practice, the contrast with other armies in the West focused not so much on the small size of the regular army—eleven line regiments after the 1821 reorganisation—as in its peripheral interest to government. Furthermore, the use of volunteers as a reserve, rather than the system of trained reservists that the Prussians in particular were to develop, weakened the army as the command ethos and practice in the American reserves did not correspond to that of the regulars; a significant difference to the situation in Prussia. Training volunteers who were capable of acting alongside regulars was an obvious response to this problem, and there were suggestions from regular officers in 1838–39 that back-woodsmen, who were used to difficult terrain, be enlisted as light infantry under regular officers; but they were not followed through. Such a scheme would have dramatically weakened the volunteer militia principle and practice.

An obvious sign of tension was the unwillingness of regular officers to accept orders from higher-ranking volunteers. When, in November 1836, Governor Richard Call of Florida was made the local military commander against the Seminole, there was public criticism from regular officers as Call was a civilian without army or militia rank and could not therefore be held to account by a court-martial. Jackson rapidly replaced Call, but tension in Florida between governors and regular officers continued.[14] The Second Seminole War also saw political tensions about America's goals, not least opposition among the northern Whigs to the removal policy towards Natives. This was linked to the concern with expansion in the South among opponents of slavery. During the war, opponents of slavery in Congress tried to cut military appropriations on several occasions. At the same time, individual careers bridged regular and militia forces. Brown and Jackson, the only two major generals retained in the Regular Army in 1815 had a militia background. Robert Patterson, who commanded Pennsylvania militia forces in the Buckshot War of 1838–39 that followed a disputed state election, and was a Major-General of volunteers in the Mexican War and again, for the Union, in 1861, had been first a militia officer (1812–13) and then a captain in the regulars (1813–15) in the War of 1812.

In 1846, the common militia's term of service was extended to six months, but this was inadequate for war with Mexico, let alone the fact that the militia was not supposed to serve abroad. Instead, the Mexican War was fought by an expanded regular army, whose authorised strength was doubled in May 1846, and further increased in February 1847, and by the summoning of 70,000 volunteer militia. This itself created problems of fighting quality and organization. The latter culminated with the removal of Major-General Edmund Gaines from his command by court-martial (in which he was acquitted) for raising volunteers without permission; although Gaines in part suffered because of his longstanding feud with Scott over seniority.

## THE TEXAN REBELLION, 1835–36

The Mexican-American war of note was that of 1846–48, but the successful Texan rebellion of 1835–36 was an important prelude. It can only loosely be described as a Mexican-American war, as it involved conflict between Texans, not Americans, and the government of Mexico (indeed some of the Texans were of Hispanic origin), and led to the creation of an independent state—the Lone Star Republic. Nevertheless, the rebellion was also crucial to American expansion into the region.

The Texan rebellion was one of a whole series of anti-centralist movements against the newly independent Latin American states, most of which failed. Thus, rebellions in Brazil—the "Cabanos" in Pernambuco in 1832–35 and in Pará in 1835–36, the "Sabinada" in Bahia in 1837–38, the "Balaida" in Maranhá in 1839–40, and the "Farraposi" in Rio Grande do Sul and Santa Catarina in 1835–45—all failed, while independence movements in the Yucatán that were fired by peasant resentment were suppressed by Mexico in 1843 and 1848. In contrast, the Texans won a rapid victory in their rebellion against an autocratic and corrupt Mexican rule that violated their assumptions of legality and fairness as much as it hit their interests. Unlike the Yucatán, the Texans could draw on foreign support; in their case, that of American migrants and sympathisers. The Texas and Latin American rebellions shared in varying degrees the element of regionalism. However, the Anglo-American element added a distinctive element: whereas *Tejanos* (Texas Mexicans) played key roles in opposing Mexico City and in the rebellion, the leading proponents of separation were Anglo-Americans, most of whom had little or no intention of truly becoming Mexican citizens.

It is appropriate at the start to turn back to the first major American-Spanish clash in Texas, that in 1812–13. This arose from the disturbances that followed the beginning, in 1810, of the struggle for Mexican independence. One of the insurgents, José Gutiérrez de Lara, took refuge in the United States where he interested influential figures in the idea of an independent Texas. Joined with Augustus Magee, a former regular officer, Guitérrez raised a "Republican Army" of about 500 men that in August 1812 crossed the Sabine River and moved on to capture Nacogdoches without resistance. The filibusters then advanced towards San Antonio (de Béxar), the capital of Texas, but, in light of a build-up of loyalist forces there instead moved south to attack and capture the weakly-defended garrison at La Bahía. Falling in October 1812, La Bahía yielded valuable munitions. Loyalist forces besieged La Bahía unsuccessfully in the winter of 1812–13, before falling back on Béxar. A far larger filibuster army, of about 14,600, advanced on the city, defeating a loyalist force nearby at Salado. This led to the surrender of Béxar and on 6 April 1813 independence was declared from Spain. However, the bitterly-divided victors lost support as a result of exactions and the harsh treatment of much of the population. On 20 June, the Republicans defeated a loyalist force at the battle of Alazan, near Béxar, but, a larger loyalist force, under Colonel José Joaquín de Arrendondo, marched north from Mexico, defeated the Republicans at the battle of Medina on 13 August 1813, captured Béxar and regained control of Texas.

This was challenged in 1819 when filibusters under James Long, rejecting the Adams-Onis Treaty, which established the Sabine River as the border, seized Nacogdoches, declared an independent republic and established outlying posts that were designed to become the focus of Native trade. These posts fell rapidly when Colonel Ignacio Pérez advanced from San Antonio, capturing Nacogdoches in October 1819. The Americans fled back across the Sabine, but a presence was maintained in Galveston Bay, where it was not easy for the Spaniards/Mexicans to operate: Long's men built a fort at Bolivar Point. In 1820, the Republic of Texas was declared anew at Bolivar Point. When, in 1821, Mexico declared independence, Long saw an opportunity for action. Sailing to San Antonio Bay, he marched inland to attack La Bahía, only to be captured by a larger force under Pérez.

Instead of becoming independent, Texas became a frontier part of an independent Mexico, from 1824 part of the state of Coahuila and Texas, with its capital at Saltillo. The attempt in December 1826 to create a Republic of Fredonia around Nacogdoches was rapidly put down in early 1827 by Mexican troops from San Antonio and militia from Austin's Colony; the rebels angered important American interests as well as the Spaniards.

The failure of the filibusters, despite the peripheral character of Texas to Mexico and the need for Spanish units in Mexico to focus on dissidence there, indicated the weakness of irregular forces, not least the difficulty of responding to setbacks or, indeed, sustaining efforts. It was possible to challenge Spanish control of the eastern borderlands near the Sabine, but San Antonio, the major Mexican center in Texas, only fell once, and that in a period of general Spanish weakness. In practice, the republic of Texas lay beyond the reach of the filibusters. However, Texas's population grew rapidly in the 1820s and early 1830s as a result of immigration from America which was initially encouraged by the Mexican government as a way to encourage economic growth. However, this rise in population made the situation volatile and led to governmental concern about the degree of central control in Texas. American immigration was stopped from 1830 until 1834. The government's attempts to prevent the import of slaves into Texas aroused ire among the settlers, but the main issue was that of control.

In 1832 and 1833 Texan conventions called for separate statehood within Mexico as well as the freedoms and liberties they regarded as their due.

Fighting began on 2 October 1835 when troops from San Antonio sought to regain a cannon they had provided for the town of Gonzales in 1831 to help it deter Native attack. The soldiers were repelled. Three days later, delegates were elected for a Texan convention. Texans speedily captured Goliad and advanced on San Antonio. On 3 November 1835, the convention, known as the Consultation of all Texans, met at San Felipe. Respecting a call for independence, the delegates created a provisional state government, which was designed to negotiate with the Mexican government. However, delegates were also sent to seek American help, and a commander, Sam Houston, appointed for the Texas army.

The Mexican dictator, General Antonio López de Santa Anna, tried to deal with the situation by force not negotiation. Similarly, in 1835, he had dealt with opposition by Francisco García, Governor of Aacatecas, by leading an expedition against him.

Santa Anna benefited from the militarised character of Mexican society and had superiority in numbers over the Texans, who declared independence on 2 March 1836. They were not prepared to accept Santa Anna's abrogation of the 1824 constitution, under which the Americans had settled in Texas, and rejected his claim that their failure to convert to Catholicism meant that their land grants were void, and that they must leave. Santa Anna left Mexico City on 28 November 1835, crossed the Rio Grande on 12 February 1836, and on 23 February reached San Antonio, where, on 11 December, the Texans under Edward Burleston had forced the Mexicans to surrender after an assault and house-to-house fighting.

The greatly-outnumbered Americans defended the Alamo mission, in the face of Mexican bombardment from 24 February. They had in fact been instructed by Houston to retreat and to add their strength (187 men) to the main army. Instead, the garrison stayed and called for help. The extensive perimeter of the Alamo was too great a defensive task for the small garrison, who also lacked sufficient munitions and food. In military terms, hanging on was a mistake; but Santa Anna was also foolish neither to bypass the Alamo nor to await the arrival of heavy artillery. In the assault, in the early morning of 6 March 1836, the Texans were overwhelmed by 3,000 Mexicans, although the Mexicans lost about 600 men killed and wounded. Although the Mexicans were present in overwhelming force, they were exposed to fire by skilled riflemen. Once they had breached the wall, the Mexicans were able to close to hand-to-hand combat and in that their superior numbers counted.

Santa Anna then divided his forces to advance further east: he did so via Gonzales while other Mexican units advanced on either flank, via Bastrop and Goliad respectively. The far smaller Texan army under Houston fell back before them in order to gather strength, but the killing of prisoners at the Alamo and at Goliad helped to stiffen resistance: 352 Texan prisoners were slaughtered in the Goliad massacre on 27 March. They had surrendered a week earlier after being found in a vulnerable position on open ground by Mexican cavalry while retreating, and holding off attack until their supplies ran out. "Remember the Alamo" was a war-cry with a point. As Houston fell back from Gonzales into areas dominated by American settlers, he looked for opportunities to mount an effective counter-attack, and was given one when Santa Anna advanced with a flying column in front of his main army in a vain attempt to seize the leading members of the Texas government. Houston turned to attack and Santa Anna moved to meet him.

In the decisive engagement, at San Jacinto on 21 April 1836, Santa Anna was defeated, although he outnumbered Houston by 1,500 to 783. A surprise Texan advance against a force that had been so confident of its superiority that it had failed to take adequate defensive preparations brought rapid victory. In their advance, the Texans benefited from a slight elevation in front of the Mexican breastworks, which gave them cover. The Texans outfought the Mexicans. The advance was followed by a devastating volley, and then the Americans closed to the kill. Lacking cohesion and morale, the Mexicans fled, only to be slaughtered: a swamp to their rear blocked retreat. The battle lasted only 18 minutes, but in it and the subsequent pursuit 630 Mexicans were killed, and 730 captured, of whom 280 were wounded. The Americans lost 2 men, with 23 wounded, although several subsequently died.[15]

Santa Anna was captured the next day. Although there were demands that he be hanged, Santa Anna was spared. On 14 May, he had to sign agreements bringing peace, withdrawing the army, and recognizing Texan independence, with the border at the Rio Grande. Although the remaining Mexican forces in Texas far outnumbered Houston's army, and indeed the force defeated at San Jacinto, their commanders obeyed Santa Anna's order to retreat, and Texas was evacuated. However, the Mexican Senate refused to accept Texan independence. Despite this, conflict was avoided bar infrequent raids, in part because western Texas was dominated by Natives, particularly Comanche. The aftermath of San Jacinto was similar to the situation in 1759, when the other single most decisive battle in North American history occurred. Outside Québec, a British army defeated a French force. However, Québec itself was not captured. Aside from the troops still in the city, substantial relief forces were approaching, and the British position was far from promising. Despite this, Québec surrendered and the relief forces turned back.

Judging Houston's strategy in hindsight is difficult as it would not have looked so promising had the other Mexican units not obeyed Santa Anna's instructions to retreat. Numbers were a problem for the Texans throughout. In an ideal defensive strategy, a more numerous and better trained Texan force would have sought to defeat the invaders in detail, concentrating first against either Santa Anna, who moved into Texas from Guerrero, or the army under General José Urrea that invaded via Matamoros. There was no such option. However, in falling back, the heavily outnumbered Houston exposed himself to the risk of a greater concentration of Mexican troops, as Urrea and Santa Anna came closer together.

The American army had been ordered to patrol the Texas border during the revolution, and did not intervene against Santa Anna. Andrew Jackson favoured restraint. General Gaines occupied Nacogdoches, but not until July 1836. Had Santa Anna been successful, then Gaines's advance was sufficiently tentative to permit disengagement. The Americans were not ready for war in 1836, and would have been in a poor position to fight one had there been a large, victorious Mexican army in Texas, albeit one at the limit of its logistical range. Gaines thus performed a valuable function in not exceeding his instructions.

Texas' success in breaking free was not an isolated episode. Other states that had been produced by the Latin American Wars of Liberation fractured. Venezuela successfully rebelled against the state of Grán Colombia in 1829–30, while Bolivia fought free in 1840–41 of Peruvian attempts to dominate her through a federation. Uruguay had been annexed by Brazil in 1816, but it rebelled in 1825. Unlike in the case of Texas, but, again, indicating what could have happened, the rebellion was not a total success, in that the Brazilians held on to the garrison towns. Furthermore, whereas America stayed out of the Texan war, Uruguay sought union with the United Provinces, the modern Argentina. This was accepted and by the end of 1825 Argentina and Brazil were at war. This wide-ranging conflict was waged without decisive advantage, the Brazilians held on to their major positions throughout the war, and the peace settlement of 1828 left Uruguay as an independent buffer.

## AMERICAN-MEXICAN RELATIONS 1836–45

The Mexican-American war of 1846–48 was a more far-flung conflict than the war of 1835–36. It arose as a result of Mexican opposition to the admission of Texas into the Union. Had the Mexicans accepted this step, then war between the two countries might have been avoided until Mexico was in a stronger state relative to an increasingly-divided America. It is interesting to speculate whether a conflict in the 1850s or early 1860s over the Mexican-ruled territory between Texas and the Pacific would have averted or accentuated divisive tendencies within America.

However, there had already been serious tensions in relations between Texas and Mexico. Aside from disputes over the frontier to the south, there was also the problem caused by Texan interest in gaining New Mexico. It was hoped that a show of force would lead the New Mexicans to reject the authority of Mexico City and, instead, join with Texas. Mirabeau B. Lamar, the President of Texas, was a keen supporter and in 1841, sent an expedition to Santa Fé. It was a disaster, in large part because of a lack of knowledge: about the route and about watercourses. In addition, the expedition was harassed by Natives and short of food. As a result, the Texans surrendered to Mexican troops without fighting. Their subsequent mistreatment inflamed relations.

The situation became more tense with reports in 1842 of plans for Native-Mexican cooperation against Texas, and orders to American commanders to try to limit Native-Texan hostilities. American forces in the region were increased. In 1842, Jacob Snively, the Texan Inspector General, won support for a retaliatory strike against Mexican caravans on the Santa Fé route. Snively's 177-strong "Battalion of Invincibles" moved into modern Kansas near Dodge City, defeating a Mexican force sent to seize them, but was in turn, in 1843, overawed by American army dragoons under Captain Philip St. George Cooke who was convinced that the Texans were on American territory. As a result, the opportunity to capture a Mexican caravan was lost. Cooke's action led to an official protest by the Texan government, but a court of inquiry cleared Cooke. In army circles, there was a lack of sympathy for independent military initiatives.

Mexico and Texas clashed on the frontier[16] and in the Gulf of Mexico, with Texan warships raiding Mexican shipping and supporting rebels in the Yucatán. On 16 May 1843, there was the full-scale battle of Campeche in which an all-sail squadron under Commodore Edwin Moore fought off two Mexican paddle-steamers that had been purchased in Britain the previous year and were armed with shell guns and officered and manned by Britons. The Mexicans had the technological lead, and theirs were the first warships to fire shell guns in action, but Tomas Marin, the Mexican commander, did not provide adequate leadership.[17] British attempts to mediate failed in early 1844.

The American annexation of Texas led in 1845 to strong pressure within Mexico for war: it was seen as a threat to national honor and as sealing the Texas revolution. The Mexicans hoped that the Americans would be weakened by internal political divisions, slave insurrection, Native American opposition, and British hostility arising from the Oregon issue, as well as the deficiencies of a small army and low quality volunteers. They were also sure of the strength of their own military. In turn, President James K. Polk and an important and vocal section of American opinion were keen on expansionism and specifically on gaining a wide Pacific coastline. San Francisco and San Diego were sought as bases for the exploitation both of the Pacific and of the western littoral of North America. Already, in October 1842, American warships under Commodore Thomas Ap Catesby Jones, who erroneously believed that war had begun, briefly seized Monterey and San Diego. The 1844 presidential campaign committed Polk to the goals of advancing to the Pacific, and the unresolved nature of disputes over Texas provided the opportunity to move to force once diplomacy had failed.[18]

## THE COMING OF WAR

American forces were sent in February 1846 into disputed territory on the Texas/Mexico border at the mouth of the Rio Grande/Río Bravo Del Norte: the Mexicans regarded the Nueces River as the border, and not only rejected the Rio Grande but also refused to receive John Slidell as American minister, and turned down the American attempt to buy the disputed territory as well as California and New Mexico for $35 million. Zachary Taylor, the American commander, made his base at Port Isabel and established a forward base at Fort Texas, later Fort Brownsville.

There was a widespread expectation that a weak Mexico would back down, but also concern about the state of American preparedness. A speech in the House of Representatives on 20 March 1846 on behalf of a Bill, backed by the Committee of Military Affairs, to raise two new regiments of riflemen, claimed that:

the present skeleton of an army, consisting of only 7,880 men, rank and file, was not sufficient, before the extension of our territory by the admission of Texas, to man our fortifications on the seaboard and on the lakes, and to give a sufficient force upon the frontier . . . we have the western frontier of Texas, bordering on Mexico, to fortify and man with forts and a sufficient number of troops to exert a moral influence upon the Mexicans in that quarter. . . . The route to Oregon must be fortified and manned . . . three stockade forts at least.

Such comments were widely disseminated by their publication in newspapers, for example for this item the *Daily Union* of 13 April. Foreign commentators were also sceptical. Richard Pakenham, the British envoy in America, wrote on 23 June 1846: "Numerous bodies of volunteers have been forwarded to Matamoros from New Orleans and other places, but apparently in a hasty and confused manner, and, as far as I can discover, without any attempt at discipline or organization. It seems difficult to imagine how a campaign undertaken under such circumstances in an enemy's country can be successful, however low an estimate may be formed of the resistance to be encountered."[19] Conflict began on 23 April 1846, when an American patrol was ambushed near Fort Brown, but both governments had already decided on war, which the United States declared, in response to the attack, on 13 May. The Mexican government under President Mariano Paredes had decided that Taylor's advance meant that a state of "defensive" war existed. On 8 March, Paredes had told Charles Bankhead, the British envoy, that America was an "indefatigable and powerful neighbor" and that he did not want Mexico to become her prey.[20] Britain was Mexico's major trading partner, and there was (unfounded) concern in America that Britain would support her.[21]

Once fighting had started, an American expeditionary force was ordered into northern Mexico. Its commander, Taylor, first, however, had to confront the advancing Mexican Army of the North, 6,000 strong, under Major General Mariano Arista. In the battle of Palo Alto, American artillery played a major role in ensuring the withdrawal of the Mexican force (8 May). The following day, at Resaca de la Palma, the advancing Americans defeated the now-entrenched Mexicans, and the latter retreated beyond the Rio Grande.

Taylor's army moved south of the Rio Grande, occupying Matamoros on the

18th. The British Vice Consul there reported on the 20th, "the Texian [*sic*] and other volunteers, who are daily augmenting General Taylor's force, are reputed to be a most unruly multitude; and the Mexicans, in order to avoid them, are all retreating to the interior."[22] Taylor pressed on to capture Camargo and to attack Monterrey, the capital of the province of Nuevo León. Taylor was outnumbered (6,200 to 7,500) and the city was a strong defensive site, but his army managed a coordinated assault from west and east, although suffering more than 500 casualties in difficult street fighting. Such street fighting in a major town was to be unusual in the American Civil War, but was more common in Europe, especially in revolutions and counter-insurgency operations, such as in Brussels and Paris in 1830, Paris, Prague and Vienna in 1848, and Budapest in 1849.

On 24 September 1846, Taylor secured his achievement by signing an eight-week armistice under which the Mexicans were to withdraw. President Polk regarded this as a failure to ensure a decisive victory and abrogated the armistice, but Taylor was aware of the problems of advancing further with his limited manpower and supplies. He captured Saltillo, capital of Coahuila, in November, but thought San Luis Potosí too far. Saltillo is about 550 miles from Mexico City.

The distances involved can, in part, be seen as the natural defences of Mexico, especially when combined with the malarial coastal lowlands that provided Mexico City with a potential degree of protection from attack from the Gulf of Mexico. In contrast, there were no natural borders to protect the Confederacy from attack in the Civil War.

The following year, Taylor lost his regulars to support Winfield Scott's attack on Vera Cruz. This was exploited by the Mexicans under Santa Anna, who had returned from exile in Cuba to take charge, and was aware, through an intercepted letter, of American plans. Santa Anna helped create a new field army, which he intended to use in order to defeat the Americans in detail. He advanced to attack Taylor, but the latter took up a good defensive position at Buena Vista, and defeated the far more numerous (15,000–4,500) Mexican attack on 22–23 February 1847, although with heavy losses: 700 killed and wounded. The previous August, Bankhead had been disparaging about Mexican courage, claiming that Paredes "will never be able to bring the Mexican troops (especially the officers) again to expose themselves in front of an American army."[23] In fact, at Buena Vista, the Mexicans launched repeated attacks, but were stopped by a firm defence, including effective artillery and a counter-attack by a Mississippi volunteer regiment under Colonel Jefferson Davis. Nearly 40 percent of the Mexican army were casualties, a percentage that reflected their determination to fight on against difficult odds. Santa Anna retreated.

## THE ADVANCE ON MEXICO CITY, 1847

American successes in 1846 had not led the Mexicans to negotiate, and the bold stroke of a strike at the Mexican centre was deemed necessary by Polk and

Winfield Scott, the Commanding General of the American army and a commander of great experience. Already, in November 1846, the American navy had captured Tampico on the Gulf of Mexico, which was an important halfway point between Matamoros and Vera Cruz. In 1847, an amphibious expedition conducted by Scott was followed by an advance on Mexico City. This reflected a force-projection capability in the Gulf of Mexico that had not been there in the War of 1812. The fleet that covered the landing included the *Potomac* and *Raritan*, sail-powered frigates; the *Mississippi*, a paddle-frigate; and a screw sloop, two other sloops, a brig, five schooners, and three leased paddle steamers.

This force projection was one aspect of a more general naval capability. The American navy dominated the Gulf, and was dominant in Pacific waters. There, ships from the Pacific and the Far East were joined by others that had sailed round Cape Horn. Guaymas and Matzatlán, on the west coast of Mexico, were captured by the navy in October and November 1847 respectively. It did not have to face Mexican warships, and the threat of large-scale Mexican privateering was not fulfilled. At sea, the Americans in 1846–48 were in a position comparable to that of Britain, not their forbears, in the War of 1812. The naval task was greater than that facing the British then, in that there was a requirement to operate in the Pacific, although that was a distant theatre that had no relationship to naval capability in the Gulf. In the latter, the usual problems of blockade—storms and resupply—were exacerbated by yellow fever.

Nevertheless, this did not prevent American attacks on the littoral. At the start of the conflict, the frigates *Potomac* and *Araitan* assisted Taylor, and landed troops at Port Isabel. In October 1846, Matthew Perry led an expedition up the Tabasco River, and he followed these with expeditions up the Vinazco River (April 1847) and the Tabasco again (June 1847). These expeditions served to make the entire littoral feel threatened, and also degraded the Mexican infrastructure. American naval power in the Gulf of Mexico, under first Commodore David Conner and then, from March 1847, Commodore Matthew Perry, emulated that of Britain in her imperial campaigns of the period: the littoral could be overawed, blockaded, interdicted, and bombarded.[24]

Scott staged an uncontested landing near Vera Cruz on 9 March 1847, the first major amphibious landing by American forces (and one achieved without casualties), and captured the city on 29 March after a short siege supported by a naval bombardment (that in its last days included the 84-gun *Ohio*) that had killed over 1,000 Mexicans. The fall of Vera Cruz gave the Americans a base, but the need to capture it had placed a question mark against the very success of the operation. A lengthy siege would have been fatal, as it would have exposed the Americans to high casualties and debilitation from disease, as the British had suffered outside Havana in 1762. Success in seizing the position would have meant little had the capture taken much time. Furthermore, if Vera Cruz had held out for any length of time, then Scott might have had to divide his forces between the siege and watching for any relief attempt. These points serve to underline the importance of his skill in producing a speedy result, but also serve to show that landing in Vera Cruz was not alone sufficient to ensure success.

On 8 April 1847, Scott advanced inland, away from the yellow fever and malaria of the coastal lowlands, on the National Road towards Mexico City. Santa Anna had created another army after his defeat at Buena Vista, but it was defeated at the pass of Cerro Gordo on 18 April, with heavy Mexican losses. Santa Anna had hoped to confine the Americans to the lowlands, and Scott's victory wrecked his strategy, forcing Santa Anna to defend his capital. At Cerro Gordo, the Americans lost 425 killed and wounded, a loss they could ill afford, but one that should be set against the Mexican army there—11,000 strong, and the Mexican casualties: about 1,000 killed and wounded and 3,000 prisoners. Although there was guerrilla warfare, which hit Scott's strength, he occupied Puebla (May 15), and used it as a base for accumulating supplies and troops. Scott's army was seriously weakened by disease, although it had left the coast, and was also affected by enlistments expiring, so that at one stage the size of the army fell to about 7,000.

In a struggle for the capital, Scott then advanced into the Valley of Mexico and defeated the Mexicans at Contreras and Churusbusco (twin battles on 19–20 August), Molino de Rey (8 September), Chapultepec (13 September), and Mexico City itself. This list gives no indication of the difficulty of the task. Mexico City was not easy to attack because the city was walled and had to be approached via raised causeways that represented choke points. Similarly, when seizing the Aztec capital Tenochtitlán in 1521, Cortés had faced serious problems in storming the causeways. In 1847, the storming of Chapultepec, which commanded important causeways, was a crucial step: this was a bold infantry storming in which American soldiers clambered up to the Mexican position in the early morning. Having taken the position, troops pressed on to fight their way into the capital. Mexico City fell on 14 September 1847, just over six months after Scott had landed. The August-September campaign cost Scott's army over 3,000 casualties. After the capture of Mexico City, Scott restored his communication links, while the American garrison at Puebla resisted attack by Santa Anna. The siege of Puebla was finally lifted by the arrival of American reinforcements.

## CONQUERING TO THE PACIFIC

Further afield, American forces had overrun Mexico's northern possessions. Troops under Colonel Stephen Kearny, Commander of the Army of the West, rapidly advanced from Fort Leavenworth to Santa Fé, which was captured without firing a shot (18 August 1846) and then to San Diego (12 December). This bland remark provides little idea of the difficulty of the task. This was due largely to the problems of crossing the desert west of the Colorado, although the initial march to Santa Fé had also been very difficult. However, Mexican opposition was also a problem. At San Pasqual (6 December), the Americans clashed with a larger force of Mexican lancers who inflicted heavier casualties before retreating. Kearny soon after barricaded himself into Snooks Ranch. Fortunately, he was able to send three men through the Mexican lines. They reached San Diego from where an American force relieved Kearny.

Meanwhile, California, which Paredes had suggested should be sold to Britain, had been lost to Mexico. American settlers launched the Bear Flag Revolt. A report of 19 June 1846 from Monterey, the capital of California, referred to:

the rapid progress, with which the North Americans are entering into this department. On Monday the 15th of present month, they took possession of the frontier of the North in the town called "Sonoma" and the mission of San Rafael; a number of adventurers, 70 men, surprised the barracks. . . . These people are supplied privately by the United States' man of war *Portsmouth*, which is in San Francisco, with arms and all necessaries, as also by land by Mr. Sutter, and an officer of the United States named Fremont, who, with his party of riflemen, overruns all the country, hoisting the star spangled banner whenever he chooses. This is the deplorable state in which this beautiful country is, and without the least hope that the superior government will take any measures to save it from the pending ruin which hangs over it, and it is likely that from such carelessness and apathy they will undoubtedly lose California; as they have done Texas. . . . The general in command Don José Castro, without troops, arms, or resources of any kind, finds himself at this moment in the most critical situation. All the authorities, as well as most of the inhabitants, leave this place today to join a few that follow the general in order to pass on to Sonoma to drive out those wicked people, which I think rather difficult. The government ought without delay to make any sacrifice to protect it with troops.[25]

The Pacific Squadron, under first John Sloat and then Robert Stockton, played a major role. It occupied Monterey (7 July), San Francisco (9 July), San Diego (29 July), Santa Barbara (4 August) and Los Angeles (13 August). Paredes told Bankhead that the settler movement was unexpected and that the government was unable to repress it.[26] On 13 August, Bankhead wrote that the fall of California had "long been expected, but I own that I did not think it would be accomplished in so short a period. Misgovernment and internal strife have done much to aid them in this enterprise, and to place in their power one of the most valuable possessions in the habitable globe, and whose resources are as yet most imperfectly known."[27]

However, the Mexican inhabitants in southern California rebelled against American control in September. They were defeated by Stockton and by the overland troops under Kearny at San Pasqual (6 December 1846), San Gabriel (8 January 1847) and Mesa (9 January). There was also an uprising in New Mexico in December 1846, which led to American counter-insurgency operations. The rebels were defeated at Taos in February 1847. Meanwhile, an American force of Missouri volunteers under Colonel Alexander Doniphan had marched south from New Mexico into Chihuahua which they captured (1 March

1847), having defeated Mexican forces en route at El Brazito north of El Paso del Norte (25 December 1846) and at the Sacramento River (28 February). These overland marches were similar to those of the French in West Africa later in the century: major distances were crossed by determined groups of men. The dry nature of the terrain was a particular problem. Supply problems helped to put an emphasis on the offensive: retreat was difficult. To a certain extent, forces in arid terrain were like squadrons at sea, coming against each other with little warning in a hostile environment where it was difficult to obtain information about opposing forces.[28]

## OPERATIONS REVIEWED

Although there was guerrilla warfare, there was nothing in Mexico to match the Spanish popular response to Napoleon. This was a testimony to the far more skilful management of the situation by the Americans, especially Scott. They avoided relying on a logistics of depredation or turning to a politics of brutality. Furthermore, California was lightly populated, while some of those who were conquered welcomed American trade. Indeed Santa Fé had been drawn into the commercial range of the United States prior to the conflict. The absence of large-scale guerrilla warfare also reflected the nature of the Mexican military and contributed to the character of the war as a series of set-piece engagements between regulars. This conformed to the nature of war taught to regulars, and was totally different therefore to the conflicts with Native Americans. The eventual peace treaty of Guadalupe Hidalgo, signed on 2 February 1848, left the United States with what were to become California, Nevada and Utah, as well as most of Arizona and parts of New Mexico, Colorado and Wyoming. Although major gains, these were less than those sought by many, including Polk. Bankhead had suggested in October 1846 that the process of transfer of protection he saw at work in New Mexico, with the Mexican population offering loyalty to their conquerors in return for protection against Native Americans and commercial benefits might well be followed in the provinces of Chihuahua, Coahuila and Nuevo Leon,[29] which would have been a significant southward extension for the United States. There had also been pressure for filibustering (unofficial initiatives), against both Cuba and the Yucatán. In a dangerous sign of independence, William Worth was ready to resign and command an invasion of Cuba in 1848, but he abandoned the idea under pressure from Polk.[30]

American campaigning was what would be subsequently described as "high tempo." Its aggressive and fast-moving character was necessary for political as well as military reasons. The Americans were helped by naval superiority, as well as better artillery, which made a major difference in battle. Horse artillery provided firepower as well as mobility. In addition, Scott's effective generalship displayed strategic insight, a skilful transfer of this insight into effective operational direction, and an ability to gain and retain the initiative. He always favoured the attack. Rather than relying on lines of infantry, Scott advocated looser formations, especially clouds of skirmishers. Scott made effective use of artillery in attack, as at Churubusco and when threatening to destroy Mexico City. He also tended to turn Mexican flanks as at Cerro Gordo, Contreras and Churusbusco, and, more generally, in the advance on Mexico City. Molino de Rey was unusual in involving a frontal assault, and the result was 781 American casualties. In practice, it proved harder to ensure flanking attacks than had been intended. Aside from difficulties in execution, there was also the issue of Mexican response. Scott showed strategic daring when, in his advance on Mexico City, he cut away from his lines of communication and pressed on despite being in hostile country and outnumbered.

This boldness horrified the Duke of Wellington: "Scott is lost! He has been carried away by successes! He can't take the city, and he can't fall back on his bases." Scott's success was to lead Wellington to revise his opinion: "his campaign was unsurpassed in military annals. He is the greatest living soldier."[31] Such boldness was more characteristic of the advances of Western forces outside the West, for example the march of a British force 785 miles from Bengal to Surat in 1778–79, or French campaigns in West Africa in the late nineteenth century, than of those of armies in Europe, although, in 1831, Field Marshal Paskievich, the Russian commander in Poland, captured Warsaw by shifting the direction of Russian attack. Instead of approaching Warsaw directly from the east, as had happened earlier in the year, he circled north of Warsaw, crossed the Vistula at Osiek near the Prussian border, and advanced on Warsaw from the west, successfully capturing it.

Size-supply ratios were one factor in Scott's favour. Smaller forces could take their supplies with them and/or seize them en route. Scott had fewer than 20,000 men, and only 10,700 effectives for his final advance on Mexico City in August–September. The supply situation was very different with larger forces. Other issues also played a part. The American conviction of superiority encouraged both operational and tactical boldness. So also did fighting a mobile opponent who could be difficult to force to an engagement. Sherman was to follow a similar policy in his march from Atlanta in 1864, but he was in a stronger position than Scott.

Initial successes in the Mexican War helped to sustain American confidence. They also ensured that there was no pressure to think through new tactics or operational methods and systems. The relatively short length of the war also had the same effect. Thus the shift in strategy to the amphibious assault on Veracruz and the direct attack on Mexico City was the change in American military policy.

The American reliance on infantry accorded with a more general long-term trend in which the battlefield value of cavalry decreased. Cavalry remained most important in reconnaissance and in action against other cavalry. Horses also provided crucial mobility for long-range movements away from rail links. While important in all these spheres, cavalry had been marginalized from battle. There were also specific problems with horses, not least their requirements in fodder and water, and the difficulty of transporting them safely by sea. Fortifications played an important role in particular campaigns, especially Monterrey and Vera Cruz, but the emphasis was on battle, with control over territory, including fortified towns, being seen as an adjunct.

Battlefield fighting quality, which owed much to the calibre of the junior officers who helped turn recruits and volunteers into effective soldiers,[32] as well as the quality of the staff work in Scott's army, has to be seen alongside serious logistical deficiencies, which reflected the weakness of the supply bureaus—the Ordnance, Quartermaster and Subsistence Departments. Slowness and other aspects of incompetence may, however, have received too much attention, as supply functioned reasonably well, given the terrain and distances involved. Problems were also posed by the determination of politicians to achieve victory at low cost and by generals who did not understand the need to work with the bureaus and within the parameters of administrative capability when posing demands. The relative brevity of the war helped ensure that pressure for bureaucratic change was limited.

The Mexicans benefited from numbers, especially against Taylor at Buena Vista, but also against Scott, and from the fighting quality of their troops, for example at Churusbusco, Molino de Rey and Chapultepec. American advances encountered serious problems, as in Taylor's attack on Monterrey in September 1846. Nevertheless, the Mexican army was poorly armed and supplied, and affected by the unpopularity of military service, and by flaws in command and equipment. No master-strategist, and lacking skill at the operational level, Santa Anna was out-generalled and the Mexicans were outfought. Defeats helped to lead to a serious fall in the morale of the Mexican army.[33] The American invasion of Mexico offered no comparison with the disastrous British intervention in Afghanistan in 1841–42.

Equally, the Americans were greatly helped by the possibility of an exit strategy. This was for two reasons. First, despite serious division, defeat did not lead to the disintegration of Mexico. Thus, a peace could be negotiated with a government that, in turn, could end the fighting on its side. Second, despite their major gains in the fighting and although there had been bold talk of annexing all or much of Mexico, the Americans did not try to annex all of Mexico nor all that they had occupied, nor, indeed, despite the longevity of Hispanic settlement in New Mexico, any real core areas. This was important in both the politics and the military dimension of the conflict. There was no equivalent to the contemporary French war of conquest in Algeria, a long, drawn out struggle in which retaining all of the occupied territory was as important as inflicting defeat. Thus, the political tasking gave the American military a goal that it could achieve and then cut short the conflict before exposing the army to the retention conflict for which it was ill-prepared, not least because the demographic challenge of holding conquered parts of Mexico was of a totally different order to that of controlling areas inhabited by Native Americans.

To indicate the challenge, it is useful to note the problems that faced the

French in Mexico in the 1860s. Mexican instability and a repudiation of international debts in July 1861 led to intervention by Britain, France and Spain in order to secure repayment. Their troops landed at Vera Cruz in December 1861–January 1862. However, the Mexicans did not change their policy and in April the British and Spaniards decided to evacuate, which they did. In 1862, however, the French sought to take this limited intervention further. French reinforcements arrived, so that by early 1863 there were 30,000 French troops in Mexico. In June 1863, the French advanced and captured Mexico City. The French Emperor, Napoleon III, encouraged the offer of the throne of Mexico, by opponents of the government of Benito Juárez, to Archduke Ferdinand Maximilian, the brother of the Austrian Emperor. However, the attempt of Emperor Maximilian to take over Mexico was mishandled and met a strong nationalist response. There was a long guerrilla war led by Juárez, with few conventional battles, and French backing, although 40,000 troops at the peak, was both insufficient and not maintained. The French benefited from naval support on both coastlines, and on land were able to seize positions, such as Oaxaca in 1865, but this did not stabilize the situation. Maximilian also had a 7,100-strong Austrian volunteer corps, but they were hit by yellow fever and only infrequently encountered the enemy. Yellow fever was a particular problem round Vera Cruz, Mexico's leading port and the key base for French intervention.[34]

After the Amerian Civil War, American pressure led Napoleon in February 1866 to decide to withdraw his forces. Juárez had already received covert support from Union forces during the American Civil War. The last French troops left in March 1867, and Maximilian, who refused to leave, was defeated at Queretaro, and shot in June. The French had been more successful in 1838 when they had staged a more limited intervention in order to punish the Mexicans for depredations against French citizens. The French had then bombarded Vera Cruz and seized a fort there.

French intervention in Mexico in the 1860s, at a time when the French themselves had considerable experience of force projection thanks to campaigns in Algeria, the Crimea and China, provides some clue as the likely fate of American forces had they not brought the Mexican War to an end. Indeed, there had been an uneasy forerunner with the time it took to negotiate peace after the fall of Mexico City. In contrast to the situation in the American Civil War after the fall of Richmond in 1865, and, instead, in keeping with that of Washington in 1814, the fall of the capital did not bring an immediate end to the war.

The war provides an opportunity for probing the impact of politics on conflict. The Mexican army and war effort suffered from many of the consequences of post-independence Mexican politics and political culture—including economic decline and regional, social and political divisions. These divisions helped ensure that many Mexicans collaborated with American troops. Given that the United States was soon to face a major civil war, it is paradoxical that it faced no such problems in the Mexican-American war. There was factionalism in the military leadership and some problems over war-finance and Whig opposition, but the

American military effort was not affected by debilitating domestic problems. The Americans did suffer difficulties in recruitment and logistics, but these did not reflect deep divisions in society. The greater professionalism of the regular army helped ensure that it was better able to give effect to offensive planning than its predecessor in the War of 1812.

There was no equivalent in America to the dictatorial policies of Santa Anna and to the opposition this inspired, nor to the rift between army and civic militia that had played an important role in Mexican politics from independence on. The civic militia played a major role in the overthrow of Santa Anna's government in 1844–45. In turn, the new government was overthrown the following winter. There were major disturbances within Mexico during the war including in June and October 1846 and February 1847, the last a civil war. These seriously affected the Mexican war effort. In what was becoming a tradition in the Hispanic world, garrisons, for example that of Mazatlan on 30 May 1846, would "pronounce" against the government and in favour of change. In July 1846, Paredes resigned in favour of his Vice-President, General Bravo, but he was rapidly overthrown by the military, plunging the country into chaos. Turmoil at the center was matched by disorder in the provinces. Thus, in November the province of Tabasco attempted to secede.[35]

Disunity in the United States over the war, its goals and its conduct,[36] was more contained, although the seeds of future division were sown. Thus, a war that saw the greatest expansion of the United States through conflict ended leaving the issue of the fate of slavery in the new territories to poison relations. In addition, the conflict, its causes and consequences, gave rise to disputes. Thus, the eventual peace terms were thought insufficiently beneficial by the Democrats, and leading to the gain of too much territory by the Whigs, who had been critical of the annexation of Texas and were suspicious about the likely consequences of increasing the number of slave states.[37] As in the War of 1812, the Northeast was particularly hostile to the conflict.

In addition, the war brought a whole series of security issues. It was necessary to secure the new territories from internal disturbance and external challenge, to define their borders, and to decide how best to rethink military tasks in response to the new gains. The American state now ruled about 60,000 Mexicans, as well as a large number of Native Americans whose relations with Mexican authority had frequently been poor. In addition, the Mormon nation in Utah had been brought within American rule, but not yet control. Last, it was unclear how far it would be possible to secure the border with Mexico, not least to prevent both continued Mexican influence, and also Native attacks on Mexico. In the peace treaty, the Americans had promised to prevent these and, more generally, they had an interest in doing so in order to reduce the volatility of the region and to ensure stability.

One response was a process of fortification. In Santa Fé, an earthwork fort was rapidly constructed, and it was supported by others including Forts Craig, Defiance, Masschusetts, Stanton and Union. These were essentially designed to provide security against the Native Americans rather than the local Mexicans, a response to the shift that rapidly occurred from regarding the latter as a possible challenge to, instead, seeing the new territories as another aspect of long-standing security concerns over Native Americans. The weakness of *revanchist* tendencies within Mexico was also important, and was to be further demonstrated by the Gadsden Purchase of 1853 in which land bought for $10 million improved the southern route to California. Furthermore, American press reports in 1858 that President James Buchanan was interested in seizing Sonora (the province to the south of the Gadsden Purchase) and other parts of Mexico seems to have been without cause. As a consequence, it was not necessary to prepare for a repetition of war with Mexico. Thus, there was no programme of concentrating troops along the Mexican border and both fortifying and training for such a conflict with a "European-style" regular army.

As with much that did not happen, it is easy to neglect the importance of this possibility and to fail to consider the resulting counterfactual. A sense of tension in relations with Mexico might have led to a repetition of American attack, but, even without that, would have encouraged pressure for a stronger federal army and would have led to its preparation for "regular" type operations. It is interesting to speculate as to the possible impact of this on the Civil War. A stronger federal force might well have played a major role in opposing secession, although not in the areas of the South that mattered as this force would have been deployed further west. Alternatively, there would have been more men available, and more relevant command talent, to act as the core for Union and Confederate forces.

Instead, the American military presence in the Southwest stemmed from, and, in turn, accentuated the importance of relations with the Natives, and also led to experimentation, for example a search for camels for the army's use. After the war, demobilisation led to an army establishment of 10,317, with all the regiments raised for the war disbanded (although the Regiments of Mounted Riflemen created in 1846 remained), but, in 1855, in response to pressure from Jefferson Davis, the Secretary of War, four permanent regiments (two infantry and two cavalry) were added, so that in 1861 the army was 16,367 strong. The cavalry were deployed in Texas in order to try to maintain order in the face of Native hostility. Robert E. Lee commanded one of the regiments.

Aside from counterfactuals, the Mexican War looked toward the Civil War in a number of strategic, operational and tactical respects; although, of course, the American army was not planning for such a conflict. The Mexican War encouraged a stress on taking war to the enemy and hitting his centre of power, in order to bring an end to the conflict, and showed that this could be achieved in part through the use of amphibious power. The war encouraged an emphasis on battle, and a stress on the value of attack. In short, the war encouraged a confidence in a high-tempo aggressive campaigning that failed to pay due attention to the possibilities that defensive firepower would both cause heavy casualties and blunt this approach and thus to the need to encourage other strategic, operational and tactical options. The Mexican War also demonstrated the importance of logistics.

Nevertheless, the years up to the Civil War were not spent basking in the glow of victory. Instead, the 1850s saw continued attempts to enhance capability, not least tactical innovation,[38] although the continued commitment to coastal fortifications, a programme expanded to cover new conquests, with protection for example for San Francisco and Fort Schuyler at the East River entrance to New York harbour (completed in 1856), was expensive and of debatable military value given advances in rifled gunnery which made projectiles more aerodynamically stable and therefore more effective. It would have been easier for attacking forces to inflict serious damage on the forts.[39]

The Mexican War, and, even more clearly, the Texan War for Independence also showed the limitations of poorly-trained forces and the need to ensure a clear command structure and adequate relations between the political and military leaderships. In Texas, these issues interacted with the problems of creating a new state. Thus, in early 1836, relations between Henry Smith, the Governor, and the Provincial Legislative Council were disastrous, with each dismissing the other. Houston was also involved in the disputes over power and authority.

This poor control structure spilled over into operational matters. In January 1836, Colonels James Fannin and Francis Johnson each claimed authority to command a planned expedition against Matamoros, near the mouth of the Rio Grande, which was seen as a way to display the effectiveness of the independence movement; and also to provide booty. Volunteers assembled at Copano, Goliad, Refugio and San Patricio, but the projected expedition lacked cohesion, momentum or adequate leadership, and the volunteers were divided when the Mexicans advanced, falling victim to attack at San Patricio (27 February), Agua Dulce (2 March) and near Goliad (19–20 March). As a result, these Texans neither contributed to Houston's army nor inflicted much damage on the Mexicans.

The limitations of the Texan volunteers would have been more cruelly exposed had Santa Anna avoided the operational and tactical flaws the Mexicans showed in the San Jacinto campaign: failing to combine in the face of the main enemy force and then showing insufficient care on the defence. This underlines the problems of untrained units and serves to emphasize the importance of the regulars in the Mexican War and the emphasis on training in the early stages of the Civil War. Tension between regulars and volunteers was seen after the Mexican War, not least in the Pacific Northwest where Governor Isaac Stevens of the Washington Territory, who had been in the army, felt that the regulars were insufficiently vigorous against Natives in 1855–56 and in response called out Volunteers and tried to formulate military policy.

## AFTER THE WAR

Success against Mexico led to greater national self-confidence, a more assertive international position, and an increase in force projection on both land and sea. National self-confidence was seen in the high hopes of economic growth and national integration that lay behind the rail boom, and in the Crystal Palace built in New York in 1853. Based on the design of the Crystal Palace built in London in 1851, this reflected America's confidence in its own economic development. In 1850, Congress decided the National Observatory should be the official prime meridian for the United States, an Act not repealed until 1912 when the Greenwich meridian was finally recognized as the zero meridian.[40]

Force-projection was seen in the Pacific, where the Americans had deployed warships for several decades. Indeed David Porter, who, in command of the *Essex*, attacked British trade in the South Pacific in 1813–1814, seized Nuku Hiva in the Marquesas as a base in November 1813, although his action was not recognized by the American government. Both the experience of the value of such deployment in the Mexican War and the new interests and possibilities that followed the annexation of California and the settlement of the Oregon dispute led to greater interest in the Pacific. This was not restricted to the eastern Pacific. After the war, the *Ohio* made its final cruise, visiting both Hawaii and Samoa, while the Mediterranean Squadron made a demonstration along the coast after foreigners, including Americans, were killed at Jaffa in January 1851.

On 8 July 1853, a squadron of four ships under Commodore Matthew Perry, entered Tokyo Bay in order to persuade Japan to inaugurate relations. After presenting a letter from President Fillmore, Perry sailed to China declaring that he would return the following year. Having wintered on the Chinese coast, itself an important display of naval capability, and made naval demonstrations in the Ryuku and Bonin Islands, which secured a coaling concession from the ruler of Naha on Okinawa, Perry returned to Japan with a larger squadron and negotiated the Treaty of Kanagawa (31 March 1854). This provided for American diplomatic representation, the right for American ships to call at two ports, and humane treatment for shipwrecked American soldiers.[41] Perry then returned to the United States, but in 1854–55 another American naval expedition, the North Pacific Surveying Expedition, greatly expanded hydrographic knowledge of Japanese waters. Aside from the Gadsden Purchase from Mexico (1853), President Franklin Pierce (1853–57) was interested in acquiring Alaska, Hawaii and Cuba.

The protection of American interests led to the landing of forces in Buenos Aires in 1852–53, Nicaragua in 1853, Shanghai in 1854, 1855, and 1859, Fiji in 1855 and 1858, Uruguay in 1855 and 1858, Panama (in the Republic of New Granada) in 1856 and 1865, and Canton in 1856. A major deployment to South America occurred in 1858, and one that was far distant from the Caribbean. As a result of disagreements with Britain and France over the treatment of their citizens in Paraguay, its dictator, Carlos Antonio López, closed the Paraguay and Paraná rivers to all foreign warships. In enforcing this policy, his forces in 1855 fired on the *Water Witch*, a lightly-armed (2 guns) U.S. naval steamer which had ascended the Paraná on a mapping expedition. The Americans did not respond rapidly, but, when they did, it was with force. In late 1858, Commodore William Shubrick cruised up the Paraná with a squadron led by the *Sabine* and the *St. Lawrence*, 50-gun sailing frigates. López apologized, paid an indemnity, and let the mapping expedition proceed. By early 1859, the American navy had eight ships deployed on the rivers of Paraguay, while the *Sabine* and *St. Lawrence* remained nearby, assigned to the South American station off the Brazilian coast. All the warships were recalled after the Civil War began.

As a result of the Mexican War, the Pacific played a role in the naval dimension of the Civil War. The Union sent an ironclad, the *Camanche*, to San Francisco in order to protect California from Confederate raids. However, the relative balance of naval infrastructure between the regions of America, and the absence of a transcontinental railway, ensured that the ship, once built in 1862–63, was divided into parts and shipped around Cape Horn before being reconstructed at San Francisco. In 1865–66, another ironclad steamed round Cape Horn to California.

The years after the Mexican War saw not only a grasping of new opportunities, but also a bitter analysis of command decisions and quality in the recent conflict. This process had begun during the war itself and is a reminder of the extent to which the heavily politicised nature of strategic direction by the government, as well as of command politics, compromised relations within the officer corps, although the frequently choleric nature of individuals also played a major role. Thus rivalry between Scott and Taylor carried over to the Whig convention in June 1848 in which Taylor was successful against both Scott and civilian candidates, in large part thanks to his victory at Buena Vista. Taylor won the presidency only to die in 1850, while Scott ran for the presidency in 1852 but lost to Franklin Pierce.[42] Scott himself was involved in a serious dispute with Gideon Pillow, a Polk appointee as a brigadier general of Volunteers. Pillow published an anonymous letter critical of Scott in the *Daily Delta* and the dispute led to a board of inquiry. Other generals were involved in bitter controversy. Accused of intriguing against Scott after a dispute over the battle at Molino del Rey, William Worth was brought before a court of inquiry, although it cleared him.

Nevertheless, the character of the war was such as to minimize dissension. It was far shorter than the War of Independence and far more successful than the War of 1812. Furthermore, the overwhelming majority of the fighting took place on Mexican soil. The war framed the military experience of America until the Civil War. Heroes from the Mexican War, such as Jefferson Davis, subsequently played a major role in command positions, Davis himself successively becoming Secretary of War, Major General in charge of the defence of Mississippi, and President of the Confederacy.

## NOTES

1. J.C.A. Stagg, "Enlisted Men in the United States Army, 1812–1815: A Preliminary Survey," *William and Mary Quarterly*, 3rd ser., 43 (1986), pp. 619–625.

2. For a key administrator, Quartermaster General from 1818 until 1860, C.L. Kieffer, *Maligned General: The Biography of Thomas Sidney Jesup* (San Rafael, 1979), and

S.J. Watson, "Thomas Sidney Jesup: Soldier, Bureaucrat, Gentleman Democrat," in M.A. Morrison (ed.), *The Human Tradition in the Early Republic* (2000), pp. 99–114.

3. M. Peterson, *The Great Triumvirate: Webster, Clay, and Calhoun* (New York, 1987); C. Sellers, *The Market Revolution: Jacksonian America, 1815–1846* (New York, 1991); M.G. Baxter, *Henry Clay and the American System* (Lexington, 1995).

4. W.B. Skelton, "The Commanding General and the Problem of Command in the United States Army, 1821–1841," *Military Affairs*, 34 (1970), pp. 117–22.

5. R.J. Spiller, "Calhoun's Expansible Army: The History of a Military Idea," *South Atlantic Quarterly*, 79 (1980), pp. 189–203.

6. Skelton, "Professionalization in the U.S. Army Officer Corps During the Age of Jackson," *Armed Forces and Society*, 1 (1975), pp. 443–71.

7. Skelton, "Professionalization," pp. 455–56; J.L. Morrison, Jr., *"The Best School in the World": West Point the Pre-Civil War Years, 1833–1866* (Kent, Ohio, 1986).

8. Skelton, *An American Profession of Arms: The Army Officer Corps, 1784–1861* (Lawrence, 1992).

9. A.A. Ekirch, *The Civilian and the Military* (New York, 1956), pp. 60–89.

10. Skelton, "Professionalization," p. 459.

11. Skelton, "High Army Leadership in the Era of the War of 1812: The Making and Remaking of the Officer Corps," *William and Mary Quarterly*, 3rd ser., 51 (1994), pp. 271–72.

12. Skelton, "The Army Officer as Organization Man," in G.D. Ryan and T.K. Nenninger (eds.), *Soldiers and Civilians. The U.S. Army and the American People* (Washington, 1987), pp. 64–66.

13. J.D. Morris, *Sword of the Border: Major General Jacob Jennings Brown, 1775–1828* (Kent, Ohio, 2000); T.D. Johnson, *Winfield Scott: The Quest for Military Glory* (Lawrence, 1998).

14. S.J. Watson, " 'This thankless . . . unholy war': Army Officers and Civil-Military Relations in the Second Seminole War," in D. Dillard and R. Hall (eds.), *The Southern Albatross: Race and Ethnicity in the South* (Macon, Georgia, 1999), pp. 9–49.

15. J. Pohl, *The Battle of San Jacinto* (Austin, 1989).

16. J.M. Nance, *After San Jacinto: The Texas-Mexican Frontier, 1836–1841* (Austin, 1963) and *Attack and Counterattack: The Texas-Mexican Frontier, 1842* (Austin, 1964).

17. E.M. Eller, *The Texas Navy* (Washington, 1968).

18. F. Merk, *The Monroe Doctrine and American Expansionism, 1843–1849* (New York, 1966); D.M. Pletcher, *The Diplomacy of Annexation: Texas, Oregon, and the Mexican War* (Columbia, Missouri, 1973).

19. Pakenham to Earl of Aberdeen, 23 June 1846, Southampton, University Library, Palmerston papers, BD/US/51.

20. BL. Add. 49968 fol. 8.

21. S.W. Haynes, " 'But What Will England Say': Great Britain, the United States, and the War with Mexico," in R. Francaviglia and D. Richmond (eds.), *Dueling Eagles. Reinterpreting the Mexican-American War, 1846–1848* (Fort Worth, 2000).

22. BL. Add. 49968 fol. 56.

23. BL. Add. 49968 fol. 46.

24. P.S.P. Conner, *The Home Squadron under Commodore Conner in the War with Mexico* (Philadelphia, 1896).

25. BL. Add. 49968 fols. 52–54.

26. BL. Add. 49968 fol. 42.

27. BL. Add. 49968 fol. 75.

28. O. Singletary, *The Mexican War* (Chicago, 1960); J. Bauer, *The Mexican War, 1846–1848* (New York, 1974); J. Eisenhower, *So Far from God: The U.S. War with Mexico, 1846–1848* (New York, 1989); D. Frazier (ed.), *The United States and Mexico at War* (New York, 1998).

29. BL. Add. 49968 fol. 177.

30. T. Chaffin, *Fatal Glory: Narciso López and the First Clandestine U.S. War Against Cuba* (Charlottesville, 1996).

31. J.A. Meyer, " 'He is the Greatest Living Soldier': Wellington and Winfield Scott Compared," *Consortium on Revolutionary Europe: Selected Papers*, 1998, pp. 240–47.

32. J.M. McCaffrey, *Army of Manifest Destiny: The American Soldier in the Mexican War, 1846–1848* (New York, 1992) and R.B. Winders, *Mr. Polk's Army: The American Military Experience in the Mexican War* (Austin, 1997). See also R. Herrera, "God's Will and the National Mission: The American Soldier and National Expansion, 1775–1848." I am grateful to Professor Herrera for letting me see a copy.

33. W.A. DePalo, *The Mexican National Army, 1822–1852* (College Station, 1997).

34. J.A. Dabbs, *The French Army in Mexico, 1861–1867* (The Hague, 1963).

35. D.F. Stevens, *Origins of Instability in Early Republican Mexico* (Durham, 1991); P. Santoni, "A Fear of the People: The Civic Militia of Mexico in 1845," *Hispanic American Historical Review*, 68 (1988), pp. 269–88, and "The Failure of Mobilization: The Civic Militia of Mexico in 1846," *Mexican Studies*, 12 (1996), pp. 169–94.

36. J.H. Schroeder, *Mr. Polk's War: American Opposition and Dissent, 1846–1848* (Madison, 1973).

37. M.A. Morrison, "The Westward Curse of Empire: Texas Annexation and the American Whig Party," *Journal of the Early Republic*, 10 (1990), pp. 221–249 and "Martin Van Buren and the Partisan Politics of Texas Annexation," *Journal of Southern History*, 61 (1995), pp. 695–724; J.H. Schroeder, "Annexation or Independence: The Texas Issue in American Politics, 1836–1845," *Southwestern Historical Quarterly* 84 (1985), pp. 137–64.

38. G.T. Ness, *The Regular Army on the Eve of the Civil War* (Baltimore, 1990); Skelton, *American Profession of Arms*, pp. 238–59.

39. S.J. Watson, "Knowledge, Interest, and the Limits of Military Professionalism: The Discourse on American Coastal Defense, 1815–1860," *War in History*, 5 (1998), pp. 280–307.

40. M.H. Edney, "Cartographic Confusion and Nationalism: The Washington Meridian in the Early Nineteenth Century," *Mapline*, 69–70 (1993), p. 48.

41. P.B. Wiley, *Yankees in the Land of the Gods: Commodore Perry and the Opening of Japan* (New York, 1990).

42. See, *Memoirs of Lieut.-Gen. Winfield Scott* (2 vols., 1864); J. Eisenhower, *Agent of Destiny: The Life and Times of General Winfield Scott* (New York, 1997); *Letters of Zachary Taylor from the Battle-Fields of the Mexican War* (Rochester, 1908).

# 6

# Civil War

## THE CONTEXT OF MILITARY HISTORY

Civil war is a traumatic experience that brings war to society as nothing else does. Some civil wars are also of wider military importance. The American Civil War (1861–65) was a major event in the military history of the West. It was the longest and largest major conflict there between the end of the Napoleonic Wars in 1815 and the beginning of World War I in 1914. The war also saw the beginning of what were subsequently to be seen as important aspects of twentieth-century total war. These ranged from the counter-societal destructiveness of Sherman's march through Georgia in 1864 to the trench warfare near Petersburg in the last winter of the war. In addition, the devastating impact of defensive firepower, taking advantage of recent advances in infantry weaponry, on mass formations, was an important sign of a major shift of tactical advantage between the offensive and defensive; a shift that put a premium on operational planning, especially on generalship.

Many of these points became clearer in hindsight, but, at the time, there was unduly little wider interest in the lessons of the conflict for the conduct of war. There were foreign military observers, and it is possible to focus on their reports and assumptions, but the war seemed eccentric to military developments in Europe. In particular, the high-tempo character of European conflict, as in the Franco-Austrian war of 1859 and the Wars of German Unification in 1864 (between Prussia and Denmark), 1866 (Prussia versus Austria and her German allies) and 1870–71 (Prussia versus France), was linked to quick victories and short wars.

The Civil War appeared very different, but there was also criticism of particular aspects of American warmaking. American generalship and staff work were treated harshly, not in the sense that they were particularly good, but rather, as the Crimean and Franco-Austrian wars revealed, that their European counterparts were scarcely better. There was also an important degree of European cultural condescension, not least an arrogant underestimate of American fighting quality. The impact of the war on European military thought was negligible on the Continent, where the leaders of professional armies and officer corps saw no lessons in a war fought by what they regarded as mass militia armies. The broader relevance of trench warfare near Petersburg became apparent only fifty years later. Furthermore, once the Civil War had ended, it became part of a military experience that was apparently made redundant by the Prussian victories in 1866 and 1870–71, each of which was far more dramatic and important than the war with Denmark, in which, furthermore, the Prussians had not been so successful in implementing their ideas.

In Britain, in contrast, there was a turn-of-the-century fascination with the war. Army staff candidates being taught at Camberley were expected to study Colonel George Henderson's *Stonewall Jackson and the American Civil War* (1898; 3rd edition, 1902); and to know the minutiae of Stonewall Jackson's Shenandoah valley campaign of 1862, in which a mobile Confederate force had outmanoeuvred and defeated larger Union forces. Henderson also produced a study of the Fredericksburg campaign. His work looked toward later British interest in the Civil War, particularly that of the influential military theorist J.F.C. Fuller, whose *Grant and Lee: A Study in Personality and Generalship* (1932) was widely cited, and reprinted in America. Three years earlier, Liddell Hart observed: "With few exceptions Continental military thinkers ignored the instructional value of the American Civil War, regarding this as a mere war of amateurs . . . an adequate study of the American Civil War would also have warned the General Staffs of Europe to expect and prepare for a long war."[1]

We will return to the issue of comparison,[2] but, first, it is necessary to focus on the particular political context that made the war different to those of German and Italian Unification, and that set the military goals. The Civil War looked to a pattern of military mobilization and tasking that focused on civil conflict, the resultant need to create military and governmental structures, and the fight for total victory. Thus the Civil War can be related to the War of American Independence, the French Revolutionary War, especially in its civil war aspects, the Latin American Wars of Liberation, and the First Carlist War in Spain.

The context was thus different to conflict elsewhere in the West, even though the weaponry might be similar. This contrast cannot be pushed too far. In one sense, the Civil War was a nationalist struggle, as were the Wars of German and Italian Unification, although, very differently, an attempt to preserve unity rather than to create a new united state. In the circumstances of America, this task proved a more formidable one than those facing Prussia or Piedmont, the initiating powers of German and Italian unification.

The Civil War involved a degree of mobilisation of resources that was hitherto unprecedented in the history of the United States, and that certainly contrasted greatly both with the War of 1812 and with the Mexican-American War. This reflected the fundamental constitutional issue at stake, the length of the conflict, and, in particular, the failure to negotiate a settlement or to maintain the conflict as a limited war. Instead, in 1862, it became an increasingly bitter and punitive struggle. In contrast, the mid-century wars in Europe did not match up to the severity or longevity of the French Revolutionary or Napoleonic conflicts.

Furthermore, the American Civil War also witnessed an intensity of loss that marked it out from international conflict, as well as from all other American wars. The Confederate Army of Northern Virginia suffered a casualty rate of 20 percent or more at each of the battles of Seven Days, Second Bull Run, Antietam and Chancellorsville, leading to 90,000–100,000 battle casualties in Robert E. Lee's first year in command (1862–63), figures that led influential scholars such as Russell Weigley, Thomas Connelly and Alan Nolan,[3] to suggest that Lee had badly damaged his own army in a mistaken quest for a decisive battle that failed to appreciate the shift away from such battles towards victory through continual pressure and overall capability. The Confederacy mobilized 80 percent of its military-age whites but, by the spring of 1865, a quarter of the white Confederate manpower-pool was dead and another quarter maimed, casualty rates far greater than those in contemporary European conflict.

## THE ORIGINS OF THE CONFLICT

High casualty rates reflected the intensity of the struggle, which began, in 1861, as the Confederacy of newly seceded Southern states sought to take over federal military posts. The most important was Fort Sumter in Charleston Harbor, as it was a clear symbol of federal control, and did not surrender. In order to prevent the garrison surrendering when supplies ran out, President Abraham Lincoln ordered that a relief expedition be sent. This provoked Confederate pressure for the immediate surrender of the fort. The bombardment of Fort Sumter on 12–13 April led to its surrender, and was followed, on 15 April, by a proclamation from Lincoln calling for 75,000 volunteers to help suppress the rebellion. Four days later, a blockade of the South was declared.

The difference between the two sides had a pronounced geographical character, more so than in many major civil wars, for example those in England (1642–46) or China (1945–49). In part, as with other such conflicts, this geographical character was a reflection of moves early in the conflict, as the initiative was seized and local opposition suppressed, but there was a more profound difference. Far from being a social or religious conflict, this was an explicitly sectional war, one in which the rationale of the struggle related to geographical units, namely the states that had seceded and were determined to fight to protect their independence and their right to make their own arrangements. This was more distinctive than slavery as there were slave states that remained with the Union: Maryland, Delaware, Missouri and Kentucky. The regional dimension was clearly present not only in that this tier of states remained with the Union, but also because, initially, the seceding states were confined to the Lower South. Between 20 December 1860 and 1 February 1861, South Carolina, Mississippi, Florida, Alabama, Georgia, Louisiana, and Texas (in that order) seceded. At a convention in Montgomery, Alabama, these states established the Confederate States of America, with Jefferson Davis from Mississippi as President. Confederate nationalism developed rapidly.

The nature of the Civil War would have been very different had these been the only states to secede, for the formation of the Confederacy divided slave-holding America with a larger number of slave-states—Virginia, Arkansas, North Carolina, Tennessee, Delaware, Maryland, Kentucky, and Missouri—all initiallly deciding not to join the Confederacy.

The regional character of the Civil War had clear implications for goals and force structure. Because of the "regionality" of the two sides, each was more coherent than was commonly the case in civil wars. As a result, there was relatively little need for internal policing and for associated military or militar-ised activity. Instead, concern and troops could be focused on the moving zone of contact that separated the Confederacy from the Union. At a very different scale, there was a parallel with the Swiss civil war of 1847 in that the cantons and federal structure of Switzerland ensured that political division had a clear geographical component and result. That war was very different to the one in America, not because of a contrast between European and American military cultures, but due to specific factors, especially that of scale in Switzerland. There, it was a case of a 25-day war between a secessionist league of Catholic cantons, the *Sonderbund*, and the Protestant-dominated Swiss Confederacy. The short conflict was swiftly won by the latter; the major battle was at Gislikon. The secessionists lacked determination and military resources. This helped lead to total casualties in the war of only 93 killed. The Confederate forces were commanded by the able Guillaume Dufour.[4]

The origins of the American Civil War in secession, rather than class struggle or ethnicity or religious divide, also made it easier to adapt governmental systems and practices of authority and community to creating new military machines. In turn, this ease lessened the need to rely on force in order to ensure local support. Thus, there was no equivalent to the widespread terrorization of insufficiently enthusiastic local people, seen, for example, in the civil conflict that followed the French Revolution and, again, in the Russian Civil War (1918–21).

Prior to the war, regional identity had become more pronounced in America. Northerners and Southerners saw themselves as different, and, indeed, there were major differences, in demographics, society, economy, and politics. Related attitudes were seen as threatening by both. Northern criticism of slavery and states rights seemed to challenge Southern identity, while, to Northerners, the South was a moral blight or at least a drag on economic progress.

Dissension developed in a geographical context, specifically over the degree to which slavery would be extended to federal territories: areas that were not yet states. This led to disputes that became more acute from 1850, when the admission of California as a free state gave the free states a majority in the Senate. Conflict began over Kansas, as a result of the Kansas-Nebraska Act of 1854 which allowed the people in a territory to determine the issue. This led to a low-level conflict between Free Soilers and supporters of slavery that helped make violence appear an option. Rival governments were established in Kansas in 1855 and, in May 1856, conflict broke out. Federal troops were deployed to end the clashes in 1856 and 1857, and their presence successfully lowered the temperature.

Tension and a sense of the imminence of widespread violence was taken further with John Brown's seizure of the federal arsenal at Harpers Ferry on 16 October 1859. Intended as the first stage of a war on slavery, to be achieved in large part by armed slaves, this rising was rapidly suppressed by Colonel Robert E. Lee and a force of Marines, but it helped raise tension in the South. Many Southerners were convinced that the insurrection revealed the true intentions of abolitionists. This was a troubling background to the election campaign in 1860, and helped accentuate the regional character of the candidacies. The election gave victory to Abraham Lincoln of the Republicans who wished to ban slavery in the federal Territories. This led to the secession of the South, beginning with South Carolina on 20 December 1860, and the formation of the Confederate States of America.[5]

As the two sides were differentiated geographically, the fate of the borderland states was particularly important. They eventually went separate ways, Virginia, Arkansas, North Carolina, and Tennessee joining the Confederacy. Lincoln's call for volunteers and his clear intention to resist secession with force, by invading the Lower South, played the major role in leading the four states to secede. They did not intend to provide troops to put down what Lincoln termed an insurrection. This secession of the Upper South greatly altered the demographic and military context of the war. Arkansas was not able to contribute much, but Virginia, Tennessee and North Carolina were each more important in economic and demographic terms than any state in the Lower South. In order, they were the leading states in white population in the Confederacy. Together, they were to field close to 40 percent of the Confederacy's forces. These states also provided half of the Confederacy's crops and more than half of its manufacturing capacity.

In military terms, the location of this productive capacity in frontier areas was a problem for the Confederacy, as they were vulnerable and thus compromised the idea of a defence in depth. However, the gain of the four states transformed the military potential of the Confederacy. The Union no longer had a common frontier with every seceding state bar Florida, and thus the Lower South became less vulnerable. It became easier to think of the Confederacy as a bloc of territory that could be defended in a coherent fashion (and that therefore required a coherent strategy in order to bring it down). The secession of Virginia and North Carolina in particular greatly altered the location of the likely field of operations in the east: militarily, the front line of the secession was no longer on the northern border of South Carolina.

However, the Union was able to gain control of Delaware, Maryland, Kentucky, Missouri, and parts of Virginia that became the state of West Virginia. As a result, the Union consolidated its superiority in resources, blocked invasion routes into the North, and exposed the South to attack. Giving Lee's willingness to march north across the Potomac in 1862 and 1863, it is interesting to consider what the military impact of having the frontier further north would have been.

Gaining control of the border states involved civil wars in microcosm: local struggles that were affected by outside intervention. As Maryland stayed in the Union, the central battleground of the war lay between Washington, which remained the capital of the Union, and Richmond, Virginia, which became the capital of the Confederacy in May 1861. Their proximity helped give a geographical focus to the conflict and also cut across the potential expansiveness derived from the area in rebellion. It offered the prospect of the rapid end to the war that Northerners sought. The importance of the loyal border states was such that when, on 1 January 1863, Lincoln declared that Union victory would lead to the end of slavery, this related only to the Confederacy.

The Civil War saw both the creation of a new military structure, that of the Confederacy, and the massive expansion of that of the American state, the Union. As such, it was a major expansion in Western military capability. The Mexican War and policing operations against Native Americans were not effective training grounds for the Civil War. Many officers had cut their teeth in the Mexican War, but it was different, both politically and militarily, to the Civil War. In 1861, the US army was only 14,000 strong and the navy had only 42 vessels in commission. Neither the Union nor the Confederacy were prepared for a major war in 1861: this was as true of the attitudes of their commanders as of the resources available; the ability to make effective use of large numbers of troops had not been developed in peacetime.

Yet, having been defeated that year at First Manassas/Bull Run (21 July), the Union reorganized its forces into the Army of the Potomac, developing a well-disciplined, well-equipped and large army. However, that, in turn, created problems because its commander, the young and brash Major-General George B. McClellan, also replaced Winfield Scott, the General-in-Chief, thus adding overall strategic direction to his command of the Union's largest field army. This further increased the focus on the Eastern Theatre and the shrinking of strategy to the goal of Richmond, although that was not immediately clear as, after First Manassas, there was a lull in the fighting in Virginia. This reflected not simply the problems of developing effective field armies, but also the lack of drive of the commanders, particularly McClellan, although his opposite number, Joseph Johnston, was not at the forefront of offensive command. Nevertheless, the Eastern Theatre was the most prominent, in part because of the proximity of the capitals, but also as the region was the focus of domestic and international attention, and contained major centres of population.

Further west, there was a very different force-space ratio, and this created both problems and opportunities for commanders. There was a greater need for mobility, and more opportunity for it. The Cumberland, Mississippi and Tennessee rivers provided the Union forces with invasion routes, but that did not guarantee success. Ulysses Grant was to create opportunities for mobility both with his advance into Tennessee in 1862 and, in 1863, round Vicksburg, the crucial Confederate fortress on the Mississippi. Once he had made the campaign there fluid, Grant gained opportunities to achieve concentrations of strength that enabled him to take successful initiatives and drive the Confederates in on the city where they could be besieged. Vicksburg surrendered on 4 July 1863.[6] Confederate resources west of the Mississippi were now cut off. Prior to the fall of Vicksburg, the American envoy in Paris had already felt able to write "The loss of this river was more injurious to the cause of the insurrectionists than the loss of many battles."[7] Beyond the Mississippi, there was also considerable diversity in the warfare. In Missouri, Confederate irregular forces waged a bitter guerrilla conflict.[8]

## MILITARY TECHNOLOGY AND ITS IMPACT

Organisational developments on both sides can be understood in two lights: the limited success in "modernising" the American military in order to be able to fight a total war, but, on the other hand, considerable achievement in mobilizing resources for war. In the former case, much of the command techniques were amateurish, specifically the limited ability to coordinate widely-spread operations, and the absence of high-grade general staff work. The armies found it difficult to assimilate new military techniques and to adapt tactics to new weaponry. Rather than focusing on the modernity of the struggle, it can be argued that, at least in important respects, it more closely resembled Napoleonic warfare than it did World War I. This has been attributed to the difficulty of assimilating new technologies, and also the character of the generalship. The generals have been criticized for a failure to appreciate the defensive strength of rifle firepower, and for focusing on the acquisition of positions rather than the destruction of opposing armies. It has also been argued that a reliance on holding fire or the effects of advances through wooded terrain ensured that the increased range of rifled muskets was not exploited. It has been suggested that a failure to advance to a bayonet assault, and instead the halting of advances in order to engage in close-range firefights, led to a failure to press home attacks that caused indecisive combats.[9] Thus, tactics, operational methods and goals, and strategy have all been found wanting.

Conservatism can be seen in a number of respects, including the weaponry used. Muzzle- rather than breech-loading rifles predominated, and this ensured that Napoleonic-style loading routines prevailed. This led to volley fire and the accompanying tactics of massing troops in the open in order to increase the weight of the fire. Artillery remained dominated by muzzle-loaders firing solid shot by direct fire, rather than breech-loaders using indirect shot.

The rifles and cannon were nevertheless more effective than those of the early 1800s. Muskets and rifles that used the mass-produced percussion cap developed in 1822 had more reliable ignition. The cap, coated with fulminates of mercury, produced a reliable, all-weather ignition system that worked when struck: there was no need for external fire, and thus detonation. Positioned over the fire hole, the cap ignited the main charge, replacing the flintlock mechanism. The dramatic reduction of misfires resulted in a great increase in fire-power. The rifled barrel of the percussion-lock rifle introduced in the 1840s, gave bullets a spin, which led to a more stable and thus reliable trajectory and, therefore, far greater accuracy and effectiveness than the balls fired by smooth-bore muskets. They were also less expensive to manufacture than earlier rifles and, unlike them, could be fitted with bayonets, an important increase in the capability of the rifle. Captain Claude-Etienne Minié's cylindro-conoidal lead bullet (1848) expanded when fired to create a tight seal within the rifle, thus obtaining a high muzzle velocity. The bullet contained an iron plug in its base and was cast with a diameter slightly less than that of the gun bore. When fitted in the muzzle, it slid easily down the bore. When the gun was fired, the charge pushed the iron plug into the base of the bullet, causing it to expand and grip the rifling of the bore. Thus it was fired on an accurate trajectory. The combination of ease of loading and accuracy was a major advance that encouraged the mass-use of rifled small arms.

This bullet was improved by James H. Burton, an armourer at Harper's Ferry, who did away with the need for the iron plug by giving the bullet a hollow base, which expanded when the charge went off, sealing the bore. This was also a less expensive bullet. The charge was fired by an external percussion cap, and this system married up the reliability of fire of the latter with the greater accuracy of the Minié bullet. The combination was deadly. The Springfield rifle, which became the army issue in 1855, had a greater effective range than its predecessors, rifling offering greater effectiveness than smoothbore; while cannon now used timed fuses; although, in neither case, did the weapon match the breechloaders that were soon to dominate battle.

The increase in the effective range of infantry fire-power had been demonstrated in Europe (but not America) in the 1850s. The casualty rates inflicted on close-packed infantry rose dramatically. In 1854, in the Crimean War, attacking Russian columns seeking to close to bayonet point, took major losses from the Enfield rifles of the British at the battle of Inkerman. The formations and tactics of Napoleonic warfare, the column attacks and bayonet tactics employed successfully by the Austrians against the Piedmontese in 1848–49 at Custoza, Santa Lucia and Novara, now seemed likely to succeed only at the cost of heavy casualties. This posed serious problems for determining how best to achieve an offensive victory, problems that have to be borne in mind when criticising Civil War generals. To adopt less dense formations, especially a development of the skirmishing line of the French Revolutionaries, cut across tradition and training, and seemed to threaten both the cohesion of units and the build up of the mass necessary for a successful attack. The Prussians were to concentrate strength on the skirmishing line, and to adopt more extended and less dense formations that were less exposed to fire, but, their example was not on offer yet, and it depended, in part, on a level of training, especially of junior officers, that the Americans (and most other powers) lacked. In 1866, massed Austrian columns proved less flexible than the more mobile Prussian companies which had been trained to move independently, albeit within the confines of a plan. The Prussian training of junior officers ensured a dynamic interaction between hierarchy and devolved decision-making, one mediated by training, that meant that small unit operations supported and harmonized with those of large forces. More specifically, they were able to respond to the problems of command created by their "lower density" battlefield with its spread out units and dispersed formations.

It was possible to mount an effective frontal attack if one side lacked rifles. Thus, in 1854, the Anglo-French force was able to make a contested passage of the river Alma thanks to their superiority in weaponry. The poorly-trained Russians suffered heavily from an absence of rifles and rifled artillery. Had there been no such superiority, the Anglo-French attack would have led to very heavy casualties.

Yet, confusedly, or, alternatively, as a reminder of the variety of war, the last conflict before the Civil War offered a different indication of battlefield effectiveness. At Magenta and Solferino in 1859, battlefield determination won victory for the French. Their infantry advances with the bayonet were successful against poorly-trained and -led Austrian troops who were unable to draw much benefit from their technically advanced rifles: there had been inadequate training in range-finding and sighting, and, as a consequence, the French were able to close and use their bayonets. Tactics were similar to those under Napoleon I. These battles were a success for dense deployments and column formations. The French gained both ground and the battle.[10]

Use of the machine gun in the Civil War was limited: the Union Repeating Rifle, or Ager Gun, was used, following on from the Colt revolving pistol in the Mexican War. This gun was followed by the Gatling gun, which was patented in 1862 and could continue firing as long as the hand-operated crank was turned. However, machine guns made scant impact. Aside from mechanical problems, high rate of ammunition usage and expense, they suffered from being considered eccentric to battlefield dispositions and tactics. This has to be related to the individuals involved. The Union's Chief of Ordnance, Brigadier-General James Ripley, was suspicious about new developments and opposed to the adoption of Ager's and Gatling's guns. Reliability and cost factors were important to him, but he also reflected the conservatism of his department. At the same time, in the Franco-Prussian War of 1870–71, the French had, in the *mitrailleuse*, an effective machine gun, but it was used neither extensively nor intelligently: the failure to develop an appropriate tactical doctrine reduced the impact of new technology.

In other respects also, technological developments brought change but not revolution. Rail brought mobility towards the battlefield, but not on it. The same was true of telegraph and command and control. In neither case had there been a leap forward: this had to wait for the internal combustion engine and radio. The absence of both limited tactical flexibility, affecting the tempo of battle. Thus, rail and telegraph enhanced the strategic and operational dimensions of war rather than the tactical.

## ORGANIZATIONAL FACTORS AND THE ROLE OF RESOURCES

Conversely, the organizational achievement of the two sides can be employed, not least in order to stress the modernity of the struggle.[11] This can be seen not only in the mobilization and support of large numbers of troops and masses of matériel, but also in the transport and control potential offered by railway, steamship and telegraph. The resulting sites and sights of activity were impressive. Munition factories, especially the federal Springfield Armory and Samuel Colt's armory at Hartford, reflected the cutting-edge of industrial organisations.

Generalship in large part related to the coordination and deployment of resources, so that manpower and supplies were in the correct place at the right moment. Thus bringing mass to bear was necessary at the strategic, operational and tactical levels, and each posed major problems. The strength of defensive firepower made the application of mass more important, and thus focused attention both on the organizational qualities of military agencies and units, and on the control and planning dimensions of leadership and command. By 1865, the Union army was about a million strong.

The railway, which had expanded greatly in the 1840s and 1850s, especially in what became the North, made a major difference to strategy and logistics.[12] It helped the North mobilize and direct its greatly superior demographic and economic resources, and played a major role in particular battles; and did so from the outset. Reinforcements under Joseph Johnston arriving by train on the Manassas Gap Railroad helped the Confederates win at First Manassas/Bull Run. The following year, Braxton Bragg was able to move his troops 776 miles by rail from Mississippi to Chattanooga, and thus create the opportunity for a Confederate invasion of Kentucky. This looked back to recent experience in Europe where, in the Franco-Austrian War of 1859 waged in northern Italy, both sides employed railways in the mobilization and deployment of their forces; in the opening stages of the war, the French moved 50,000 men by rail to Italy, thus helping to gain the initiative.

In the Civil War, rail junctions, such as Atlanta, Chattanooga, Corinth and Manassas, became strategically significant, and the object of operations. In turn, operational plans depended on using or threatening rail links, as in the campaign that led to the battle of Second Manassas/Bull Run (28–30 August 1862), when, on 27 August, "Stonewall" Jackson hit the Union supply route along the Orange and Alexandria Railroad, destroying the supply depot at Manassas Junction. McClellan's successor as commander of the Army of the Potomac, Ambrose Burnside, proposed in late 1862 to move south along the Richmond, Fredericksburg and Potomac Railroad after he had captured Fredericksburg.

Man-made landscape features created for railways, such as embankments, played a part in battles. Jackson concealed his men in an abandoned cutting for an unfinished railroad at Second Manassas/Bull Run, and subsequently used it as a defensive position. The North's dependence on railways led to the South raiding both them and the telegraph wires that attended and controlled them, as with John Morgan's raids in Tennessee and Kentucky in 1862. Similarly, in 1864, Union cavalry in the Atlanta campaign raided the Atlanta, West Point, and Georgia Railroads. After a raid on the Macon and Western Railroad failed, Sherman moved his army to cut it, and forced the Confederates to abandon Atlanta.[13]

New transport and control capabilities created the problem of a new standard of achievement. The difficulty of the task can be underlined, not least the contrast with that facing the Prussian military: the latter had had more time to prepare and had more compact zones of deployment and operations. The Union created U.S. Military Railroads as a branch of the War Department, although this did not fully exploit the powers of the President under the 1862 Act which gave him the authority to take control of the railways. U.S. Military Railroads also built and repaired track and bridges, providing a quickly-responsive system to enhance transport links as the exigencies of the war required. Nevertheless, logistical problems continued to be serious, and it proved very difficult to supply adequately forces taking part in active campaigns. The organisational sophistication of the combatants should not be exaggerated.

There were also important developments in the infrastructure of government. The Union created a National Bank and introduced income tax and paper currency. Combined with the greater buoyancy of the Northern economy, these measures helped stabilise the finances of the Union: unlike the Confederacy, it could raise substantial loans without causing damaging inflation. More generally, the wealthier Northern society coped better with the burden of supporting the war.

The ambiguity of the evidence for military modernisation can be seen by considering conscription, which is commonly seen as an aspect of the modern planned total war that characterised the two World Wars in the twentieth century. Both the Confederacy and the Union adopted conscription and it can be seen as a major shift in the relationship between state and citizenry. Individual and states' rights were infringed. The Confederacy went much farther down this road than the Union. Central government was more intrusive in the former case and included tax in kind, impressment of supplies and other measures.

However, in practice, the impact of conscription was far less than in either

World Wars. In the Confederacy, there were occupational exemptions, as well as the all-important racial limitation: only white males were conscripted. In the end, 21 percent of the one million Confederate troops were conscripts. In the North, conscription applied to men aged twenty to forty-five (seventeen to fifty in the South), although it was possible to pay a commutation fee of $300 (a vast sum) or hire a substitute. However, the draft produced only 46,000 conscripts and 118,000 substitutes (out of 2.1 million troops). These figures possibly minimized its impact as the draft encouraged volunteering as in other episodes of conscription.

The American Civil War is far from alone among nineteenth-century conflicts in that not only is it difficult to judge their modernity, but also the competence of the protagonists; although in the case of the Civil War there was the unprecedented nature of the struggle. As a consequence, it is scarcely surprising that there were no adequate preparations. At the same time, the war revealed a lack of appropriate strategic and tactical doctrine. However, that was also true of other struggles, for example the Crimean War, where strategy occurred almost by accident, there was a lack of purposeful planning, and the British and French were fortunate that the Russians lacked modern weapons. In addition, in the winter siege of Sevastopol, the troops experienced terrible conditions, especially a lack of adequate food, clean water, shelter and clothing, that helped to lead to very heavy losses from disease, and that were not matched in the Civil War. In both cases, it is possible to underrate the achievement of deploying, supplying and controlling large forces, and also the extent to which each war ended with a victory. In both wars, the struggle lasted longer and took more lives than had been anticipated, but these are apt to be characteristics of war. In the Franco-Austrian War of 1859, the French suffered from the poor military leadership of Napoleon III, who did not match his famous namesake in strategic or tactical skill.

In the Civil War, the ability of both sides rapidly to create battle-winning armies able to further strategic plans was critical. This culminated with the command of Grant, who was appointed General-in-Chief of the Union Army in 1864. He added a strategic purposefulness and impetus to Union military policy, and subordinated the individual battle to the repeated pressure of campaigning against the Confederates. The near-continuous nature of the conflict from his advance in May 1864, which led to the Battle of the Wilderness (5–6 May), combined with heavy casualties, gave the war in the Virginia theatre an attritional character, and ground down the outnumbered South, which had a smaller army.

Rather than pause or withdraw, after the battle, with its failed attempt to outflank the Confederate centre and to break through their centre, the Union forces pressed on towards Spotsylvania Court House, where the two sides fought it out around the Confederate entrenchments from 8–21 May. Having failed to break through, Grant again tried to turn the Confederate flank, losing heavily in front of Confederate breastworks at Cold Harbor on 3 June before besieging Petersburg.

The availability of large numbers of troops in America, made it possible to recover and to continue after heavy casualties, in both attack and defence; although the large numbers created serious problems in training, supply and command. The North not only had a 2.1 to 1 edge in manpower (in terms of those who fought), but also a formidable advantage in manufacturing plant, railway track, and bullion resources. This made it easier to equip the large numbers that were raised. For example, nearly 1.5 million Springfields were manufactured, a total that reflected the productive and organizational capability of contemporary industry, and one that could not be matched in the South. The North also had a far greater capacity to raise both tax revenue and loans, and thus finance what was, for America, a conflict of unprecedented expense. War bonds provided about two-thirds of the cost of the war, and the financial strength and stability of the North permitted the issue of close to $457 million of Treasury notes, which held their value well. The first American income tax was imposed. The North did not need to finance the war by borrowing from Europe. The ability of the federal government to raise the necessary sums rather than the need to rely, as in the War of Independence, on the individual states, marked the major advance in the warmaking capability of the government, specifically the potential for a centralized monetary system. The situation was very different in the South, and there inflation was far worse. This exacerbated the problems caused by a major fall in real wages, and led to hardship as well as the spread of barter.

In his Farewell Address to his soldiers, in April 1865, Lee argued that they had been "compelled to yield to overwhelming power," a theme that was extensively to be taken up, for example by Jubal Early, a Confederate general, in an 1872 address at Washington and Lee University. Reviewing the 1862 campaign, William Dayton, American envoy in Paris, informed the French foreign minister that November that the Confederacy was running out of men and money: "equality of strength . . . has existed nowhere except on certain battlefields, and especially between the two great armies in Virginia. Here the insurgents have advanced and retreated. . . . Here at least they have shown equality of strength, but everywhere else the permanent gain has been with the armies of the Union."[14] The Northern advantage can be seen in many unexpected areas. Thus, although the South was agricultural, it had only 300,000 draught animals compared to the North's 800,000. The North's agricultural strength was formidable and, in part, rested on an ability to respond to new possibilities, specifically agricultural machinery. As a consequence, wheat crops rose in 1862 and 1863, and wheat, corn, beef and pork exports rose, even though about a third of the agricultural workforce served in the army, and indeed had to be fed there. Supply problems in the Confederacy were far more serious.[15] They encouraged Lee to march into the North in 1862 and 1863: he hoped to gain food, shoes and other supplies.

The resources issue has encouraged a focus on the nature of Southern white strategy, and it has been argued that the shortage of resources exacerbated the inherently divisive social character of the South. This has been seen in a double sense: first, that a shortage of resources, especially food and footwear, hit morale and reduced the operational effectiveness of many soldiers, and, secondly, that the impact on the home front of shortages and of other economic pressures, particularly high inflation, hit military morale, encouraging high rates of desertion. In short, it has been suggested that military factors contributed to a loss of Confederate will, but that home-front factors were decisive. Had it not been for the latter, the desertion rate would have been lower with important operational consequences. This has been linked to the "class" character of the South, with the soldiery and the home front seen in terms of "plain folk," whose interests were neglected by a plantocracy that directed the war and were, to a certain extent, insulated from its most savage consequences.[16] There were indeed serious social tensions, although that is characteristic of all conflicts that place heavy demands on the home front.

It is important not to overestimate the sophistication of the organization on either side. They cannot be described as war machines, if that is intended to suggest predictable and regular operating systems that could be readily controlled and adapted. Furthermore, organization was not only a matter of raising and moving resources. It also involved their effective use on the battlefield. In this sphere, both sides experienced major limitations, with the Union lacking the advantage it had in overall resources. Training was inadequate. The problem of the effective use of resources was seen in particular, with infantry-artillery coordination, which was later to be very important in twentieth-century conflict, not least in the success of the British in 1918 on the Western Front. By these later standards, there was woeful inadequacy in all armies in the mid-nineteenth century.

More generally, there were serious deficiencies in the operational dimension of war. Resource strength was applied through the "filter" (i.e., choke-point) of logistical systems that, in the particular circumstances of campaigns, had only limited capability. This was true not only of the campaigning in the West, where distances were great and logistical infrastructure limited, but also in the East, where the greater numbers of troops put a heavy burden on supply systems. As another aspect of operational limitations, it proved difficult to secure adequate tactical concentration and co-operation on the battlefield.

This was true of both the Union and the Confederacy. Such concentration was required for success in attack and for turning battlefield advantage into victory. Too many assaults were uncoordinated between units and arms (infantry, cavalry, and artillery), and this was also a problem for the counter-attacks that were the standard response to opponents' success on the battlefield. Moreover, a preference for linear formations made it harder to retain unit coherence on the advance, to resist flanking attacks, and to switch from firepower to shock attack: in attack, the line lacks the mass and impetus of the column. For these and other reasons, it was difficult to achieve a decisive tactical triumph. Defeats did not lead to the destruction of the defeated army; unless they were the case of the fall of surrounded positions, such as Vicksburg. In addition, an emphasis by many commanders on flank movements, rather than frontal advances, helped ensure that defeated armies were pushed back, not shattered. Furthermore, the arduous, and frequently lengthy, character of a successful fight tended to leave the victor unable to mount an effective exploitation, not least in the face of intact withdrawing forces. This also encouraged cautious generalship in the aftermath of battles.

Organization was made even more important by the lengthy character of individual battles. Gettysburg for example was fought over three days. The deficiencies of organization in part reflected the rapid expansion of the armies and the consequent lack of appropriate training on the part of soldiers and officers. The deficiencies of generals were not counteracted by effective staff structures, for these were lacking; in marked contrast to the situation in the Prussian army. The nature of the terrain, often heavily wooded and with a low density of roads and tracks, did not help in tactical coordination or in operational execution. Conversely, heavy casualties suffered in counter-attacks might ensure that withdrawing forces that had rested on the defensive had suffered heavy casualties, and were thus in poor shape to resume fighting.

Before using the contrast with Prussian warmaking to create an American exceptionalism, it is worth noting that a lack of adequate planning and of command coherence could also be seen in the Crimean War, and in the Franco-Austrian War of 1859 in which the high commands of both sides largely lost control of the course of battles, as at Magenta and Solferino. Neither was to be the masterpiece of Napoleonic envelopment that was held up as an ideal. Instead, they were more attritional in character. The French also encountered problems with transporting and supplying their forces.

Organizational requirements in the Civil War were very varied. One such was cartography. This was a conflict in which government and public demand for information affected mapping, not least by creating an immediacy of public mapping. Field commanders used maps extensively, although, certainly at the outset, they were affected by a shortage of adequate maps. Commercial cartography could not serve military purposes, and thus the armies turned to creating their own map supplies, part of a more general shift between commercial and military sources that affected military cartography in the century. By 1864, the Coast Survey and the Corps of Engineers were providing about 43,000 printed maps annually for the Union's army. That year, the Coast Survey produced a uniform, ten-mile-to-the-inch base map of most of the Confederacy east of the Mississippi. This was an instance of the more general process within the West by which war increased the capability of government by creating demands that only government direction could satisfy.

Technology served the cause of war, lithographic presses rapidly producing multiple copies of maps. The production of standard copies was crucial, given the scale of operations, especially the need to coordinate forces operating over considerable distances. This was true not only of campaigns, but also of battles. The scale of the latter was such that it was no longer sufficient to rely completely on the field of vision of an individual commander and his ability to send instructions during the course of the engagement. Instead, in a military world in which planning, and staff specifically for planning, came to play a greater role, maps became far more important. Surveyors and cartographers were recruited for the war, creating problems for private producers, who were also affected by the impact of military demands on the availability of paper, cotton, fabric, boards, and glue. Government intervention could be more direct: some maps were withheld from sale because they were seen as of potential value to opponents.

Cartography also reflected public interest in the war, not least the wish of those "at home" to follow the movements of relatives and others. Newspapers were expected to provide maps, and were able to do so because of the presence of military correspondents and recent advances in production technology in printing and engraving: steam-powered rotary printing presses and wood-engraving. The development of illustrated journalism paved the way for the frequent use of maps. Military correspondents sent eyewitness sketches that were rapidly redrawn, engraved and printed. In addition, publishers issued a large number of sheet maps. The scale of production was vast: between April 1, 1861 and April 30, 1865, the daily press in the North printed 2,045 maps relating to the war. Conversely, in the South, there was a severe shortage of press operators, printers, wood-engravers and printing materials, all of which combined to ensure that the appearance of maps in Confederate newspapers was infrequent.[17]

The difference in cartographic production reflected the stronger and more flexible character of the Northern economy. However, superior resources alone were not enough to guarantee Union success. The Confederates had to be beaten in the field. Furthermore, the resource situation was not always so favourable for the Union as might appear. Thus, superiority in manpower, did not readily translate into trained troops on the battlefield, let alone the right battlefield. Advancing into the Confederacy, the Union had to detach steadily more troops to occupy territory and to protect steadily longer supply lines, which were harassed by Confederate guerrillas. This posed serious problems for Union strategists. It reflected the asymmetry of the grand strategic aims of each side: the Confederacy ultimately had only to fend off the Union, which did not require its conquest, whereas the Union had at least to crush Confederate military power and probably to occupy considerable swathes of the Confederacy in order to force it back into the Union.[18] Defeat at Gettysburg did not end Confederate options and motivation.

The weaker power was helped by having the more modest goal; while, in terms of the history of the United States, its stronger counterpart had an unprecedented task. In some respects, there was a parallel with the Mexican War, in that the Mexican unwillingness to negotiate forced the Americans both to defeat, repeatedly, their armies and to overrun much of Mexico. However, the Confederacy was more united than Mexico, mounted a more sustained effort, and was in a position to inflict blows on core Union areas.

Unlike the Union, in neither 1866 nor 1870 did Prussia have to conquer its opponents. Indeed, unlike the Union, Prussia and the Prussian army were not really up to the task of conquering their opponents. After successes in the decisive battles fought near the French frontier in 1870, the Prussians encountered difficulties as they advanced further in France, not least supply problems and opposition from a hostile population. More generally, the resources for the total conquest of Austria and, later, France, including possibly resisting a war of *revanche* mounted from the French colony of Algeria, were not present. Such a conquest was not the option the Prussian government or Moltke sought; they wanted a swift and popular conflict, with relatively low casualties. The rate at which resources were used up militated against a long war and political support for it was lacking. The difference in goals helps explain the contrast between the Civil War and the Wars of German Unification.

## THE WAR AT SEA

Superior resources certainly played a major role at sea. They were overwhelmingly at the disposal of the Union navy, although it had to face the uncertainties created by new technology and the pressures of building large numbers of ships. The government yards were in the North, but they were not up to the task of building the new navy that was now required. Already private contractors had played a major role in building the engines for the six steam frigates authorised in 1854. In the Civil War, private contractors played a major role on both sides.[19]

The inconclusive duel between the *Monitor* and the *Merrimack* (renamed the *Virginia* by the Confederates) in Hampton Roads on 9 March 1862, was the first clash between ironclads in history, although that was because the three European navies that already had commissioned ironclads (Britain, France, and Italy) had not been at war with each other. In Hampton Roads, cannon shot could make little impact on the armoured sides of the two ships even though they fired from within 100 yards. There was only one casualty in the engagement. In the Civil War, Confederate mines sank seven armoured Union ships, compared to only one lost to fire from shore batteries. February 1864 saw the first effective attack by a submersible, mounted in Charleston Harbour when the *Hunley* sunk the Union screw sloop *Housatonic*, although she herself sank soon afterward, probably as a consequence of the stresses created by the explosion. Later that year, the first successful torpedo boat attack occurred in Albemarle Sound, North Carolina, when, with a spar torpedo fitted to a steam launch, the Union sank the ironclad *Albemarle*.

The potential of ironclads had been shown, on 8 March 1862, when the *Virginia* attacked the wooden warships blockading Virginia, employing ramming to sink one and using gunfire to destroy another. During the war, the capability of ironclads increased. Whereas the *Monitor*, a ship that symbolised the power of the machine,[20] had had two guns in one steam-powered revolving turret, the Union laid down its first monitor with two turrets in March 1863, and converted one ship to a three-turret monitor. By 1866, 41 one-turret and 9 two-turret monitors had been completed, although the three-turret *Roanoke* rolled too badly to be effective. It represented an advance in goals for the monitors, as it was designed for the high seas, whereas most monitors had too shallow a draught for this end.

However, much of the naval action did not involve ironclads nor other aspects of new naval technology. Instead, wooden steamers played a major role, especially on inland waterways. In 1862, Farragut led such a force to take New Orleans, overcoming the single Confederate ironclad and two substantial forts in defence. Yet, on the waterways, the Union also added iron armour to many of its ships. Some were "tinclads," with only thin iron armour, but others, the "city class" built at St. Louis, had 2½ inch thick armour. The Confederate loss of New Orleans and Memphis in 1862 reduced its ability to build or convert warships for service on the Mississippi and other inland waterways, although the mobilisation of the Confederate economy and the adaptability of the available manufacturing resources led to building ships at other river shipyards such as Selma and Shreveport. This permitted the construction of ironclads at places away from the coast and major rivers, and thus not as vulnerable to capture by Union forces.[21] However, it was quite an ordeal for the Confederates to get their ironclad *Tennessee* down the Alabama River from Selma to Mobile Bay. The impact of Union amphibious capability and control of the littoral was also seen in May 1862, in the Peninsula campaign, when, as Union forces advanced, the Confederates scuttled the *Virginia* on the 11th.

Most of the naval conflict involved clashes between warships and shore defences, or, as in the War of Independence and the War of 1812, between individual ships. The dispersed nature of the Confederate fleet, and Southern interest in blockade-running and privateering ensured that larger actions were uncommon. To a certain extent, Confederate force structure and goals can be seen as prefiguring those advocated by the *Jeune École* in France, particularly in the 1880s. Rather than focusing on conflict between battle fleets, they argued that France should respond to British naval power by emphasising commerce raiding, the *guerre de course*, a strategy that required fast cruisers. The torpedo boat was seen as a way to undermine British battleships. In contrast, although it did not create a deep-sea fleet, because it did not need one to fight the South, Union goals looked towards the command of the sea pressed by Alfred Thayer Mahan, especially in his important *The Influence of Sea Power upon History, 1660–1783.*

The last major action in the Civil War was in Mobile Bay on 5 August 1864 when four Confederate ships were defeated by eighteen Union ships, despite the help of mines which claimed one ironclad. The single Confederate ironclad was bombarded into surrender. Again, the fortifications at the Bay's entrance were the principal Confederate defensive asset.

It would be mistaken to present New Orleans and Mobile as naval battles only and to neglect the coastal assault aspects of both actions. Indeed, the chief obstacle to Farragut's passage of the head of the Mississippi was not the paltry Confederate naval force, but Forts Jackson and St. Philip. The same was true of Mobile, where Forts Gaines and Morgan could have kept the Union squadron out of the Bay. Once they were successfully passed, a Union victory was assured. Vicksburg was not reduced when bombarded from the Mississippi by Farragut in 1862, and Charleston also resisted Union bombardment the following year. However, both had unique geographical advantages, and it is possible to point to numerous successful coastal and river assaults by Union warships, as at Port Hatteras, Port Royal, Fort Henry, Island No. 10, Memphis, and Fort Fisher, although the first attack on the last was unsuccessful.

The Union navy turned from being a small force of deep-sea sailing ships to a far larger and more varied navy that was powered by steam and included many coastal gunboats able to mount the blockade declared in April 1861 and to support amphibious attacks. Ultimately, it became the second largest navy in the world, with (figures vary) 650–675 warships, including 49 ironclads. This was a massive organisational development. The blockade mounted by the Union fleet demonstrated the continued strategic value of seapower: 295 steamers and 1,189 sailing ships were destroyed or seized. The Union blockade, while permeable by small, fast steamships until late in the war, did grievous economic harm to the Confederacy. Most of the blockade-runners were eventually sunk or captured, although not before large quantities of arms had gotten through.[22] At the same time, Confederate privateering was a threat to Union commerce. Clashes between Confederate privateers and Union warships occurred over a vast range: including off France both and Brazil in 1864. The following year, the *Shenandoah*, the first composite (iron and wood) hulled cruising warship wrecked much of the New England whaling fleet in the northern Pacific and it was there that the last shots of the war were fired.

Blockading capability had a number of secondary consequences. For example, immigrants to the United States went to the North: over 800,000 in 1861–65. Many were liable for military service. Union control of the Atlantic ensured that this flow continued.

Alongside blockade, the Union fleet provided an amphibious capability that was useful in specific instances, and also tied up large numbers of Confederate troops in coastal defence. Furthermore, the strength of the Union navy helped to keep Lee from fighting near where warships could make a direct impact, although this was not true of operations in the Mississippi valley. The Union's seaborne and riverine campaigns were more than incidental to the conflict's outcome. Union boats played a major role on the Cumberland and Tennessee rivers in the critical campaign in western Tennessee in February 1862. Productive and military capability were closely linked. Thus, David Dixon Porter both created a shipyard at Cairo, Illinois, where a river fleet was built, and led the Mississippi Squadron effectively during the Vicksburg campaign. Similarly, operations on the river Paraguay played a major role in the War of the Triple Alliance of 1864–1870. The ability of the Brazilian fleet to gain control of the rivers, and to arrive off Asuncion in 1868, were crucial to the fate of the struggle.

The rapid demobilisation of the Union fleet after the Civil War was an important event in naval history. So also, earlier, was the avoidance of British entry into the war. Relations had been tense, as the British government expressed sympathy for the Confederacy, although it did not wish to get involved in the war. The British fleet in North American and Caribbean waters was strengthened. However, opinion within Britain was divided,[23] there were powerful voices for caution, and, to Confederate disappointment, war was avoided. On 9 February 1863, the House of Representatives was warned "unless some success in a short time crowns our arms, does not every man in this House feel that the nations of Europe will essay to intervene in our affairs," and indeed in early 1863 the French government pressed the Union to negotiate with the Confederacy, only to have the approach rejected by the Union, which insisted on unconditional surrender.[24] Convinced that independence for the Confederacy was best, the French envoy complained in March 1863 that: "American politicians were timid. They sought to sail with the current—they followed public opinion, they did not attempt to lead it. Now separation was an idea too repugnant to the pride of the people to be willingly admitted, and those Americans who themselves entertained it were afraid to announce it boldly. 'Impulsion' from abroad might be eminently useful in such a case." The envoy argued that the war might end if Britain and France recognized the Confederacy and that it was worth seeking Russian support, but his British counterpart retorted that Britain was against interfering by force.[25]

British entry would have transformed the situation at sea. American strength should not be exaggerated, as their ironclads were not really suited for distant service on the high seas, while their ships were also inferior in battle conditions, because their naval ordnance had too low a muzzle velocity to be effective against British armor, while American armor was inferior because of the incapacity to roll thick iron plates.[26]

Resources were important in securing the Union's naval superiority, but that superiority could not be applied to determine the war on land. It was the Union army that was the war-winning tool. To look for parallels, Anglo-French naval superiority over Russia in the Crimean War did not lead to the defeat of the latter. Instead, it provided a lift that permitted an invasion of the Crimea, but the Russians had to be defeated there on land. Second, France was far stronger at sea than Prussia, but was unable to employ this strength to prevent the Prussian victory in 1870–71. The more powerful naval power prevailed in the American Civil War, but not in the Franco-Prussian War.

On the other hand, it is very unlikely that the Union could have done so well had the Confederacy been superior at sea. It would have been very risky for the

Union to mount coastal attacks, and, as a consequence, the Confederacy would have been able to concentrate its forces on the landward frontier with the Union. Conversely, Union forces would have had to be dispersed along the eastern seaboard. In more specific terms, attacks on the North by Lee would have been more threatening could they have been combined with naval operations in the Chesapeake, the Delaware or further north. It would have been more difficult for the Union forces to dominate the Mississippi as they could only have attacked the valley from the north. Furthermore, the Northern economy would have been crippled had the Confederacy been superior at sea.

## THE WAR ON LAND

The successful application of military power was Grant's achievement, and his remorseless and skilful determination had led him to win the Mississippi war by capturing Vicksburg in July 1863.[27] This can be underlined by a consideration of the failures in the East of his well-resourced predecessors. These failures also show the role of contingency in determining the outcome of operations. McDowell's advance on Richmond from the north was blocked on 21 July 1861 at First Manassas/Bull Run, a clash in which neither commander behaved adroitly and in which the fate of the struggle hinged not on planning but on the arrival of fresh troops. In that, the Confederates benefited from operating on interior lines, and their reinforcements decided the battle with an attack on the Union flank. The battle ended with the flight of the Union forces who suffered heavier losses, although the Confederates failed to exploit their victory in large part because they had been exhausted and disorganised by the battle.

McClellan's advance on Richmond along the James River in May 1862 after a landing to the east of the city could have been a decisive blow. However, McClellan was no Moltke (the Prussian Chief of the General Staff); he organised for battle but could not win it. In so far as he was "the Young Napoleon" that he was termed, the pertinent comparison was with Napoleon III, who was to be defeated by Moltke, not the famous Napoleon I. McClellan lacked Moltke's fixity of purpose and ability to give rapid operational effect to strategic planning, and also greatly overestimated Confederate strength, which led him to accentuate his natural caution. In both 1866 and 1870, Moltke showed the value of winning the initial attacks and gaining the initiative to an extent that deprived the opposition of tempo.

McClellan showed little ability to learn from his mistakes, and was unable to develop an effective strategic partnership with Lincoln; instead, McClellan presented himself as a general held back by incompetent civilians, yet another aspect of his eagerness to clutch at excuses for inaction. A different general might have ended the war by capturing Richmond. Nashville and New Orleans had already fallen to Union forces in early 1862 and most of Tennessee had been overrun. On April 6–7, Grant had defeated a surprise Confederate counterattack at Shiloh that had initially seemed likely to end in victory, but that had been hit by the death of the Confederate commander, Albert Sidney Johnston, and by the arrival of Union reinforcements.[28]

Instead of adding to the picture of Confederate defeat, Lee reversed the pattern of retreat set by his predecessor, Joseph Johnston, who was wounded on 31 May at the battle of Seven Pines. Lee succeeded in blocking McClellan's cautious advance in the Seven Days battles (26 June–2 July 1862) and went on to regain the initiative.[29] This helped stiffen Northern views about the war, persuading politicians about the likelihood of a difficult conflict, and thus the need for a more intractable war, in goals and methods. Initially, instead, the Union had made no attempt to abolish slavery, both because Lincoln feared the impact of such a policy on sections of Northern opinion, particularly in the loyal border states, and because he hoped that this would weaken support for secession in the South.

McClellan, who had advocated modest war goals, as part of a generally conciliatory Union approach,[30] was replaced that November after the battle of Antietam, and Union goals and methods became more radical. The Union became committed to the emancipation of the slaves and more willing to attack Southern society in other respects as well. The high casualties in the repeated battles in the east from Seven Days to Gettysburg (1–3 July 1863) both reflected and encouraged a sense that the war would be a massive struggle that would require unprecedented determination and ruthlessness. The task of conquering the South, an area of more than 750,000 square miles, was formidable, and this posed questions for political and military goals, as well as strategy and operational effectiveness.

The last has been found wanting in numerous detailed studies of particular engagements. Poor planning and an inability to implement plans, especially the coordination of units and the interaction of moves with a planned time sequence, repeatedly emerge, as do command flaws. The basis for a systematic process of effective and rapid decision making was absent, as was one for the implementation of strategic plans in terms of timed operational decisions and interrelated tactical actions. Put differently, "the mid-nineteenth century was the heyday of loose command arrangements."[31] This encouraged incoherent strategies and piecemeal tactics that led to battles without overall direction. This was not only true in America. In the First Carlist War (1833–40), a civil war in Spain, morale, experience, surprise, terrain and numbers were crucial in battle; and all were as important as effective tactics, if not more so; these were not campaigns that left much room for a complex strategy or for sophisticated tactics by complex formations. Coordination in America was handicapped by the role of the individual states in raising and officering units on both sides. On the Union side, the regular establishment was increased, but the bulk of the army was comprised of volunteer units organized by the states and funded by the government. Their officers frequently had uneasy relations with those who served, or had served, in the regular army.

Allowing for such problems, there was still woefully poor control in many battles. Thus, at Antietam, McClellan failed to coordinate the attacks on the Confederate left, right and centre; rather as the Italians launched uncoordinated attacks when they were defeated by the Austrians at Custoza in 1866. The breakthrough, on the Confederate right on Antietam Creek, came too late. In the Peninsula campaign in 1862, Confederate units failed to coordinate their attacks at Mechanicsville (26 June), Savage's Station (29 June) and Glendale (30 June). More generally, whereas Napoleon I made effective use of separately operating corps and Moltke was able to achieve the concentration of his forces prior to battle, American commanders found that effective coordination of both corps and armies often eluded them; although their opponents were often more successful in adapting to circumstances than those of Napoleon and Moltke had been.

Specific command problems included the difficulty of getting subordinate commanders to carry out their orders. This can be seen as bringing a welcome flexibility to the implementation of plans, but wilfulness was as much the issue. This was seen with Braxton Bragg's invasion of Kentucky in 1862, which was wrecked, in part, because of the failure to cooperate by his senior corps commander, Leonidas Polk, and the theatre commander, Edmund Kirby Smith. In many engagements, it is both sides that are found wanting.[32]

This was a reflection of the fact that the United States was an unmilitaristic society which had hitherto not needed to create massive armies, especially in the heat of war. Poor planning had a particularly serious impact on offensive operations, both operationally and tactically, as it made it difficult for units to provide adequate levels of mutual support. In contrast, the Prussians had developed a system of General Staff work and training at a General Staff academy that was given much of the credit for victory in 1866 and 1870. Training of staff officers gave the Prussian army a coherence its opponents lacked; the Americans conformed more to the French system of muddling through. Prussian staff officers were given an assured place in a coordinated command system. Officers from the General Staff were expected to advise commanders and the latter were also expected to heed their chiefs of staff. This system of joint responsibility provided a coherence that rested on the reputation of the staff system, and it contributed to a high level of forward planning.

With very limited antebellum background in staff training and doctrine, and no attempt on either side to standardise the situation during the Civil War, American generals lacked this integrating staff system. Instead, they developed staffs that reflected their personalities. Lee and McClellan failed to develop staffs up to the challenge of moving and controlling large forces and providing effective operational planning, but Grant was able to scrutinise his subordinates' practical capability in order to develop an effective staff. This sustained Grant's generalship and the fighting quality of the Army of the Potomac in 1864–65.[33] Nevertheless, the command on both sides was organizationally deficient, compared to that of the Prussians, and more dependent on individual ability and initiative; a dependence that was inherently divisive. Each side lacked an effective high command, although the background was radically different to that in Prussia.[34]

Generalship was not notably better on either side, although Gary Gallagher has suggested that "Lee's accession to command probably lengthened the conflict by more than two years."[35] Lee strengthened his position by using both a flexible defence and entrenchments in a way that the French did not seek to match in 1870. Although Lee and his subordinates were effective in the eastern theatre, Confederate generalship further west was poorer. Conventionally, it has been argued that Lee failed to offer an overall strategy for the Confederacy, and, instead, focused excessively on Virginia, but this interpretation has been challenged by recent work suggesting that he had a good understanding of the general strategic situation.[36]

The generals of both sides had much in common: many had been educated in West Point and had served in the Mexican War. The legacy of the prevalent interpretation of the Napoleonic wars encouraged an operational emphasis on interior lines and defeating opponents in detail; while there was a tactical stress on turning the opponent's flank. In the Second Manassas/Bull Run campaign, Lee sought to attack the Army of Virginia under John Pope while the Union forces were divided between that and the Army of the Potomac, while Pope tried to destroy Jackson's corps while it was separated from that under Longstreet. At the same time, the interpretation of Napoleonic tactical success combined with the example of the Mexican War and contemporary ideas of heroism to encourage many officers and men to put a stress on gallant advances and charging and storming enemy positions. These ideas failed to take due note of recent improvements in firepower technology and, anyway, of the strength of close-range massed fire; although it is equally pertinent to suggest that most generals were aware of this strength but could see no other way to achieve their goals. Attacking reflected more than cultural factors. It also seemed the way to force engagements and to win ground.

However, flanking movements by units whose speed was no greater than that of defenders frequently led to frontal assaults on defenders who had rapidly altered deployment. Speed and surprise could not be readily achieved with inexperienced troops and commanders. In the battle of Fredericksburg (13 December 1862), Burnside proposed to turn Lee's right in order to cut his direct route to Richmond. In practice, the Union forces attacked positions on the Confederate right, were inadequately supported, and were repelled. Instead, the battle came to focus on frontal attacks on the Confederate left, which fell victim, with heavy casualties, to well-positioned musket and cannon fire. The following month, Burnside tried to move round Lee's left only for the "Mud March" to be brought to a halt by heavy rain.

The following year, Burnside's successor, Joseph Hooker, planned to outflank Lee's left, before trapping Lee between this column and Fredericksburg. Initial operational success was lost, however, as Hooker responded cautiously to engagement with the Confederates (1 May 1863). Instead, it was Stonewall Jackson's Second Corps that made the most successful flank move, turning the Union right before launching an effective attack (2 May). After a subsequent Union advance was checked on 4 May, Hooker retreated to the other bank of the Rappahannock River, proving that superiority in men and matériel could not yet be translated into an effective army capable of defeating the Army of Northern Virginia; and, specifically, able to bring Union force to bear, and to outfight their opponents.

Due to defensive firepower, massed frontal attacks on prepared positions became more costly and unsuccessful, as the Union, in particular, discovered at Second Manassas/Bull Run (29–30 August 1862), and the Confederates at Corinth (3–4 October 1862), Stones River (31 December 1862–3 January 1863), Gettysburg, and Franklin (30 November 1864). Such assaults were also costly in less prominent engagements, such as Glorieta (28 March 1862) where the unsuccessful Confederate attempt to conquer New Mexico and then press on to Colorado, Utah and southern California took heavy casualties from Union artillery and infantry firing from behind an adobe wall.[37] However, at this stage the Union troops were forced to withdraw due to problems on their flanks, although they were subsequently successful.

Combatants that were successful in battle could nevertheless suffer heavy losses and failure in frontal assaults that were part of the operation. Furthermore, battles that ended with the opponent retreating after frontal attacks on their positions, as with the Confederate attacks at Mechanicsville (26 June 1862) and Malvern Hill (July 1), should not necessarily be seen as vindications for those attacks. In neither of these cases did the Union forces need to retire. Similarly, in the War of the Triple Alliance of 1864–70, frontal assaults on entrenched Paraguayan forces led to heavy casualties, as with the Argentian attack at Curupaity (1866) and the Brazilian attacks at Ytororó (1868) and Itá-Ybaté (1868). In the end, envelopment proved a more effective technique.[38]

In the Civil War, the effectiveness of the defence was increased by the manoeuvrability of riflemen within the relatively compact battlefields. This permitted the ready presentation of new defensive fronts, although that required adequate intelligence and skilled generalship. At Second Manassas/Bull Run, Pope failed to respond adequately to the arrival of Longstreet's troops on his flank and was therefore driven back by Longstreet's attack.

Most of the casualties inflicted by rifle fire in the war resulted from long-range, accurately-aimed defensive fire from behind entrenchments and log breastworks. Both sides learned the necessity of throwing up entrenchments as a consequence of fighting each other to a costly draw at the battle of Antietam (17 September 1862). There, the Confederate defenders had taken heavy casualties because they were not entrenched. Bayonets and rifled muskets were increasingly supplemented by, or even downplayed in favor of, field fortifications and artillery—a sign of the future character of war between developed powers.[39] Such fortifications became more common from 1863, although artillery was important from the outset.

The Union enjoyed a major advantage in artillery, and it was carefully developed in the Army of the Potomac by Henry Hunt, from September 1862 the Army's Chief of Artillery. Hunt had played an important role in pre-war developments, helping to revise light artillery drill and tactics, and, in December 1862, was ordered to organise the army's Artillery Reserve. He played a major role on the battlefield, especially at Malvern Hill and Gettysburg, and in the siegeworks at Petersburg. Union artillery had more and better equipment than that of the Confederacy, but was also well trained.

The strength of entrenched troops through firepower became greater as the war continued, not least because the artillery did not find an effectual way of suppressing it, arguably in fact not until the British on the Western Front in 1918. As a result, the Union assault on the Confederate lines at Cold Harbor on 3 June 1864 was a bloody disaster.[40] Attacking in columns, not lines, which Union forces increasingly did in 1864 and 1865, was designed to reduce the target for defensive firepower and to increase the speed and mass of attack.

In 1862, the Seven Days battles had started a series of Southern advances and victories in the east that affected the political as well as the military development of the struggle. Lee was a figure around whom the Confederates could rally, and this was important in helping to create a Confederate "nation" from people who stood for states' rights. He understood that Confederate public opinion had a preference for taking the initiative, not responding to Northern moves, and that it sought offensive victories. This has led Gary Gallagher to reject the notion that Lee was an old-fashioned general. Instead, he suggests that Lee understood the implications of large-scale conflict between democratic societies and was by that standard "a modern warrior . . . plotting a strategy designed to erode Northern popular will before it exhausted inferior Confederate resources." The way Lee fought and won was very important to public opinion, North and South.[41] His advance across the Potomac into Maryland in September 1862 was designed to shock Union opinion by carrying the war to the North and inflicting defeat there. It also obliged the Union forces to follow, and thus reduced the threat to Richmond.

The measure of Lee's success in turning the tide of the war can be grasped by considering the failure of the French to do the same when the Prussians advanced on Paris in September 1870. Relying on new draftees, troops from Algeria, *Gardes Mobiles*, and American arms shipments, the French assembled armies to relieve the city, leading to a series of battles from early October to late January 1871. Moltke was of course a more effective general than McClellan and the Prussians also benefited greatly from the prestige and confidence they had gained in their earlier victories and from the disorientation of their opponents, which included the revolutionary Paris Commune. The French also discovered, as the Americans had done in 1861, that rapidly raising large forces created serious problems of supply, training and command. These were made much worse because France was already experiencing defeat, division and dislocation. Numbers alone could not suffice: it was the way in which men were integrated into already existing military structures that was crucial, as the Prussians showed, and this could not be done quickly or easily given the demoralized state of the French army. Despite its setbacks in early 1862 (which were less in scale than those of the French in the initial battles), the Confederacy avoided any comparable political or military crisis, but, equally, Lee's successful generalship brought a reversal in the flow of the war that his French counterparts could not achieve.

Equally, it proved impossible to win lasting success from Lee's victories, not least because the Union army remained in being. Defeated Union forces did not respond to Lee's victories by removing themselves from the campaign into fortified inactivity, as the French commander Bazaine did in Metz after the battle of Gravelotte-Saint Privat in 1870. The heavy losses of the Army of Northern Virginia forced Lee to be cautious in exploitation; and he was less able than Moltke to press on to new tasks. Furthermore, success in an individual battle was not going to bring the destruction of the opponent's military strength. Conversely, Lincoln also needed to build up Union morale, and, as a result, sought a stunning victory.

Drawing attention to the role of public opinion and army morale in helping to explain Lee's offensives and to the political value of offensive victories, does not imply that all of Lee's attacks can be thus justified. There is, in particular, criticism of Lee's decisions at Malvern Hill (1 July 1862), where frontal attacks led to 5,000 casualties without inflicting serious harm, Antietam and, even more, Gettysburg.[42] In some respects such attacks corresponded tactically to the attacks the Prussians, by superior operational skill and manoeuvre, forced on the Austrians in 1866 and the French in 1870; although, certainly at Gettysburg, the Confederates had the choice of withdrawing from the battlefield without serious tactical, operational or strategic danger or loss. As Carol Reardon has ably shown, however, the contemporary, like the subsequent, perception of the battle was shaped and reshaped by emotion and selective memory.[43]

There are parallels in operational terms with the Prussians. At the operational level, Moltke and Lee were able to use dispersed forces to outmanoeuvre more concentrated and slower-moving opponents. There was also a tactical unevenness. Moltke was aware of the hazard of closely-packed frontal attacks, and criticised them in an essay of 1864, "Remarks on the Influence of Improved Rifles on the Attack," but the Prussians could still mount such attacks and take heavy casualties, as (against Moltke's orders) at Langensalza in 1866, and at Gravelotte-Saint Privat in 1870. In both cases, the Prussians were still successful, in the first case as a result of the convergence of more numerous Prussian forces, and in the second because the French were pushed back and totally lost the initiative. Grant would have understood the point: the price of success could be heavy casualties. There was a contrast. Grant defeated Lee with an attritional pounding, whereas Moltke won a victory of manoeuvre, but then Moltke was blessed with foolish opponents. In the Civil War, it was possible for the invading army to manoeuvre so that its opponent attacked, but that was not a guarantee of success for the army resisting this attack.

In the Civil War, the impact of politics on strategy had been shown at the outset when political pressure in the North for a rapid advance on Richmond to destroy the Confederacy by seizing the capital, led to a departure from the plan drawn up by Winfield Scott, the General-in-Chief. He, instead, had called for an advance down the Mississippi to bisect the Confederacy, combined with a blockade. Termed the "Anaconda Plan" by the press, this was intended to save lives and, by increasing support for a return to the Union, encourage the Confederacy to peace or, failing that, put the Union in the best state for further operations. Scott's emphasis on planning, the indirect approach, training, and a delay in the offensive until the autumn of 1861, fell foul of the pressure for action. Without success, he opposed McDowell's proposal to attack the Confederates at Manassas Junction that July. Scott sought strategy—"a war of large bodies"—but what he termed "a little war by piece-meal" prevailed.

Throughout, the debate over military strategy was closely related to the political strategy of the conflict. The British envoy wrote on 10 March 1863:

Some of the leaders of the Democratic Party, who were active in opposing the government at the elections, five months ago, are loud in their declarations that the war must be vigorously prosecuted, and bitter in their denunciation of foreign intervention.

In fact, the opposition to the war which showed itself at the elections was based on the belief that the South might really be induced by conciliation and concessions to come back to the Old Confederation, and foreign mediation was regarded, by those who favoured it, as a means of reconciling the pride of the South to reunion. But these illusions have been dispelled. Overtures are believed to have been secretly made to the South by some of the leaders of the Democratic party, and to have been contemptuously rejected. It has, at any rate, become apparent to all the world that the Confederates are resolved to accept no terms short of an unqualified admission of this independence. The majority of the people of the North are weary of the war, but they have not yet brought themselves to endure the idea of losing any part of the old territory of the Republic. Military successes at this moment might induce them to make another vigorous effort to recover the seceded states by force.

It seems however to be generally admitted that everything depends upon the military events of the next few months. There is no longer even a semblance of unanimity in the North. There is a violent opposition in many parts of the country to the Emancipation measures or, as they should perhaps be rather called, declarations; and there is a resistance, almost amounting to mutiny, in the part of a large proportion of the army, to the enlistment of negro regiments . . . the popular feeling which in this country is almost always at first in favour of violent measures, the Administration has hitherto been very unsuccessful in its military measures, and the unpopularity which this has brought upon it, gives influence to a large party which opposes it on the score of its being weak and inefficient. Lastly, there is a peace party, which will acquire great importance, if military reverses increase the distaste for the war. Undoubtedly, if the Federal Administration can exercise the powers conferred upon it by the late Congress, it may pursue its own course, regardless of public feeling. But the impression appears to be almost universal that unless the administration can gain popularity and reputation by some military success, it will not venture to attempt to put the new measures into execution, or that, if it does attempt to do so, it will provoke in some of the states a resistance which it will be unable to suppress.

As usual everything is supposed to depend upon some particular events, and the fate of the Republican party and of the country is represented as hanging on the capture of Vicksburg and Charleston, and on the result of the election for Governor in the state of Connecticut.[44]

The role of counterfactual possibilities is illustrated by the relationship between Lee's successes and Northern war-weariness. The latter might have became stronger and this could have led to greater pressure for peace. Thus, in the autumn of 1862, there was a possibility that Democrats might capture the House of Representatives and press for peace. Had Lee's invasion of Maryland maintained its initial dynamism that September, and Lee outmanoeuvred McClellan, instead of dividing his army in the face of the Union forces who had managed to acquire a copy of Lee's orders, then the elections might not have gone for the Republicans. In March 1863, the British envoy reported that the expiry of enlistments in the North or the growth of demands for peace might slacken pressure for the war. Again, Lincoln had a particularly strong need in the early summer of 1864 for an appearance of success. The heavy casualties in Grant's unsuccessful "Overland" campaign and the initial failure to capture Atlanta hit civilian morale in July and August. Lincoln feared that he would not be re-elected. His opponent, McClellan, wanted reunion as the price of peace, but McClellan's running mate, George Pendleton, was a Peace Democrat, and the platform pressed for an armistice. However, a series of Northern successes in the Petersburg and Atlanta campaigns and the Shenandoah Valley let Lincoln back in; Atlanta fell to Sherman on 2 September.[45]

## "TOTAL" WAR

The Franco-Prussian War was "total" in one extent, in that Moltke's systematised warfare offered a hitherto unprecedented degree of methodical effectiveness. However, the scale (on both land and sea), duration and mobilisation of resources of the American Civil War provided a different degree of totality. In November 1862, the American envoy in Paris told the French foreign minister "neither principle nor policy will induce the United States to encourage a "servile war," or prompt the slave to cut the throat of his master or his master's family."[46] Nevertheless, the willingness to seize and, even more, destroy civilian property was very marked. Whereas McClellan opposed attacks on private property, Grant pressed it from the spring of 1862 in order to hit Confederate supplies and, thus, warmaking. Similarly, Major-General John Pope, Commander of the

Union's Army of Virginia in 1862, agreed with the Republicans, not McClellan, and claimed that it was legitimate to confiscate rebel property and move civilians who refused to take the oath of allegiance. His army destroyed a large amount of property and thus made its presence in Virginia especially unwelcome.

This was declaring war on an entire people. It was not novel, and had been employed in counter-insurgency warfare in Europe earlier in the century; but the Americans were certainly not used to it, although they were willing to apply such techniques against Native Americans. The combination of such techniques with the more conventional conflict of the war was arresting in a struggle on this scale. In February 1863, the British envoy reported on the Union garrison at Port Royal holding prisoner a non-combatant while the Confederacy held a Union officer captured in Florida who was threatened with trial for inciting slaves to rebel. The Union commander had declared that civilian prisoners were hostages for the safety of Union officers and that Confederate officers would be answerable with their lives if the Union officers were killed, a breach of the rules of civilised warfare that the Union commander claimed was a response to a breach by the Confederate commander. Lord Lyons commented: "It shows the danger, which seems to be daily increasing, that the present war may degenerate into a contest, in which, under the guise of retaliation on both sides, the usages of civilized warfare will no longer be observed."[47] Ordinary soldiers came increasingly to press for a more ruthless war as well as for more radical war aims.[48]

A more ruthless war also served some operational ends. A harsh approach to private property enabled Grant to live off the land. He used this in order to manoeuvre round Vicksburg, rather as Scott had done in order to capture Mexico City in 1847; although Scott was willing to purchase supplies. Sherman destroyed $100 million worth of property as he set out to destroy the will of Confederate civilians in 1864 by making "Georgia howl," although morale had already been badly hit by the loss of Atlanta and much property had already been lost or damaged as a result of the demands of the Confederate war effort. His march in November and December 1864 did indeed, in his words, "cut a swath through to the sea." This was ideological warfare. Sherman set out to punish the Confederates and to cripple their morale, as well as to destroy their infrastructure; and, as a result, sought a decisive victory.[49] His soldiers shared his objectives.[50] The Great Valley of Virginia was devastated by Philip Sheridan in 1864; South Carolina suffering similarly, at Sherman's hands, in February 1865.

The ability to spread devastation unhindered across the Southern hinterland helped destroy Confederate civilian faith in the war, and also made the penalty and limitation of guerrilla warfare apparent. Sherman had also destroyed the strategic reserve and economic resources provided by the size of the Confederacy. Slavery was also badly hit: thousands of slaves used the opportunities of Sherman's advance to escape their masters. The prestige of white rule was lost with that of the Confederacy. The British chargé des affaires reported in December 1864, as Sherman neared Savannah: "if Sherman's plans are brought to a victorious end it will have if not a material certainly a moral result as a march for upwards of three hundred miles across the enemies country without serious molestation must argue that beyond the Confederate armies at present on foot but little can be spared in other quarters."[51] Sherman did not only destroy civilian morale and any notion of defence in depth. In addition, the movement of his army north from Savannah was an instance of the indirect approach that has been overshadowed by Grant's successes against Lee in Virginia: Sherman's advance threatened Lee's rear. Columbia, South Carolina, was occupied on 17 February, North Carolina was entered the following month, and Raleigh was occupied on 13 April. This contributed to the situation in which Lee was defeated without his army being destroyed. Liddell Hart gave Sherman rather than Grant, the credit for overthrowing the Confederacy. He saw Sherman's advance as a decisive instance of the value of the indirect approach.[52]

In their different ways, Sherman and Grant ensured that the uncertainty of war undermined the Confederacy. They managed risk and uncertainty; while their opponents came, in 1864, to experience it. The tempo of Union operations exploited the uncertainty of conflict and directed it against the Confederacy's military as well as its socio-political underpinning. Sherman's advance was also the culmination of the long series of Union triumphs in the western theatre. In 1862 and 1863, these had not prevented Lee from advancing in and from Virginia, and, to a considerable extent, it had been possible to trade space in the West for time with which to attack in the East. This potentially war-winning formula had failed, in the East, not across the Appalachians, but it was only after that that the Union forces were able to exploit their success in the West in order to attack what could otherwise have been the defence in depth in the East.

Another aspect of "totality" was suggested by the character of warfare round Petersburg in 1864–65, at once attritional and prefiguring the siege tactics of World War One. The first recorded battlefield appearance of barbed wire (originally devised to pen cattle in) occurred at Drewry's Bluff in May 1864. Edward Porter Alexander, a Confederate artillery general, recorded of the trenches near Petersburg:

the enemy promptly built a strong line of rifle pits, all along the edge of the dead space with elaborate loop holes and head logs to protect their sharpshooters, and they maintained from it a close and accurate fire on all parts of our line near them. . . .

We soon got our lines at most places in such shape that we did not fear any assault, but meanwhile this mortar firing had commenced and that added immensely to the work in the trenches. Every man needed a little bombproof to sleep in at night, and to dodge into in the day when the mortar shells were coming.[53]

Trench warfare did not originate at Petersburg. For example, the Anglo-French force that besieged Sevastopol in the Crimea in 1855 had to face a type of trench warfare that was different to earlier sieges. The Russian army was strongly entrenched outside the town, making able use of earth defences, and supported by over 1,000 cannon. The Allies fired 1,350,000 rounds of artillery ammunition during the siege. Nevertheless, the trenches near Sevastopol can be seen as an aspect of a traditional siege rather than as a development of field entrenchments as in Virginia in 1864. The entrenchments there, for example at the lengthy battle of Spotsylvania in 1864, looked towards those in World War One, although the more fluid nature of operations ensured that they were less developed. There were parallels between trench warfare in 1864–65 and in World War I, for example defensive firepower, the limited value of cavalry, and sappers laying mines, but the great difference, at least in so far as the Western Front was concerned, was that in America there was no equivalent to the Channel and Switzerland to anchor the trenches at each end. As a result, the trenches could be outflanked, as Grant did with Lee in 1865. Lee could not put trenches all the way around Richmond, or he would have been starved out, and, to the west, the land went on all the way to the Pacific.

Furthermore, the purpose of entrenchments was different in the two conflicts. It was not necessary to resist lengthy bombardments by heavy guns firing plunging shots, as in World War I; nor indeed was there reinforced concrete with which to protect positions. Trenches in Civil War battlefields were shallower, and designed to protect against non-plunging shot. In contrast, the siege of Petersburg was drawn out, the trenches were deeper, and the trench systems more complex.

## THE LEGACY OF THE WAR

The direct legacy of the American Civil War was political rather than military. There was a swift return to civil peace, legitimacy, and unity. There was not only no powerful revanchist movement for Southern Separatism, but also, in order to win, the Union had not embarked on a radicalizing process akin to that which eventually affected England in the Civil War, or France in 1793–94. The United States remained a united state dominant in the Western hemisphere and without the source of division that an independent Confederacy would have provided. This was crucial to global history: the century was to close with Britain and the United States the two most powerful countries in the world.

However, the disbandment of the forces raised for the Civil War, so that the army fell to 29,000 men in 1871, ensured a lack of continuity that meant that the military lessons learned were not retained. Furthermore, the United States did not embark for another fifty years on a great power war that might have kept such lessons pertinent. Instead, prior to the outbreak of war with Spain in 1898, the American military engaged in conflict with Native Americans, a very different experience in terms of practice and relevant doctrine.

In the 1860s, American politics and society were not stamped with the marks of a permanent militarization, and, in the short term, there was a lack of promotion in the much reduced army, and an emphasis on peacetime profession-alism.[54] The potential had been very different. Jefferson Davis was determined to fight on after Lee's surender at Appomattox on 9 April and, to that end, he headed for the Trans-Mississippi region, only to be captured in Irwinville, Georgia, on 10 May. Joseph E. Johnston, commander of the other major Confederate force in the field, that in North Carolina, had already surrendered to Sherman at Durham Station, North Carolina, on 20 April. Richard Taylor, who commanded the last Confederate force east of the Mississippi, surrendered at Citronelle, Alabama, on 4 May. In the Trans-Mississippi, Kirby Smith's army surrendered on 26 May. There was to be no guerrilla war. Davis had proposed one in a proclamation after the fall of Richmond:

Relieved from the necessity of guarding cities and particular points . . . with an army free to move from point to point . . . operating in the interior of our own country, where supplies are more accessible, and where the foe will be far removed from his own base . . . nothing is now needed to render our triumph certain but the exhibition of our own unquenchable resolve.[55]

Such a conflict would have been difficult for the Union forces. Alongside pressure, not least from within the military, for demobilisation, there would have been the problem of containing guerrilla action from across the extent of the South, not least given the nature of much of the terrain and cover. The problems the British faced in the Carolinas in 1780–81 offer an interesting indication. So also does the First Carlist War in which the Carlists created a successful guerrilla army in their Basque-Navarre heartland that made full use of the mountainous terrain in order to seize the initiative, although they were far less successful when they left the mountains and sought to capture cities. The success of the Cuban rebels in 1868–78 in taking advantage of the rugged terrain to ambush Spanish forces forced the Spaniards to turn to conciliatory promises as well as reinforcements in order to end the rebellion.[56] Guerrilla warfare had indeed characterised the American Civil War where terrain was difficult and the number of regulars limited.[57]

Lee, however, ignored Davis's call. He felt that such a policy would lead to chaos, with guerrilla bands lacking discipline and direction and forced to live on civilians. Such warfare would also have tested socio-cultural assumptions and practices, both the belief in honourable conflict held by Lee and the Christian gentlemen who dominated the Confederacy, and white supremacy over blacks. A recent comparison of the Confederacy with South Africa, where guerrilla opposition to the British in the Boer War (1899–1902) helped ensure that when the war ended, Britain conceded a self-governing status that enabled the maintenance of a whites-only franchise, puts the stress on social, not military factors: "The Boer decision for guerrilla war in 1900 did not threaten existing class and status relationships among whites to the extent that would have been the case if the Confederacy had made a similar decision in 1865."[58]

As an index, however, of the extent to which the verdict of the war was unacceptable to many, a large number of Confederates was to migrate to South America. It is not known how many went, and figures vary from 8,000 to 40,000, with 20,000 possibly the safest estimate. Most of the exiles went to Brazil where they were encouraged by the Emperor, Dom Pedro. These *Os Confederados* did not, however, serve as the basis for any attempt to challenge the war's verdict.[59]

In the former Confederacy, the structure of a militarised occupation was rapidly created. The South was divided into the divisions of Atlantic, Gulf, Mississippi and Tennessee, each under the command of a major general (a technique employed in England under Oliver Cromwell), and these were subdivided into military departments. The military were responsible for a range of tasks, mostly civil, but including the military task of disarming local militia and preserving order. The latter was particularly necessary in some areas. Thus the guerrilla warfare of Appalachia left a legacy of vendettas and feuds.[60] The troops were also a restraint on any attempt to mount organised resistance or to resort to low-level seditious behaviour.

At least initially, politics ensured that this task was potentially enlarged. Although Lincoln's Vice-President and successor, Andrew Johnson, wanted a rapid return to normality, at least in the shape of Southern self-government and re-entry into the Union, the majority in Congress disagreed. They pushed through the Reconstruction Acts of 1867 which dissolved the Southern state governments (they had passed racist "black codes") and reintroduced federal control. This gave the army the potential role of preserving the federal order against local opposition. The difficulty of this task was exacerbated by the unpopular nature of the new state governments that were created on behalf of the "carpetbaggers": Northern adventurers; at least unpopular as far as the bulk of the white population was concerned. The army was expected to support the new governors and the new order. This involved protecting government buildings, blacks and polling places. In March 1863, the French envoy had suggested to his British counterpart that the war would end with the independence or subjugation of the South: "Either event would make so great a change on this Continent as to amount to a revolution." If subjugation, "the hatred between the two sections of the country could never now be appeased. The North could govern the South only by force, and by establishing a rigid despotism there. This would at once destroy all the elements which had produced the strength and the prosperity of the Americans. It was freedom—the "spontaneity of individual action" which had made the Americans what they were."[61]

The army was not simply a latent presence in the South. It also was the agency for the new order. Thus, in Galveston, a centre for occupation forces, Major-General Gordon Granger announced emancipation for Texas slaves on 19 June 1865. The army played an important role in the Bureau of Refugees, Freedmen, and Abandoned Lands, which answered to the War Department. Its commissioner from 1865 to 1872 was Major General Oliver Otis Howard, a West Point graduate who had played an important command role throughout the Civil War, losing an arm at the Battle of Seven Pines. He was responsible for looking after the freed slaves, and also dealing with confiscated and abandoned properties. The army also played a major role in restoring infrastructure, building bridges and running railways.

The military support for this new program was modest: about 20,000 troops from 1867, and far fewer in the 1870s as securing the West became the central issue for the Army. As a consequence, even had it been willing, the Army was not in a position to support Reconstruction once it was challenged by widespread violence against blacks. The foundation of the Klu Klux Klan, a Confederate veterans movement, in 1866 was followed by several thousand lynchings, although not all of them were by the Klan.[62] In 1866, the army intervened to prevent a pogrom, if not massacre, of the black population of New Orleans. White militias that had been created after the Civil War were disbanded by the government in 1867, but whites clashed with the black militias recruited by Radical Republican state governments. Bodies such as the White Brotherhood and the White League challenged Reconstruction, the White League tried to seize control of New Orleans in 1874, and by 1877 the black militias had been disbanded or lost control.[63]

By then, the Republican governments in the South had been overthrown, in part by the threat of mob violence, in every state bar Florida, Louisiana and South Carolina. It was only in these states that the troops sent to support Reconstruction remained (and there were now very few). As a result of complex political manoeuvres after the 1876 presidential election, in which disputed returns to the electoral college from these states were crucial, a compromise awarded the presidency to the Republican candidate, Rutherford B. Hayes, a volunteer who had risen to be a Major General in the Union army, but only in return for withdrawing the troops from the three states. This led to the fall of their Republican governments,[64] and the new, more limited role for the army was underlined by the Posse Comitatus Act of 1878 which banned the use of the military in law enforcement.

In addition, northern politicians and public opinion came to support reconciliation. Lee received good obituaries in the Northern press, and in 1898 the surviving Confederate generals were made U.S. generals.

Thus, changing political parameters ended the prospect of a situation in which the Army would have been a long-term occupation force, with a task focused on controlling civilians, and possibly even low-level counter-insurgency work. This was another example of the extent to which important military developments were far from inevitable.

This political tasking was matched externally where the Americans did not attack the French in Mexico, nor invade Canada, as the British feared. Nevertheless, the military capability built up and shown in the Civil War had a major effect on other powers, and also gave force to American political demands. The Monroe Doctrine could be revived. Already, in 1861, Secretary of State William

Seward had suggested war with France and Spain over their Caribbean policy in order to unite America. In 1863, Lincoln became concerned about the buildup of French forces in Mexico, their capture of Mexico City, the subsequent move of French units towards the American border in order to suppress opposition in northern Mexico, and the nature of French intentions. It was reported that France saw its presence in Mexico as a bar to American dominance of the region. This led Lincoln to press for the dispatch of a Union force to the Texas coast. After the Civil War, American pressure, which included moving troops to the Rio Grande in 1866, helped lead the French to leave Mexico.[65]

In 1866, such pressure also led the Spaniards to end hostilities with Peru and her ally Chile that had begun in 1864: the Spaniards had occupied the Chinca Islands, from whose guano (bird droppings) Peru derived much of its income, and had also bombarded Callao and Valparaíso. In May 1864, Seward had pressed the British envoy about Spanish conduct, had suggested that the two states co-operate in order to settle the dispute, and had said that the United States would complain about Spanish policy in the New World, including the annexation of the Dominican Republic in 1861. The American tone was tough: "it might be impossible for the government of the United States to restrain the indignation of the country."[66] The Spaniards abandoned the Dominican Republic, which had indeed turned out to be a fruitless commitment.

In 1867, America annexed Midway and bought Alaska and the Aleutian Islands from Russia for $7,200,000, although critics condemned this as "Seward's Folly." Russia's Pacific ambitions were directed to the opposite shore of the Pacific where in 1858–60 they had acquired the Amur Valley and the nearby Pacific coastline from China. Seward also suggested gaining Hawaii, the Dominican Republic, and the Danish West Indies, and building a canal across Central America. Such plans did not seem unrealistic in the aftermath of the Civil War. The Americans had again demonstrated force projection in September 1864, when the corvette *Jamestown* had cooperated with British, French and Dutch warships in acting against batteries erected by the Prince of Nagato that had threatened the use of the Straits of Shimonoseki by foreign shipping.[67]

Had the tension between America and the French over Mexico spilled over into conflict then this might have made it harder to pacify the South. Several prominent Confederates found shelter with Maximilian. In 1865, John Bankhead Magruder became one of his Major Generals. However, the possibility that Mexico might become a base for Confederate revanche was lost.

The Civil War was followed by a political stabilisation to north and south (and, eventually, after their conquest, with the Native Americans as well). This helped ensure a shift in American military priorities in the late nineteenth century. Like Britain and Japan, the United States was not threatened over land, and so all three could concentrate their defence spending on their navies. In contrast, both the army and fortifications became lesser priorities. This shift has been related to changing political priorities within the United States, but the suggestion here is that the role of contingent circumstances has to be stressed, specifically the ability to win the Civil War without going on to create long-term military commitments in the South or in Mexico or Canada. Furthermore, the Americans had not yet developed the practice of intervening militarily in Central America or the Caribbean.

## COMPARISONS WITH EUROPE

The Civil War took far longer than the individual wars of German and Italian Unification, but it was far more decisive. The Confederacy ceased to exist as an independent state, a very different fate to that of Denmark, Austria and France. In the Franco-Austrian War of 1859, the French did not press on to attack the powerful Austrian fortresses of the Quadrilateral and conquer the Venetia, which was left to Austria. The Union forces had no such limited option. Aside from leading to the total fall of the Confederacy, the Civil War transformed the relationship between the federal government and the states. Similarly, there was a major social change, with the ending of slavery and the freeing of four million slaves; again, there were no comparisons in the European wars. Nevertheless, the relative length of the conflicts greatly impressed contemporaries. Although the Napoleonic Wars had been lengthy, subsequently Western commentators had become used to short wars and to decisive campaigning. Indeed Scott's advance on Mexico City fitted into this analysis. As a result, it was easy to overlook the magnitude of the task facing the North and to regard the war as lengthy, indeed overly lengthy.

To a certain extent, as already suggested, this was reasonable. Due, in large part, to mismanagement, the opportunity to seize Richmond in 1862 had been lost, while, at Antietam, McClellan failed to commit his reserve, which could have broken the Confederate centre, and subsequently failed to disrupt Lee's retreat, both immediately after the battle, and later while the Confederates were retreating across the Potomac. As with George Washington's retreat after the battle of Long Island, there was an opportunity to wreak havoc on an army having to organise a difficult retreat from a vulnerable position; and it was not taken in either case.

However, the North's task was made more difficult, because, in contrast to the situation facing the Piedmontese in 1860 and the Prussians in 1866 and 1870, it was the more poorly-commanded army, that of the Union, that had to mount the strategic offensive. Bar for the unexpected success of Lee in regaining the initiative, the pattern of the Civil War appeared likely to be that of a short conflict that might match that of the Prussians, or of the French against Austria in 1859: Union victory in a war of the frontiers, that, in the case of the Civil War, would lead the Confederacy to abandon the struggle to maintain independence.

Even then, a war of the frontiers was a more formidable challenge in America. Union success in early 1862 was so farflung and extensive that the "frontiers" have to be understood in different terms to those of say the Metz and Sedan campaign of 1870. For example, the advance of Halleck's army as far as Corinth, Mississippi, was a dramatic demonstration of the extent to which initial successes had provided the basis for long-distance advances. The latter were seen in 1863 and 1864, and these gave the Union both the Mississippi axis and that from Tennessee via Atlanta to the Atlantic. There were long advances in Europe, for example those of Garibaldi fighting his way through Sicily and southern Italy, or Russian forces suppressing nationalist revolutions in Hungary in 1849 and Poland in 1863. Neither, however, matched the logistical challenge and the opposition faced by the Union forces. More generally, there was a contrast in circumstances with the Wars of German Unification that reflects credit on both sides in the Civil War.

Deficiencies in command and control by Austria and France enabled the Prussians to outmanoeuvre them. The Americans should not be thought inadequate in comparison. Moltke himself was increasingly sceptical about the potential of the strategic offensive, because of increases in defensive fire-power and the size of armies. This was to be amply displayed in the German nemesis in World War I; and the Civil War offered important lessons that looked to the future. There was also an important contrast. In World War I, the Germans suffered from their failure to keep or create an open campaign zone with room for manoeuvre and a tempo permitting the retention of the initiative. This operational immobility did not characterise the Civil War.

It is valuable to look for parallels and comparisons between the Civil War and conflict in Europe, if only, in part, to focus on the contrasts that emerge. To that end, it is important to note that it is too limited to see the Wars of German Unification as defining European warfare and thus as providing a ready frame of contrast with the Civil War. Instead, this paradigm model should be rejected, and it is necessary to stress the variety of mid-nineteenth century European warfare. The same was true of twentieth-century warfare, not least that of the last fifty years. As a result, it is clear that the term modernity needs to be employed with far greater care than when it was seen to describe the total warfare of the two World Wars. "Modernity" today can be seen as encompassing cutting-edge high technology preparations for conflict between "super-powers," as well as the "limited" warfare waged by those powers, and the diversity of conflicts involving lesser states. From the perspective of modern America, with relatively small forces of regulars prepared for conflict with other major powers, principally China, as well for expeditionary-style limited conflicts, it is possible to look back to American military history in the period 1775–1865 and to see precursors of modernity, not only in the Civil War but also in the earlier regular army with its conflicts with Native Americans and with the challenge of British power. The comparisons cannot be pushed too far, but they serve to underline the danger of assuming a clear path towards modern war.

## NOTES

1. Liddell Hart, "Strategy and the American War," *Quarterly Review* (July 1929), pp. 118, 130, London, King's College, Liddell Hart Archive, Liddell Hart papers 10.5/1929/1; J. Luvaas, *The Military Legacy of the Civil War* (Lawrence, Kansas, 1999).

2. On which, see S. Förster and J. Nagler (eds.), *On the Road to Total War: The American Civil War and the German Wars of Unification, 1861–1871* (Cambridge, 1997), and, less successfully, P. Howes, *The Catalytic Wars: A Study of the Development of Warfare, 1860–1870* (1998).

3. Eg. A.T. Nolan, *Lee Considered. General Robert E. Lee and Civil War History* (Chapel Hill, 1991), p. 105.

4. J. Remak, *A Very Civil War: The Swiss Sonderbund War of 1847* (Boulder, Colorado, 1993).

5. B.H. Reid, *The Origins of the American Civil War* (1996).

6. W.E. Grabau, *Ninety-Eight Days: A Geographer's View of the Vicksburg Campaign* (Knoxville, Tennessee, 2000).

7. PRO. FO. 5/877 fol. 149.

8. M. Fellman, *Inside War: The Guerrilla Conflict in Missouri During the American Civil War* (New York, 1989).

9. P. Griffith, *Battle Tactics of the Civil War* (New Haven, 1987); Reid, *Civil War in the United States. 1861–1865* (2000).

10. J.M. Black, *Western Warfare 1775–1882* (2001), pp. 121–29.

11. E. Hagerman, *The American Civil War and the Origins of Modern Warfare* (Bloomington, Indiana, 1988); R.A. Doughty, I.D. Gruber and others, *The American Civil War: The Emergence of Total Warfare* (Lexington, Mass., 1996); D.E. Sutherland, *The Emergence of Total War* (Fort Worth, 1996).

12. R. Pickenpaugh, *Rescue by Rail: Troop Transfer and the Civil War in the West* (Lincoln, Nebraska, 1998).

13. D. Evans, *Sherman's Horsemen: Union Cavalry Operations in the Atlanta Campaign* (Bloomington, Indiana, 1996).

14. PRO. FO. 5/877 fol. 150.

15. W. Blair, *Virginia's Private War. Feeding Body and Soul in the Confederacy, 1861–1865* (New York, 2000).

16. D. Williams, *Johnny Reb's War. Battlefield and Homefront* (Abilene, 2000).

17. D. Bosse, *Civil War Newspaper Maps of the Northern Daily Press: A Cartobibliography* (Westport, 1993) and *Civil War Newspaper Maps* (Baltimore, 1993).

18. P. Maslowski, "To the Edge of Greatness: The United States, 1783–1865," in W. Murray, M. Knox and A. Bernstein (eds.), *The Making of Strategy. Rulers, States, and War* (Cambridge, 1994), p. 236.

19. B. Anderson, *By Sea and by River: The Naval History of the Civil War* (New York, 1962); K. Hackemer, "Building the Military—Industrial Relationship. The U.S. Navy and American Business, 1854–1883," *Naval War College Review*, 52 (1999), pp. 89–111 and *The U.S. Navy and the Origins of the Military Industrial Complex, 1847–1883* (Annapolis, 2001).

20. D.A. Mindell, *War, Technology, and Experience aboard the USS "Monitor"* (Baltimore, 2000), e.g., p. 15. For uncertainty about what ironclads could achieve, K. Hack-

emer, "The Other Union Ironclad: The U.S.S. *Galena* and the Critical Summer of 1862," *Civil War History*, 40 (1994), pp. 226–47.

21. W.N. Still, *Iron Afloat: The Story of the Confederate Armorclads* (Nashville, 1971).

22. R.M. Browning, *From Cape Charles to Cape Fear: The North Atlantic Blockading Squadron during the Civil War* (Tuscaloosa, Alabama, 1993).

23. F.L. Owsley, *King Cotton Diplomacy* (Chicago, 1959); K. Brauer, "British Mediation and the American Civil War: A Reconsideration," *Journal of Southern History*, 38 (1972), pp. 49–64; H. Jones, *Union in Peril: The Crisis over British Intervention in the Civil War* (Chapel Hill, 1992); R.J.M. Blackett, *Divided Hearts. Britain and the American Civil War* (Baton Rouge, 2001).

24. *Daily Globe*, 9 Feb. 1863; PRO. FO. 5/877 fols. 93, 146.

25. PRO. FO. 5/879, fols. 52–57.

26. J.F. Beeler, *British Naval Policy in the Gladstone-Disraeli Era 1866–1880* (Stanford, California, 1997), pp. 199–200.

27. J.R. Arnold, *Grant Wins the War* (New York, 1997).

28. C.P. Roland, *Albert Sidney Johnston* (Abilene, 2000).

29. S.W. Sears, *To the Gates of Richmond: The Peninsula Campaign* (New York, 1992); S.H. Newton, *Joseph E. Johnston and the Defense of Richmond* (Lawrence, Kansas, 1999).

30. Reid, "Rationality and Irrationality in Union Strategy, April 1861–March 1862," *War in History*, 1 (1994), p. 38; M. Grimsley, "Conciliation and Its Failure, 1861–1862," *Civil War History*, 39 (1993), pp. 317–35.

31. Reid, *The American Civil War and the Wars of the Industrial Revolution* (1999), p. 41.

32. W.J. Wood (ed.), *Civil War Generalship: The Art of Command* (Westport, Conn., 1996); Gallagher (ed.), *Three Days at Gettysburg: Essays on the Confederate and Union Leadership* (Kent, Ohio, 1999); S.E. Woodworth, *Six Armies in Tennessee: The Chickamauga and Chattanooga Campaigns* (Lincoln, Nebraska, 1998), and *No Band of Brothers: Problems of the Rebel High Command* (Columbia, Missouri, 1999); A. Castel, *Decision in the West: The Atlanta Campaign of 1864* (Lawrence, Kansas, 1994); G.C. Rhea, *The Battle of the Wilderness, May 5–6, 1864* (Baton Rouge, Louisiana, 1994); T.B. Buell, *The Warrior Generals: Combat Leadership in the Civil War* (New York, 1997); M.A. Palmer, *Lee Moves North: Robert E. Lee on the Offensive* (New York, 1998).

33. R.S. Jones, *The Right Hand of Command: Use and Disuse of Personal Staffs in the Civil War* (Mechanicsburg, 2000).

34. A. Jones, *Civil War Command and Strategy: The Process of Victory and Defeat* (New York, 1992).

35. Gallagher (ed.), *The Richmond Campaign of 1862* (Chapel Hill, 2000), p. xi.

36. J.P. Harsh, *Confederate Tide Rising: Robert Lee and the Making of Southern Strategy, 1861–1862* (Kent, Ohio, 1998) and *Taken at the Flood: Robert E. Lee and Confederate Strategy in the Maryland Campaign of 1862* (Kent, Ohio, 1999).

37. D.E. Alberts, *The Battle of Glorieta. Union Victory in the West* (College Station, Texas, 1998), p. 120.

38. H.G. Warren, *Paraguay and the Triple Alliance: The Postwar Decade, 1869–1878* (Austin, 1978), pp. 8–26.

39. Gallagher (ed.), *Antietam: Essays on the 1862 Maryland Campaign* (Kent, Ohio,

1989) and (ed.), *The Fredericksburg Campaign: Decision on the Rappahannock* (Chapel Hill, 1995).

40. R.W. Maney, *Marching to Cold Harbor: Victory and Failure, 1864* (Shippensburg, Pennsylvania, 1995).

41. Gallagher, "An Old-Fashioned Soldier in a Modern War? Robert E. Lee as Confederate General," *Civil War History*, 45 (1999), p. 321, and *The Confederate War. How Popular Will, Nationalism, and Military Strategy Could Not Stave off Defeat* (Cambridge, Mass., 1997), pp. 58–59, 115.

42. Gallagher, " 'If the Enemy is There, We Must Attack Him'": Robert E. Lee and the Second Day at Gettysburg," in Gallagher (ed.), *The Second Day at Gettysburg: Essays on Confederate and Union Leadership* (Kent, Ohio, 1993), pp. 1–32.

43. C. Reardon, *Pickett's Charge in History and Memory* (Chapel Hill, 1997). See also M.H. Blatt, T.J. Brown and D. Yacovone (eds.), *Hope and Glory: Essays on the Legacy of the Fifty-fourth Massachusetts Regiment* (Amherst, 2001) and N.L. York, *Fiction as Fact. The Horse Soldiers and Popular Memory* (Kent, Ohio, 2001).

44. PRO. FO. 5/879 fols. 163–65.

45. PRO. FO. 5/879 fols. 58–59; M.J. Forsyth, "The Military Provides Lincoln a Mandate," *Army History*, no. 53 (2001), pp. 11–17.

46. PRO. FO. 5/877 fol. 149.

47. PRO. FO. 5/877 fols. 139–41.

48. J.A. Frank and B. Duteau, "Measuring the Political Articulations of United States Civil War Soldiers: The Wisconsin Militia," *Journal of Military History*, 64 (2000), esp. pp. 71–76. For their experience, G. Linderman, *Embattled Courage: The Experience of Combat in the American Civil War* (New York, 1989).

49. C. Royster, *The Destructive War: William Tecumseh Sherman, Stonewall Jackson, and the Americans* (New York, 1991); M. Grimsley, *The Hard Hand of War: Union Military Policy Toward Southern Civilians, 1861–1865* (New York, 1995); V.D. Hanson, *The Soul of Battle: From Ancient Times to the Present Day. How Three Great Liberators Vanquished Tyranny* (New York, 1999).

50. J.T. Glatthaar, *The March to the Seas and Beyond: Sherman's Troops in the Savannah and Carolinas Campaigns* (Baton Rouge, Louisiana, 1995).

51. PRO. FO. 5/964 fols. 210–11.

52. LH. 10.5/1929/1, pp. 127–28.

53. Gallagher (ed.), *Fighting for the Confederacy. The Personal Recollections of General Edward Porter Alexander* (Chapel Hill, North Carolina, 1989), pp. 435–36.

54. M.R. Grandstaff, "Preserving the 'Habits and Usages of War': William Tecumseh Sherman, Professional Reform, and the US Army Officer Corps, 1865–1881, Revisited," *Journal of Military History*, 62 (1998), pp. 521–45.

55. N.A. Trudeau, *Out of the Storm: The End of the Civil War, April-June 1865* (Boston, 1994).

56. J.L. Tone, "The Machete and the Liberation of Cuba,"*Journal of Military History*, 62 (1998), pp. 14–15.

57. S.M. O'Brien, *Mountain Partisans: Guerrilla Warfare in the Southern Appalachians, 1861–1865* (Westport, 1999).

58. G.M. Fredrickson, *Why the Confederacy did not fight a Guerrilla War after the fall of Richmond: A Comparative View* (Gettysburg, 1996), p. 29.

59. E.C. Harter, *The Lost Colony of the Confederacy* (College Station, 2000).

60. O'Brien, *Mountain Partisans*, pp. 184–87.

61. PRO. FO. 5/879 fols. 49–50.

62. R. Hofstadter and M. Wallace, *American Violence: A Documentary History* (New York, 1970), p. 223; A.W. Trelease, *White Terror: The Ku Klux Klan Conspiracy and Southern Reconstruction* (New York, 1971); S.V. Ash, *When the Yankees Came: Conflict and Chaos in the Occupied South* (Chapel Hill, 1995).

63. O. Singletary, *Negro Militia and Deconstruction* (Westport, 1984).

64. V. DeSantis, "Rutherford B. Hayes and the Removal of the Troops and the End of Reconstruction," in *Region, Race and Reconstruction: Essays in Honor of C. Vann Woodward* (1982), pp. 417–50.

65. PRO. FO. 5/950 fols. 19–22.

66. A.J. and K.A. Hanna, *Napoleon III and Mexico: American Triumph over Monarchy* (Chapel Hill, 1971).

67. PRO. FO. 5/965 fols. 112–14.

# 7

# Political and Social Contexts

The current trend for emphasising the role of cultural factors (in the widest sense) in assessing military capability,[1] rather than technology, encourages revived interest in the nature and impact of the political and social contexts of military activity. These are important not only in their own terms, but also as they offer a way to approach the question of American military exceptionalism. From its inception as an independent state in 1776, America was the largest republic in the world, and it swiftly became a democratic empire that challenged the prejudices and suppositions of European commentators. This political distinctiveness had consequences that require probing, but first it is necessary to consider how the fight for independence affected the creation of the American military system. A ready contrast is offered with the lengthy Dutch struggle to win independence from Spain in the late sixteenth and early seventeenth century, as that led the independent Dutch state, the United Provinces, a federal republic, to have a large army that was little different from those of other Western European states.

## BEFORE INDEPENDENCE

Prior to independence, the Americans already had a considerable military tradition, born out of fighting both Native Americans and the Bourbons. Troops from New England had been responsible for the capture of Louisbourg, a major French base, in 1745. American troops had also played a prominent, although less happy, part in operations against Florida and other Spanish possessions in and around the Caribbean.[2]

Given the military aptitude of so many Americans, it could be argued that the British government was foolish not to entrust the bulk of the defence of North America to the colonists. This would not have been a practical option in Canada, where much of the population was Catholic and of French origin (especially prior to the Loyalist immigration after the War of American Independence), but, elsewhere in North America, there appeared to be no great need for British troops. Had such a course been followed, it is possible that there would have been no war for independence or, if a conflict had broken out, that it would have ended rapidly with British forces defeated by well-trained and well-armed American units; although much would have depended on the strength of Loyalist sentiment. Instead, the British government had preferred to rely on British regulars. Some British officers loathed the American troops, and thought them incompetent, a judgement that the French and Indian War did not bear out, but one that reflected the view that many regulars held of militia. This view might have received some support from recent work arguing that many Americans did not have guns, while those who had did not make much use of them, a powerful qualification of what is presented as the mythology of the gun in American public culture,[3] but the research on which the thesis is based has been subject to considerable and powerful criticism.

Paradoxically, the British position within North America after 1763 might have been less difficult, had Britain been in a more exposed international situation. Conflict with France, Spain, or both, came close in the late 1760s and, again, in the Falkland Islands crisis of 1770, but it was avoided, and in 1770 the hostile leading French minister, Choiseul, was dismissed. His successor until 1774, D'Aiguillon, sought co-operation with Britain, and this gave British policymakers a margin of opportunity to turn to other issues, especially imperial finance and control. This is a reminder of the need to locate American military history in a wider context that cannot simply be discussed in terms of factors particular to America.

## WAR OF INDEPENDENCE

Opposition to a standing army, British or their own, was part of the American ethos. The Americans were wedded to the seventeenth-century English polemic against standing armies, a polemic that was out of fashion in Britain by the mid-eighteenth century, but one that reflected earlier opposition to what was seen as tyranny, whether from Stuart kings or from Oliver Cromwell. George Washington observed in 1777 that he understood how Americans could be against a standing army in times of peace, but not how this could extend to wartime. However, the powerful anti-authoritarian character of the independence period affected the Continental Army, and indeed the fledging American state. The acceptance of the theory of "natural rights" or "natural law" in the Declaration of Independence questioned the legitimacy of all authority, especially central authority, be it British or American. The discrediting of executive power was also important, as was the decision to choose a plural rather than a single-nation interpretation of independence. This was reflected in the use of "they" rather than "it" when referring to the United Colonies, or, later, the United States, for many decades after independence.

The creation of a national army did not free military operations from the views of state governments. This was accentuated by the degree to which the army had to turn repeatedly to the states for their assistance, especially with manpower and supplies. The initial force that had blockaded Boston was essentially a New England army, which dissolved in the autumn of 1775, only to have to be built up again that winter. Following an agenda that was true also of other revolutionary struggles, Congress sought to create a broader-based army, focused at first on a one-year term of service. The British decision to send more troops in 1776 led Congress to vote to raise eighty-eight battalions, with an intended strength for 1777 of about 75,000 soldiers. Men were offered enlistments for the war, with the eventual reward of 100 acres and 20 dollars, or service for three years. At first, voluntary enlistment sufficed, but, eventually, conscription was necessary: drafts from the militia for a year's service, although South Carolina and Rhode Island did not introduce conscription. Thus the states played a major role in raising troops, while, as men could avoid service by paying a fine or providing a substitute, the rank and file were largely drawn from the poorer sections of the community. They sought material benefits, bounties and wages, rather than glory, although that does not imply an absence of convictions and patriotism, which were further fostered by military service, as was group cohesion.[4] As with the forces of Revolutionary France and the unsuccessful Polish uprising of 1794, most of the officers were men of property. Conscription badly failed to provide the anticipated numbers of troops.

Unlike the situation in Revolutionary France, George Washington was obliged to deal with a form of government in which Congress could do little more than request men, funds and supplies from the states. The response varied considerably. Virginia was a state that provided much support for the revolution, but, when, in April 1777, Congress recommended drafts from the militia to fill the Continental Army, Jefferson opposed them, arguing that they would be very unpopular. That November, the General Assembly of Virginia resolved that county lieutenants should collect clothing for the Continental troops raised in the county and send them to the army, but little was sent. In 1779, when a boat with 5,000 stand-of-arms imported for use by the Continental Congress arrived in Virginia, the arms were seized by the state government, leading to a serious dispute.[5] There were riots against the draft in Virginia in 1780. In the winter of 1777–78, General Anthony Wayne blamed what he saw as a lack of support from Pennsylvania on anti-military feeling in its government.[6] Benjamin Lincoln found the South Carolina militia unwilling to accept the command of Continental officers, while, in October 1780, Horatio Gates, his successor as commander of the army in the south, found his orders to the North Carolina militia countermanded by the state's Board of War. Gates had to threaten officers who obeyed the Board with dismissal, and pressure from the North Carolina legislature played a role in his removal from command.[7] In New York State, in early 1781, several local committees stirred up opposition to the impressment of supplies by the army. The strong sense of state identity and interests restricted any attempt to lessen state power in favour of Congress, while hostility to uncontrolled army activities was well developed.

The struggle for independence was also affected by the strength of individualism. Troops drifted off: desertion implies furtively sneaking away, but Americans, for the most part, just walked out of camp, unlike in Revolutionary France. Desertion was an issue of individual rights.[8] The militia suppressed or inhibited Loyalists, but local communities were not therefore disciplined to provide what was deemed to be necessary by Congress and the army. From their perspective, these communities were obstinate and individuals were selfish, so that the collective cause was undermined, with serious consequences for the war-effort.

However, the demands of the war-effort were onerous. This has been underappreciated because it is the papers of generals in the Continental Army and politicians eager for independence that have been most extensively studied and published. Their general perspective was that those who did not provide sufficient support were selfish hinderers. However, the colonial ethos has to be considered. Lack of intercolonial co-operation was deeply engrained, as can be seen from the failure of coordinated efforts between 1689 and 1760.

Furthermore, the war hit the economy hard, while the specific demands of supporting the Revolutionary war effort placed a severe strain on economic activity. The financing of the war by the over-issue of paper currency, the value of which rapidly deteriorated, posed many problems for those who sought to trade products or services, and helped to sap economic confidence. Overissue led to a reluctance to accept American currency or bills, which affected both the economy and military activity. Indeed, some Revolutionary firebrands, such as Richard Henry Lee, refused to accept Continental money from their own dependents. In July 1780, Gates complained that his troops were having to steal food in North Carolina, because the people were unwilling to accept Revolutionary money or credits.

Possibly most critical was the demand for manpower which pressed hard on a society that benefited from few labour-saving devices; and those were largely provided by animals which were also needed for the war effort. Family and communal economies, and thus the war effort as a whole, were dependent on the time-consuming and arduous tasks of breaking the soil, sowing, hoeing and harvesting, and the absence of men in the army threatened the ever-precarious balance of household economies. It was scarcely surprising that desertion was a serious problem. In addition, impressment of horses was necessary. This led to the hiding of horses and wagons.

The image of an armed citizenry resisting the redcoats is well established, although it has recently been challenged. Indeed, many white Americans were freer to possess firearms than the population of much of Europe, who were denied firearms in order to secure the hunting rights of their social superiors. In Normandy, under an edict of 1766, a simple denunciation by a noble could lead to a peasant's house being searched and the culprit jailed for three months without recourse to the ordinary courts. No such social regime prevailed in America, although fishermen and some farmers had little need of muskets and there were not many American gunsmiths. The Revolutionaries were faced with severe shortages of firearms, especially in the first year of the revolution. Furthermore, knowing how to load and fire a weapon no more made a man a soldier than giving him a uniform. Also, many militiamen left the family musket or shotgun at home for defence and hunting game, hoping to receive a weapon in camp. Many militiamen were issued with weapons which they took home with them.

Despite the vitality of the American agrarian economy, the demands of the war proved difficult to meet, while problems with credit and transportation further exacerbated the situation. The rations established by Congress in 1775 for the rank and file were generous: one pound of beef, three quarters of a pound of pork or one pound of salt fish daily; one pound of bread or flour daily; one pint of milk daily; three pints of peas or beans weekly; one-half pint of rice or one pint of Indian meal weekly; and one quart of spruce beer per man or nine gallons of molasses for one hundred men weekly. However, the gap between aspiration and reality that was such a characteristic feature of eighteenth-century government was rarely wider than in the case of the conditions of troops on active service. At Valley Forge in 1778–79, the soldiers dined on "fire cakes," a baked flour-and-water paste. In the South, rations were often rice or "johnny-cake," or hoe cake, mixed quickly from flour and water and baked over a fire on a hoe.

The war was fought largely through credit, not taxation, although the unreliable nature of the credit itself constituted a form of taxation, while commandeering was a very direct form. In Maryland, the local authorities sought to requisition half of every household's extra blankets during the first winter of the war, paying for them in paper currency, and later, similarly, a pair of shoes from every housekeeper. In early 1780, Congress devised a new system under which individual states were to be asked to provide specific supplies which would be credited towards their portion of Congress's debt. This did not work well, because of the growing exhaustion of the population, the reluctance of the states to subordinate their priorities to those of Congress, and their own problems with credit-worthiness. In consequence, the army was in a very bad state in 1780. This led generals such as Greene to criticise politicians and civilians, reflecting a tension between the civilian political control that characterised the Revolution and the sense among generals that they could handle matters better.

Many soldiers took more direct action. Indeed, it is remarkable that there had not been widespread mutinies earlier. This could be attributed to the troops' certainty of the justice and necessity of their cause, but it may also have owed much to the relative ease of taking leave without permission. There had been disturbances in 1777, when an unpaid New England brigade had refused to join the main army in Pennsylvania, and in 1780, when two hungry Connecticut regiments had to be prevented from ravaging New Jersey, but, in January 1781, both the Pennsylvania line and three New Jersey regiments mutinied.

Nevertheless, there was far less violence within the Revolution than was to be the case in France in the 1790s. Although, in the War of Independence, America, like France in the 1790s, was both invaded and affected by civil war, the treatment of Loyalists was less savage than that of Royalists in France: in America, the tumbrils never rolled. However, that did not imply an absence of violence: pre-war intimidation of Loyalists was quite common, and, during the conflict, Revolutionary councils and militia could be quite harsh in their dealings with Loyalists, and were very much so in the Carolinas in 1781–82, although their treatment of them varied considerably.

American society was less mobilized for war than that of Revolutionary France was to be, and more respect was paid to private property and pre-existing institutions. This was in part because there was less of a social contest in the American Revolution than in its French counterpart. French local government was reorganized institutionally and geographically, provincial assemblies being a major casualty, and the Church was despoiled. In America, there was no equivalent centralization; indeed, avoidance of centralization was a principle of American revolutionary ideology. In one sense, the Revolution was made possible by the existence of relatively mature political institutions in the colonies/ states that did not need replacement. By and large the same people who ran the colonial governments would run the new state governments. Nor was there any comparable attempt to export the Revolution, certainly not outside British America. Before their respective revolutions, America lacked a strong identity comparable with that which France enjoyed, and in America, unlike France, there was to be no source of revolutionary activity able to terrorize those who supported the Revolution but had alternative, less centralist, views of how the new state should be organized.

Rather than treating such differences as immutable, however, it has to be recognised that had the British been more successful, the Americans might well have resorted to more revolutionary military methods, such as guerrilla warfare, as they did in the South. Alternatively, the Americans might have continued to rely on field armies, as the French Revolutionaries did, but those who took power could have taken a harsher attitude toward states rights and private property. The consequence might have been a very different American public culture, one that stressed the national state more than the individual citizen, and obligations more than rights. This might have engendered a public ethos that was more genuinely egalitarian than that of freedom and property that was to be expressed in the constitution; although the ideological underpinnings of the Revolution were so strong that it is possible that the Revolution would have been abandoned by many, if not most, Americans in the face of such a compromising of their principles. However, military exigencies had a potential for authoritarian politics, as was shown by Andrew Jackson in the War of 1812 when he approved the hanging of seven militiamen for desertion or disobedience, and, after the departure of the British from New Orleans, continued to insist on martial law, ordered the deportation of French-speaking residents, and jailed a critical newspaper editor and federal judge.[9] Henry Knox, a keen Federalist, pressed hard for a stronger federal government and a national military establishment while heading the War Department in 1785–94. In 1783, he had aroused concern by founding the Society of Cincinnati as a body for officers from the War of Independence and their descendants. This was seen as a threat to the Confederation government.

To turn from the Revolution to subsequent American history, the military can be defined functionally as the arm of the state. As elsewhere, this involved the use of force against what were seen as enemies both internal and external; and the two categories often overlapped. During the independence struggle, Loyalists were the prime internal enemy, but, thereafter, as the formal borders of the state expanded, Native Americans were the major category. On and over the southern border, this overlapped with hostility to the inchoate world that weak Spanish authority made possible, and that Americans both exploited and sought to order. Thus, the Republic of the Floridas, created by a multinational revolutionary force under Sir Gregor MacGregor on Amelia Island in 1817, defeated Spanish attempts to regain the island, but was overcome that year by American forces who saw the republicans as pirates.[10] The Canadian border constituted a marked contrast, as the Canadian colonies were more ordered and under greater imperial control.

## OPENING UP AMERICA: EXPLORATION AND COMMUNICATIONS

Ordering the American world also involved the military taking a central role in the process of opening up the new lands. This entailed exploration, mapping, classification, and the creation of new routes for communications. These military activities helped to give a shape to the territories over which America had acquired sovereignty that the new state could grasp and use.[11] The army played a decisive role in the organisation of territorial governments, not only in performing essential police functions that made settlement possible, but also in the crucial role of patronage and contracts that provided the "loaves and fishes" for early political development in the newly-organized territories.

Military exploration enjoyed considerable government backing. In 1803, Jefferson persuaded Congress to finance an expedition up the Missouri. After Congress agreed, Jefferson's interest was further raised by the Louisiana Purchase that spring. The expedition was entrusted to Meriwether Lewis, Jefferson's private secretary and an army captain, and his former commanding officer, William Clark. Their Corps of Discovery reached the Pacific in November 1805, before arriving back in St. Louis in September 1806 with much information on what they had traversed, particularly route maps. This expedition did not establish any base, but it whetted American interest in expanding to the Pacific.

Other officers led expeditions elsewhere. In 1805, the self-serving General James Wilkinson, Governor of the Louisiana Territory, sent Lieutenant Zebulon Pike to assert American claims to the Mississippi Valley and to press Native Americans to accept American rule. The following year, Wilkinson sent Pike from St. Louis to find the source of the Red River, which was seen as the southern boundary of the Territory. Pike was given secret orders to chart the route to Santa Fé, which Wilkinson hoped to seize from the Spaniards for his own ends. Pike reached the Rockies, but was captured by the Spaniards, although that gave him an opportunity to report on New Spain and Texas when he was returned.

The pace of government-sponsored exploration picked up after the War of 1812. In 1819, the Secretary of War sent Colonel Henry Atkinson towards the Yellowstone in order to enforce control, although what, to the Americans, was enforcing control in the areas ceded by the Louisiana Purchase was, to the Natives, simple aggression. Due to a lack of supplies, as well as ill-health in the expedition, it only got as far as Old Council Bluffs, Nebraska, but an ancillary scientific expedition, under Major Stephen Long, pressed on. He took with him across the Great Plains a botanist, a zoologist, a geologist, an assistant naturalist, a landscape painter and two assistant topographers. Edwin James, who replaced the botanist and the geologist in 1820, became the first botanist to reach the alpine flora on Pike's Peak, and left much detail on fauna, geology and Natives in his account published in 1822–23.[12]

Long's expedition benefited from the existing network of forts, travelling out via Fort Osage and returning to Fort Smith, but it journeyed far beyond this network, bringing in a mass of information. This was not the end of the process; nor of the military's close involvement. In 1832, Captain Benjamin Bonneville, who had been given leave from the army, led an expedition into the Rockies, instructed to acquire "every information which you may conceive would be useful to the Government," specifically about Native military techniques. He built a fort on the Green River, and, from there, explored the mountains, sending out a mountain man, Joseph Walker, who found a route to San Francisco Bay via the Great Salt Lake. Bonneville was court martialled for overstaying his leave, but, again, a soldier had greatly contributed to knowledge of the West.

This process was pushed much harder the following decade; a major part of the process by which the 1840s saw a determined and self-conscious attempt to expand American power. The institutional framework and cohesion for this purposeful exploration was provided by the Army's Corps of Topographical Engineers, which was created in 1838, when the Topographical Bureau was placed under the army (topographical engineers were always part of the army, although expanded and organised as a fully-fledged staff corps in 1838). This Bureau was supplemented by the Coast Survey which produced, among other works, the *Report on the Physics and Hydraulics of the Mississippi River* (1861). The

Topographical Corps played a major role in the exploration and mapping of the West.[13] They also played an important role in providing maps for the war with Mexico.[14] Military surveyors used Native maps and geographical information, but only to a limited extent;[15] they were concerned to locate, understand and utilize the lands they surveyed in the context of an expanding state: localities acquired meaning with reference to this project.

Army engineers also played a major role in exploration of routes for a transcontinental railway, as with Lieutenant Amiel Whipple's survey of a possible southern route in 1853. The Pacific Railroad Survey Act of 1853 ensured political and financial backing, and the pace was encouraged by competition between the sponsors of particular routes. The resulting Pacific Railroad Surveys were published as Senate Executive Documents.

More generally, army engineers played an important role in developing transport links. A Supreme Court decision that placed interstate commerce under the federal government led, in 1824, to the General Survey Act and to the assignment of the surveying of routes for canals and roads to the Corps of Engineers. Also in 1824, an Act gave the Corps authority to improve waterways, and this led to an extensive role in harbour works, such as the construction of jetties, lighthouses and piers, and in "improving" rivers, by dredging and other means to regularize river channels.[16]

The relationship between army engineers and the development of America's transport infrastructure was also seen in many careers, although criticism of overly close links between officers and individual companies led to a requirement that they resign if they accepted posts in these companies. Thus, Henry Halleck, a West Pointer who went into the Engineers, became President of the Pacific and Atlantic Railroad, returning to the army in 1861 where he proved a poor field commander, but an effective organiser. McClellan and Burnside were also West Pointers who moved from the army to the railroads, before returning to military service in response to the Civil War. Joseph Hooker was a West Pointer who became Superintendent of Military Roads in Oregon in 1858–59, and, subsequently, a Civil War commander.

The exploration of the West was pressed hard by the supporters of American expansion. This can be seen in the early career of John Charles Frémont, who became a lieutenant in the Topographical Corps in 1838. Having already taken part in surveying expeditions, he married the daughter of Thomas Hart Benton, Senator for Missouri and a keen and influential supporter of expansion to the Pacific. In 1842, Benton persuaded Congress to allocate funds for a Topographical Corps expedition to the Rockies. Frémont led this expedition that year, following in 1843–44 with another to the Great Salt Lake and then along the Oregon Trail before turning south into California. In 1845, Frémont crossed Mexican territory to California where, in December, he was ordered out by the Mexican authorities. He refused, raised the American flag, left for Oregon, and returned, in June 1846, to help lead the Bear Flag Republic of settlers. Frémont then in 1846–47 played an active role in the American conquest of California.

Frémont's career at this point was a major instance of the interaction of exploration and conquest.[17]

This was taken further in other careers in the Topographical Corps. In 1849, James Simpson's exploration of what was to be northwest New Mexico and northeast Arizona was as part of John Washington's punitive expedition against the Navajo. Simpson was able to explore the Canyon de Chelly only after Washington had defeated them. This trip was not one of simple control and exploration. Simpson also advised on the route for a rail line from Texas to the Colorado River and then California. In 1851, Captain Sitgreaves followed Simpson, both in being part of an expedition to control the Navajo and in seeking information about the region, not least with reference to the rail route. They had several skirmishes, especially with Mohave and Yuma in the Colorado Valley, but greatly added to information about Arizona, although without finding an acceptable rail route.

Military purposes encouraged further exploration in the region in 1858–59. Concern about the possibility of war with the Mormons in Utah led to efforts to find first a river route to the Great Basin via the Colorado River and then to explore the route from Santa Fé. In the first attempt, the prefabricated paddle steamer USS *Explorer* rapidly fell victim to the rocky bed of the Colorado, a good example of the extent to which riverbeds across the world limited the potential of steam technology for river transport. However, Lieutenant Joseph Ives led the expedition up the Colorado, and, via the Grand Canyon, to the Painted Desert and then Fort Defiance. They had not discovered a river route, but had greatly increased American knowledge of the Colorado River.

There were casualties in the struggle for information; and the exploration for rail routes had its losses. Captain Warner was killed by Pit River Natives in northeast California in 1849. Lieutenant John Gunnison, who set off in June 1853 from Fort Leavenworth to find a route between the 38th and 39th parallels, was killed with seven of his men by Ute at Sevier Lake. However, Lieutenant Beckwith, who took over the mission, found two acceptable passes over the Sierra Nevada the following year. Further north, Isaac Stevens, a former army engineer, explored a route from St. Paul to the Pacific Northwest in 1853, while, to the south, in 1853, Whipple explored a route from Fort Smith through Arizona into southern California, and, in 1854, Lieutenant John Parke another from San Diego to El Paso, through the recent Gadsden Purchase, and Captain John Pope, later a Civil War general, from there to the Red River. Lieutenants Williamson and Abbott explored railway routes in the Pacific states.

Thus, the military played an important role in the process of gaining knowledge and consolidating control over lands ceded to America. In order to appreciate the nature of this mission, it is useful to turn to the striking *Atlas of Native History* (Davis, 1981), by Jack D. Forbes. This is a dramatic repudiation of the conventions of American historical cartography. Forbes consciously rejected the appropriation of the Native American past, an appropriation that was true of both nomenclature and territoriality. He employed the "names used by the native peoples themselves" and sought to "present real political conditions," ignoring "the claims of white governmental units" which, Forbes argued, had come to compose a "mythological map." The very titling of the maps represented a conscious rejection of past cartographic traditions; and contents matched titles. The map of "The United States Area as it really was in 1820," depicted Native groups as well as European-American states, for example the Maskogi Confederation between Georgia and Alabama. The map included a note "By 1820 U.S. troops had occupied parts of North Florida." The map for 1845 did not carve up North America into, for example, Mexico, Canada, and the area gained by the Louisiana Purchase. For the 1845 and 1861 maps, no European frontiers were shown west of the line of white settlement; instead, forts and isolated areas of settlement were depicted.

## MONOPOLIZING FORCE

These points might suggest that this section should be located in the chapter on warfare with Native Americans and, in part, that is correct. However, the use of the military for expanding control (including knowledge) was also an aspect of the more general context of military activity. Most significantly, the process of expansion, especially its militarization, was effected by federal troops. As with much that appears obvious, this does not attract attention, but, in fact, it was not inevitable. Across much of the West in the early modern period, there had been a considerable use of agencies and individuals outside the control of the state in order to raise, control, and supply, troops and warships. This was lessened from the mid-seventeenth century, as governmental control over the military increased, but there was still a range of independent and autonomous forces within the Western system, such as mercenaries, irregular troops, privateers and pirates.[18] Nevertheless, societies within the Western world that offered different models of socio-military organization to that of the state and that resisted, such as Highland Scotland, Corsica and the Cossacks, were subjugated.[19]

American military development from 1775 to 1865 can be discussed in this context, with Native Americans in part seen alongside societies such as Highland Scotland, although in America there was the added complexity of different types of public military authority: in particular, there was a fundamental divide between federal and state military organisations. In America, however, there was also a range of independent elements. These reflected, in particular, the rate of gun ownership and the possibilities created by frontiers, not simply the external frontier, but also "inner frontiers" where sedentary society gave way to less orderly milieux.[20]

Part of the military history of the period, a "silent" part, was the marginalisation of the possibilities created by such independent elements. This can be presented in mechanistic terms, by suggesting that the very presence of an advancing frontier both attracted the "marginals" who were unhappy with governmental authority, and also moved them further away from centres of settlement and power. Most of the conflict with "marginals" can be seen as an aspect of law enforcement, but there was also a degree of political rivalry. This looked back to colonial-period clashes between governors and opponents, for example the Regulator movement in North Carolina in 1771, which had been defeated at the battle of Alamance. In particular, tension between the easterners/tidewater who dominated legislatures and westerners/backwoodsmen who felt ignored played a major role in the years before and immediately after independence; although the extent of the resulting violence in American society should not be exaggerated.

## SHAYS' REBELLION

There was widespread tension in 1786–87, including in New York, Pennsylvania and Virginia. Two thousand militia were used in 1786 to overawe New Hampshire farmers who were protesting against the Assembly. In 1786–87, the tension between easterners and westerners seen in many states culminated in Massachusetts in Shays' Rebellion, when the heavily debt-ridden farmers of the central parts of the state, many of whom were veterans of the War of Independence, rebelled in order to stop the confiscation of their property to pay debts and taxes they could not meet. However, the rebellion was put down by Massachusetts volunteers who had successfully defended the Springfield Arsenal. The clash there, on 25 January 1787, was a brief one. About 1,500 Regulators armed with pitchforks and other weapons of limited effectiveness confronted the 4,400 strong volunteer militia force under Benjamin Lincoln and dispersed after Lincoln's men opened fire, including cannon fire. The Regulators retreated but were unable to recoup their strength because, on 4 February, having marched through a snowstorm, Lincoln's force came up and surprised them. One hundred and fifty were captured and the remainder fled. Isolated violence continued on the Massachusetts–New York border, but it was no longer deemed of wider importance. An armed demonstration was not to be converted into a civil war. Discontent continued but not so as to pose any military challenge or any serious political difficulties.[21] Lincoln's career benefited from his role in suppressing the rebellion. He was elected Lieutenant Governor of Massachusetts in 1788.

The role of Massachusetts volunteers, rather than federal troops, in suppressing the rebellion reflected the absence of a significant standing army. It was also a consequence of Massachusetts' longstanding autonomy in military matters. Thus, in 1779, the General Court of Massachusetts acted unilaterally, without Congressional assent or assistance, when sending a substantial force to Castine. In 1786, the federal government tried to respond to the Massachusetts disturbances. The decision of Congress, on 20 October, to recruit 2,040 troops was explained with reference to the crisis with the Native Americans in the Northwest, but it owed much also to concern about Massachusetts. The number raised fell far short of this figure, although regulars were sent to Springfield. The rebellion was suppressed by the militia, and the Act was repealed on 4 April

1787. Indeed, at the Constitutional Convention, Elbridge Gerry of Massachusetts proposed that the constitution restrict army size to 2,000 or 3,000. The rebellion indicated the extent to which the federal government was not seeking excuses to develop a powerful military. Far from it. Massachusetts wanted federal troops to replace the local forces that had been raised to confront the rebellion, but Congress was unwilling.

In 1787, the largely ineffectual Daniel Shays fled to Vermont. There, Ethan Allen was seeking to press his case for Vermont statehood, if necessary as a British colony. Had he succeeded, this would have created a significant military problem, as, prior to the War of Independence, Allen's Green Mountain Boys had been effective in resisting New York settlement in the New Hampshire Grants (now Vermont). However, the British did not provide the necessary support, Allen died in 1789, and, in 1791, Vermont joined the union as the fourteenth state.[22]

## THE WHISKEY REBELLION

Three years later, the Whiskey Rebellion, which centred on west Pennsylvania but spread over twenty counties, again revealed the lawlessness of frontier areas, but now showed that the federal government was better able to respond. The excise tax on spirits introduced in March 1791 created widespread dissatisfaction and led to a populist response akin to that seen in the last decade of British colonial rule. However, this discontent focused on rural areas, rather than on major towns. Tax collectors and their allies were again tarred and feathered. There was scant sympathy for the government's desire to use taxes to help address the national debt and to support the federal government. Conflict broke out in the summer of 1794, with an attack on an excise inspector's house that was resisted with the aid of soldiers. As tension mounted, about 6,000 men attended a meeting at Braddock's Field near Pittsburgh, but they did not use the opportunity to take any political or military initiatives, and, instead, dispersed.

The federal government was unwilling to accept any loss of control. George Washington called out the militia and sent commissioners to offer amnesty in return for promises of submission. The failure of this approach led to the dispatch of militia and volunteers from Maryland, New Jersey and east Pennsylvania. Marching to Pittsburgh, they did not encounter any real resistance: insurgent leaders fled or were arrested. The march involved logistical rather than fighting problems. However, the successful suppression of the rebellion showed that the federal-state military system could respond rapidly and effectively to a crisis. The "Rebellion" itself was not a formidable challenge, but its suppression helped to increase the power of the federal government.[23]

In the War of Independence, the revolutionaries had overthrown established political patterns, but the organized use of force had been brought under the control of the new government and, after 1783, the military was used to suppress opposition. This process was to be repeated in Latin America, but there it proved difficult to end civil conflict and the habit of contesting government through violence. It is important to consider how far the political and military histories of America would have been different had the insurgents in Shays' and the Whiskey rebellions been successful. This might well have led to pressure for a stronger federal force capable of enforcing government power; or, conversely, there might have been a "balkanisation" of America akin to that in Mexico where local militias and strongmen enjoyed great power in the 1820s. Despite the sense of crisis that affected many politicians and commentators, American nationalism was not defined in terms of civil war.[24]

## MAINTAINING CONTROL

In America, troops in frontier regions inherited from the British the task of enforcing regulations on relations with the Native Americans. This led them to fall foul of whites who tried to sell alcohol or to seize land. Another aspect of "frontier" resistance can be seen in the Kansas Territory in the 1850s as disagreements over extending slavery escaped government control.

Independent military initiatives in America varied greatly. They included not only the filibusters who extended American power in the Gulf Region in the 1800s and 1810s,[25] and those who pressed into Texas, but also American supporters of rebellion in Canada in 1837–38, as well as the Mormon state in Utah, and John Brown's seizure of the federal arsenal at Harper's Ferry in October 1859. Although very different, they shared a willingness and ability to employ force outside, and if necessary against, the views of federal government. Such defiance led to far-flung commitments for the military. In the early 1830s, the army removed squatters from Georgia and Alabama, while, in 1837–38, the use of the army to suppress filibustering on the Canadian border led to tensions with civil society, including militiamen, as the army was ordered to enforce the Federal Neutrality Acts of 1818 and 1838. American officers served as the representatives of an unpopular national policy.[26] Had British rule collapsed in Canada then the resulting disorder would have created political problems and, possibly, military tasks for the Americans.

One aspect of military history is the extent to which the state sought and succeeded in limiting independent initiatives. In the case of America, the army's task was eased by a number of factors, including the size of the country, which permitted a degree of defiance of state authority; toleration of gun ownership, so that the military did not need to take part in any attempt to disarm the population; and the small size of the army, which limited its possible commitments.

## THE MORMON CONFLICT

Nevertheless, there were tensions, and they could easily have led to serious conflict. The Mormons were pledged to struggle in order to achieve the Kingdom of God on earth or at least, eventually, in Utah. Joseph Smith formally organised the later Church of Jesus Christ of Latter-day Saints in 1830, and communities were established, first in Kirtland, Ohio, and then in Independence, Missouri. The frontiersmen drove them first from Independence and then from the state, and the Mormons moved to Illinois where Smith was murdered in 1844, a reminder of the extent to which violence served political ends. The Mormons themselves had organised a private militia, the Nauvoo Legion, answerable only to Smith, and a secret society, the Sons of Dan, that was like a secret police.

The Mormons' willingness to resist by force of arms helped them survive. However, the state authorities said that they could not protect the Mormons and this encouraged them to move west. Smith's successor, Brigham Young, established the Mormons in Utah in 1850, and it initially proved possible to reconcile Mormon ends with the lightness of federal control in the vast lands of the West. Young became governor of the Territory of Utah.

However, there were tensions over Young's hopes for the extent of what he termed the "state of Deseret" (the latter a reference to the honeybee, not a corruption of desert). Furthermore, Young sought to prevent non-Mormons from arriving, only to find this goal fall victim to the development of the West and Utah's position on the Oregon Trail. In addition, Mormon claims, both political and other, especially the public endorsement of polygamy in 1856, and the treatment of non-Mormons, proved incompatible with federal pretensions, leading to claims by federal officials that the Mormons were in a state of rebellion. Mormon firmness was strengthened by a religious revival. The Republican party condemned polygamy in 1856, declaring it a "barbarism" equal to slavery and in 1857 President James Buchanan decided that the Mormons were in rebellion.

This led, in 1857, to the appointment of a non-Mormon to succeed Young as Governor, and to the dispatch of 2,500 troops under General William Harney, and, subsequently, Colonel Albert Sidney Johnston, to provide necessary support. Brigham Young presented this as "a hostile force who are evidently assailing us to accomplish our overthrow and destruction," and prepared a response including a withdrawal from northern Utah into the mountains. Mormon militia burned three of the supply trains of the army in early October, although they were instructed not to take life. This helped to delay Johnston's force, which had anyway been sent too late in the year. Winfield Scott had argued in May that it was already too late that year to send the expedition. Scott warned that the Mormons could deploy 4,000 men, and argued that such a challenge, and the need to protect supply lines, would require a very large American force. This warning was not heeded, but the first American troops did not depart for Utah from Fort Leavenworth until 18 July. Johnston failed to occupy Utah, as planned, in the autumn of 1857 and, instead, had to winter near Fort Bridger. A Mormon group slaughtered 120 migrants en route to California at Mountain Meadows. Captain Stewart Van Vliet who was sent to Salt Lake City in September 1857 in order to demand supplies for the army, reported that the Mormons would not help, and that they would fight to stop the army entering

Utah, if necessary responding with a scorched earth policy and taking refuge in the mountains where they had stored food and could destroy American forces.

War was avoided as the result of an agreement in 1858, in which Young lost the governorship, the Mormons were pardoned, and the army stayed outside Salt Lake City, instead establishing Camp Floyd nearby. This helped support emigrant trains on the Oregon Trail. In 1861, Utah lost territory to Colorado and Nevada, although plans to partition it were abandoned. The Civil War, in which Utah sought to follow a neutral policy, led to the withdrawal of the federal troops, but, in 1862, California troops under Colonel Patrick Connor, who had been dispatched to protect routes through the territory, arrived. Distrusting Young, Connor built Fort Douglas to threaten Salt Lake City, and encouraged opposition to Mormon authority. Utah lost territory to its neighbours in 1863 and 1864, but, as in 1861, this was not cause or consequence of conflict. It was near Ogden, Utah, that construction gangs on the Central Pacific Railroad met the Union Pacific line on 10 May 1869, completing the first trans-continental railway line.

The willingness to send an expedition against the Mormons, combined with the dispatch of a squadron to Paraguay in 1858–59, indicates the readiness of the Buchanan administration to use force, not least to use the army for political purposes against countries and people on the margins of American society. This looked towards the employment of troops under Lincoln to preserve the Union, although Buchanan's use of force against South Carolina, if it can be considered as such, during the secession winter of 1860–61, was limited to resupply. Lincoln attacked the notion of state sovereignty as an answer to the slavery question by asking whether Utah was to be admitted into the Union if its constitution tolerated polygamy.[27] Utah did not become a state until 1896 and only after polygamy had been abandoned as an essential doctrine in 1890.

War with the Mormons was avoided in 1858, and, as President, Lincoln had other concerns than Utah, but the tension from 1857 on was a reminder of the potential that frontier regions offered for conflict, although, on the other hand, opposition in both Kansas and Utah was constrained by the arrival of the army. As one of the central functions of a military is preserving the authority of the state, then one of the major might-have-beens in American military history relates to the likely consequences had there been what was seen as a major internal challenge prior to 1861. It would have been very different in scale to the Confederacy, but might still have posed a major military problem, not least because of the small size and limited preparedness of the army. Again, politics plays a major role, in that the federal structure of America made it easier to accommodate differences between states, as many governmental and political functions were both the prerogative of the latter and reflected local wishes, not central government instructions. There were also surprisingly few examples of attacks on troops. In the Kansas disturbances, only one soldier was killed in action, although about 200 civilians died.

## FORCE AND SLAVERY

This benign account does not make allowance for those excluded from representation, including, in particular, Native Americans and slaves. Major attempts were made to limit the availability of firearms to the latter. Thus, those plotting what was to be known as Gabriel's conspiracy in Richmond in 1800 had first to consider how to acquire guns, horses and swords. In the event, the plan was betrayed by other blacks before the rising could take place.[28] There were no major slave risings: nothing to compare with Brazil, let alone Haiti. Thus, military tasking was not greatly affected by episodes such as a rising in Louisiana in 1811, the abortive Denmark Vesey conspiracy in 1822, which included a plan for the seizure or destruction of Charleston, or Nat Turner's rebellion in Virginia in 1831, in which about sixty whites were killed. The British envoy reported from New York on 30 August 1831: "Accounts have been received from Virginia of an insurrection of the Blacks in that state. It is understood that from two to three hundred are in the field variously armed, and plunder and murder have already taken place in every part where the insurrection holds its sway."[29] The rebellion was rapidly suppressed. It was only in 1811 that regulars fought slaves.

However, there was long-standing concern about escaped slaves in the backcountry. Thus, the Dismal Swamp on the Virginia–North Carolina border was a source of raids, especially in 1775–78, while the swampy inlets and islands along the Virginia and Carolina coast were only imperfectly under control. Georgia also had both coastal and inland swampy areas that resisted the authority of settled white rule. Ex-slaves who had served the British army took refuge in swamps along the Savannah River, fortifying a camp at Bear Creek and staging raids until 1786 when a militia expedition suppressed them.[30] In 1814, Viscount Sidmouth, one of the leading British ministers, received a proposal suggesting that the British change the politics of America by turning to the slaves:

From the great armed force now on service, abounding in military skill and judgement, arising from their own glorious establishment I venture to suggest the sending an overwhelming military force into the Chesapeake—say, not less than 25,000 men—to land in such parts of Virginia and Maryland, as may be thought most advisable. Terms . . . to be sent to the American Executive; which, if not speedily complied with; then, Proclamations to be issued, declaring Virginia and Maryland as conquered countries, with consequent emancipation from slavery to all of its inhabitants, under such regulations etc. as may be considered politically advisable, leaving the other American states to make their own peace, and settle into any kind of government they may prefer . . . the great body of Negroes (surpassing that of the white inhabitants) rejoicing in their liberation from slavery might soon be embodied as a military force, in aid of our own, if wanted.

Distributing among the emancipated slaves, one third or one half of that land, whereon they had been treated as slaves; in order to afford them a future maintenance, may be considered moral, as well as political justice, and independent of this future free labour, to be paid them by their employer, as it might be on the portion of land left with the proprietor, if he chose to remain and occupy it under a new system of government established for Virginia and Maryland. Or for work performed for any other employer.

The establishing of Virginia and Maryland into a separate government would operate on the other states in making them more peaceably disposed towards this country, and the bulk of the inhabitants being black, or people of colour, would (under the protection of Great Britain) secure it from again becoming united to the other states.

It would operate in effecting a valuable and strengthening connection with Canada from the back lands of Virginia, and would open the navigation of the Ohio and Mississippi.

All this and much more might be thus achieved to the great and lasting benefit of this country, if the present crisis or favorable moment is embraced, while so large a disposable force is afloat to strike a death blow to Mr. Madison's politics, which aimed at taking a most base and cowardly advantage of our situation.

Our numerous gallant officers and soldiers could not be sent a finer climate and country for support, when connected with Canada, or ultimately be provided for better than by permitting them to settle therein that chose it as a conquered country like unto Canada, instead of being disbanded and difficult to find a maintenance at home.[31]

Also in 1814, Sir Alexander Cochrane of the British navy suggested the use of black troops in British operations against America, specifically that "about one thousand men half black troops ought to be employed upon the coast of South Carolina and Georgia—that possession be taken of Cumberland Island . . . a force so situated acting upon the flanks of the enemy on their southern boundary will operate much in favour of the Indians and disoblige the Georgians to keep troops for home defence."[32] The end of the war cut short such plans. Offshore islands, nevertheless, were a problem for the American state. Thus, in late 1814, Commodore Daniel Patterson, with his warships carrying troops, attacked the pirate Jean Laffite's stronghold on Grand Terre Island, Louisiana, and captured the Baratarians' ships.[33]

Florida posed a bigger problem than Georgia as ex-slaves there could shelter from American raids under Spanish rule. Thereafter, escaped slaves caused a problem for the army in the Second Seminole War in Florida as they co-operated with the Seminole. They were certainly a more serious military challenge than Nat Turner's rebellion.

In Florida, the continued vitality of the Seminole and their (understandable) unwillingness to accommodate the American state as the Cherokee did, ensured that ex-slaves could find "space" for their activities. This was less the case further north as the pace of white settlement increased. Settlement brought far more men for militia and volunteer units able to act against those seen as threatening law and order. In addition, the terrain became increasingly "known" and it was thus harder to live outside what was seen as society. Roads were built, units of authority, such as counties, established, courts and jails constructed, and terrain mapped. As a consequence those seen as banditti, whether white or black, were brought under control, or they found it expedient to follow the frontier.

Mention of slavery serves as a reminder that the military history of the period was far from co-terminous with violence, and the same relates to social and gender relations. Force and violence played a major role in society, but mostly outside the concern of government, and, in so far as they were regulated, outside the scope of the army. Had there been a major slave rising or widespread social violence, the situation would have been different; and Harper's Ferry was an indicator of the first. Again, this serves to emphasise the "silent" military history of the period. Action against slaves involved a number of pseudo-military activities that are a reminder of the extent to which there was a continuum. Thus slave patrols involved a degree of organised tracking and other military-type activities; learning to hunt, ride and shoot for more than the table. This helped to raise the military skills of many Southerners, although it did not prepare them for a combat situation in which the other side could inflict serious casualties. However, the relatively high level of pseudo-military skills also helped ensure during the Civil War that opposition in the South to the conflict led to violence.[34]

## THE NAVY AND MARGINALS

Action against "marginals" also involved the navy. Again there was a range of duties including the protection of trade against privateering and piracy, and action against the slave trade: in 1807 (with effect from 1808), Congress had banned the trade. There were extensive operations offshore and ashore Cuba, Puerto Rico, Santo Domingo and the Yucatán. Thus, Robert Stockton served in the Mediterranean in the 1810s and 1830s, while John Sloat commanded the *Grampus* against piracy in the Windward Isles in 1823–1824. This reflected not only a new commitment, but also a new organisational structure: the West Indies Station, which was aimed at pirates. In 1822, Commodore James Biddle commanded a squadron of fourteen ships in the West Indies, although the largest were two frigates. Farragut won notice in 1823 in command of a shore party in Cuba while on anti-slavery duties. There were also landings on Cuba in 1822, 1824, and 1825, the last in co-operation with the British. Far further afield, in 1831, a frigate and a sloop were ordered to Sumatra to punish pirates who had captured an American ship and killed some of the crew. A force was landed and stormed a fort at Quallah Battoo. In the winter of 1838–39, another force was landed to attack Sumatran bases from which American ships had been attacked. This was a testimony to the range of American commerce. In 1843, sailors and marines from four American warships landed on the Ivory Coast in order to act against those who had attacked American shipping, and also to discourage the slave trade.

In May 1857, Charles Henry Davis, commander of the USS *St. Mary's*, arranged the surrender of William Walker, an adventurer, and his followers who had been attempting to seize control of Nicaragua. That November and December, American warships under Commodore Hiram Paulding landed marines and thwarted another attempt by Walker on Nicaragua. Walker had landed at Punta

Arenas, but was arrested by an American landing party. This was disapproved of by Lewis Cass, the Secretary of State, Walker was acquitted in an American court on the charge of violating American neutrality laws, and Paulding was forced to retire. Walker was the best example in mid-century of filibustering. He launched expeditions against Baja California, Sonora, Nicaragua and Honduras, all of which employed chartered ships operating out of San Francisco, Mobile or New Orleans. Only in 1857 did the navy intervene to stop him. Walker's last expedition, to Honduras in 1860, ended in disaster after his men deserted him. Walker placed himself under the protection of the captain of a British naval vessel operating off the Honduran coast, but the captain turned him over to the Hondurans, who executed him in September 1860.

## THE "MORALITY" OF MARGINALISATION

The American naval presence in the Mediterranean, the Caribbean, and further afield encouraged and reflected a moralistic presentation of American power. Opponents were inferior, morally so as pirates or slavers, and, at least subliminally, by extension as ethnically different. Slavers were white, as were most pirates, but they were generally presented as North African, Hispanic or half-castes. There was thus an ethnic component to American power that matched its moralistic purpose.

"Marginals" could still be incorporated into the American military and, in part, as a consequence, into new definitions of citizenship. This took several forms, including the use of Native Americans and of blacks. It is also possible to see the use of frontiersmen as, in part, a recruitment of marginals that was linked to their role in American society. Furthermore, immigrant and artisan or trade groups formed volunteer militia companies.

Free Blacks were defined as marginal in military terms with their recruitment to the army prohibited in 1820 by Secretary of War John C. Calhoun, although in the War of Independence they had served in the Continental army and navy and in state militias. Blacks were not allowed to serve in the army in the Mexican War (although about 1,000 served in the navy), but they played an important role in the Civil War, contributing powerfully to the Union cause.[35] In early 1863, the dispatch by the Khedive of Egypt of black soldiers from the Sudan in support of the French forces in Mexico was seen by Lincoln as an example for the Union.[36] Nearly 200,000 blacks served in the Union army, and they performed a range of non-command functions: at least thirteen served as chaplains.[37] As a consequence, it can be argued that blacks earned freedom on the field of battle, rather than having it bestowed on them, although the political chronology and context of the issue might suggest a different approach.

However, attitudes to Natives and blacks were seen, even by those favourable to them, in terms of trusteeship, not equivalence. American civilisation was presented as superior. Despite the powerful evangelical emphasis on shared humanity, the end of the slave trade did not mark the close of the powerful racism of the period. Slavery continued, American slavers profited from demand in Brazil and Cuba, and racism was not restricted to the world of slavery. Racism drew on notions of an inherent racial hierarchy that was based on ideas of sharply distinguished races, and on supposed differences between the races that could be classified in an hierarchical fashion, and whose genesis was traced back to the sons of Adam. Race was also linked to alleged moral and intellectual characteristics, and to stages in sociological development. This encouraged a sense of fixed identity as part of a compartmentalised view of mankind, an essentially divisive approach, rather than an acceptance of an inherent unity and of shared characteristics. Compartmentalism led to classification, with religious and biological explanations of apparent differences between races. They were linked to the idea that species of animals had been separately created by God.

Aside from the assessment of the inherent characteristics of non-Westerners, a belief in progress, and in the association of reason with Western culture, led to a hierarchy dominated by Westerners, and thus a treatment of others as inferior. Thus, although monogenesis—the increasingly influential theory of the descent of all races from a single original group—can be seen as a more benign theory than polygenism, and as one that could contribute to a concept of the inherent brotherhood of man, it was also inherently discriminatory. It was assumed that the original ancestral group had been white, and that climate, diet, disease, and mode of life were responsible for the developments that led to the creation of different races. Characteristics and developments were understood in terms of the suppositions of Western culture, and this led to, and supported, the hierarchisation already referred to. Among "advanced" thinkers, notions of brotherhood were subordinated to a sense that Enlightenment and Revolutionary ideas and movements originated within the Western world. Irrespective of the nobility of outsiders, their societies appeared deficient and defective, and thus inferior. This can be seen in writing on history and sociology, in which whites were seen as more advanced economically and socially, while Natives were presented as debilitated and as concerned with self-gratification,[38] not a practice that recommended itself to theorists of the period.

Attitudes to Natives and blacks encouraged notions of separate development: Natives were to be moved beyond white settlement, while freed slaves were to be sent to Liberia. Their "savagery" meant they were separate from Western civilisation. For Jefferson and other patriots, Natives were at an earlier stage of historical development and could only share in the future of North America if they changed "into civilized republicans and good Americans."[39] Jefferson was very interested in Native American linguistics, but insistent that the "merciless Indian savages" of the Declaration of Independence, make way for settlers, in pursuit of America's destiny.[40]

Whether such attitudes can be referred to helpfully as violent is unclear, but they certainly accorded with principles and practices of expropriation that rested on force, and sometimes used it directly. This can be seen not only with the treatment of those people brought under American sovereignty, but also with those reached by American power. The New England Congregationalist missionaries who arrived in Hawaii in 1820 established schools, trained native teachers and provided literacy, but they also encouraged the destruction of temples and images of gods, and the abolition of traditional religious taboos.[41] New England traders co-operated with the king and aristocracy in Hawaii to force people to cut sandalwood in the wet uplands, a process that affected traditional subsistence patterns. Organised by Boston merchants, the first American circumnavigation of the world, begun in 1787, was intimately linked with trading with societies that did not want Western control: Captain Robert Gray obtained furs on the northwest coast of North America, sold them in Canton, and bought tea which he sold in Boston. Other fur trade voyages followed: fifty fur-trade voyages to the northwest coast were made by Americans between 1795 and 1804. This trade was not free from tension. In 1792, Gray clashed with the Kwakiuts in Queen Charlotte Sound, while the Russians regarded the Americans in the Pacific as interlopers. Trade was both destructive and enriching for the Natives, who were already decidedly mercantile before white contact.[42]

Western commercial activity also had a demographic impact. Alcoholism and smallpox were brought to the northwest coast. The whalers who came to Hawaii brought diarrhoea, influenza, measles, smallpox, tuberculosis, venereal disease and whooping cough, hitting the population very hard. Local sexual mores ensured that syphilis was particularly devastating to Native society.[43] New systems of economic activity was often harmful to the environment. Whereas Native whaling in the northern Pacific does not appear to have depleted whale stocks, the situation was very different when Western whalers arrived. Without any interest in conservationist methods or ethos, they embraced inefficient methods that killed many whales but failed to bring in large numbers of those they had harpooned: instead, many died and fell to the floor of the ocean.[44]

It may seem fanciful to discuss such practices in a book on America as a military power, but, in fact, they throw light on attitudes to the wider world that help explain the context within which Americans acted. The use of violence was constrained by cultural factors, but there was still no sense of equivalence. Thus, in the Second Seminole War, the American commander, in 1837, ordered blacks hanged if taken prisoner in combat (although the order was rescinded before it apparently had effect), while, in 1839, bloodhounds were obtained from Cuba to catch the Seminole, although, due to congressional concern, they were only used when leashed and muzzled. It was considered acceptable to seize Natives under flags of truce and to rely on hostage-taking.

## THE TREATMENT OF THE SOLDIERY

Ironically, it is also possible to see the ordinary soldier and sailor as "marginals," admittedly less so than blacks, Native Americans or Mormons, but, nevertheless, a group that was regarded as a problem and that required policing. This could be seen in the harsh discipline used in both army and navy, a discipline that reflected and strengthened hierarchical divisions within the forces. Recent immigrants and those in a poor economic position were heavily represented in both army and navy. This was true of provincial forces raised for the French and Indian War, of the Continental Army, the First Regiment of 1794, and thereafter.[45] In the post-1815 army, a large percentage of the ordinary rankers was made up of recent immigrants, particularly from Ireland and Germany, and this introduced an "ethnic" and sometimes religious division between the rankers and not only their officers but also many militia and volunteer units.

Gustavus Otto, a German immigrant who enlisted in 1848, complained about the severity of the Wisconsin winter and about the drudgery of garrisons having to obtain their own firewood, water and hay: "we were plagued much with the hardest labour . . . we had to procure from a distance of 2 miles wood, hay, and water, where one's life was not safe one minute not to slip and fall down with the wood, which we had to throw down from the bluffs."[46] The parlous conditions of military service[47] were commented on by British travellers,[48] and, more seriously, hit recruitment and encouraged desertion, mostly in the early stage of military service when it was hardest to adjust to. In 1814, it proved impossible to raise the sailors necessary for the campaign on the Great Lakes, and, instead, as in 1813, they had to be taken from the bluewater fleet. Desertion was especially serious in the 1820s and early 1850s, periods of economic boom when there were many other opportunities for employment. Yet desertion was not only a problem then. Between 20 percent and 25 percent of the soldiers in the Continental Army deserted during the War of Independence and the rate was higher for the First Regiment. In December 1830, the British envoy drew on the report of the Secretary of War when writing about "the prevalence of desertion in the regular army . . . which amounted last year to 1,000 men, or one sixth of the whole force." In December 1831, the item was reiterated: "Desertion continues to increase, and it is computed that in this year 1,400 desertions have taken place."[49]

Desertion in turn led to distrust of soldiers by their officers, and a heavy stress on discipline. Combined with poor pay, unacceptable food and accommodation, and boredom, especially the isolation of frontier postings, this ensured that military service remained unattractive,[50] and thus an expedient for marginals, not only recent immigrants but also those who were distrusted in their communities, possibly as a consequence of criminal activities. They were more prepared to make the difficult adjustment to military life. The banning of flogging in the navy in 1850 was scant amelioration of the situation. Desertion affected both Civil War armies: rates exceeded 10 percent.

Desertion at least lessened the danger of a military mutiny over conditions. Furthermore, the extent to which soldiers and sailors were "marginals," especially recent immigrants, ensured that, even had they been inclined, generals and officers were not in a position to stage insurrections. As with much that did not happen, such a comment might appear anachronistic, but the position in America was markedly at variance with the situation across much of the West, particularly in Latin America, but also in Europe. For example, in Portugal an unsuccessful liberal plot in 1817 was led by a general, and in 1820 the revolution was begun by the Oporto garrison. In Spain, there was a long series of military conspiracies and attempted coups after the expulsion of the French forces, including in 1814, 1815, 1817, 1819, and 1820. In Piedmont, in the kingdom of Sardinia, radical garrisons led the revolution of 1821. In Russia, elements in the army launched the unsuccessful Decembrist Revolt in 1825.

These uprisings are a reminder of the degree to which military power could pose a threat to governments. The extent to which this was the case was a product of political culture rather than some particular stage on the trajectory of military development. However, rather than treating America as exceptional, it is worth noting that in Britain there was no significant military dissidence between the naval mutinies of 1797, which were mostly about conditions, and the Curragh Mutiny of 1914 when officers indicated a willingness to defy government policy in Ireland.

Aside from peacetime desertion in response to conditions, it is worth noting that the circumstances of wartime service were frequently grim. For example the soldiers who fought in the Black Hawk War of 1832 faced bad food, marches and sleeping in mud and rain, and vicious mosquitoes.[51] The people of the age did not expect modern standards of comfort, including those judged appropriate for the modern military, and a workforce much of whom worked on the land was accustomed to exposure to the elements. Nevertheless, it is still difficult not to be very impressed by what soldiers and sailors faced and overcame.

## WOMEN

A last mention of "marginals," although, in this case, not of a group that had to be coerced or overawed by force, must include the roughly half the population that were female. Contemporary attitudes ensured that military service was restricted to men and, indeed, seen as an aspect of their distinctive character. Women, however, were involved in war, and suffered heavily from it. There was the personal loss: of fathers, sons, husbands, sweethearts, and friends, losses that frequently left women bereft both materially and psychologically. Widows could be forced into vagrancy and prostitution. Even if soldier members of the family survived, their absence made it harder to manage farms and to cope with the challenges of life. Furthermore, male absence pushed more tasks onto women, both in agriculture and in industry, so that in the North in the Civil War, the percentage of jobs held by women rose from about a quarter to about a third, but with considerably lower wages.

The number of women killed or raped in war was low; although the situation was very different for Native Americans. As far as other Americans were concerned, the practice of bombarding towns increased the risk of civilian casualties. Nevertheless, it was excused on the grounds of military necessity. Thus, the Union bombardment of Fredericksburg on December 11, 1862 was defended by arguing (correctly) that Confederate forces used the cover of private houses.

## CONCLUSIONS

To return to the theme of the role of the military in overawing, resisting, and suppressing "marginal" forces, it is worth noting that however weak the army (and navy) might seem, they helped to keep the federal government in control of the results, if not always the process, of expansion. With the exception of Utah, there were no significant problems with autonomous groups moving beyond the bounds of American sovereignty or adopting an independent position within those bounds. Nor, prior to 1861, was sectional rebellion an issue. There was no equivalent to the frontier rebellions Mexico had faced in Texas and California, and that the British in Canada faced in Manitoba in 1870 and 1885.

It is noteworthy that actual military challenges to federal authority in the United States were limited, but the political and cultural context that helped mute and contain such violence was itself tremendously volatile. The possibility that a fragile and vulnerable union was always on the verge of collapse may, paradoxically, have acted as a powerful deterrent to extra-military adventurism. The cult of the Founding Fathers focused on the necessity of preserving the union. In addition, Manifest Destiny helped to incorporate particular elements that sought expansion, especially in frontier regions, with the national political culture.[52] At the same time, a growing conservatism in many aspects of American life, especially in its institutions, had an important impact. Thus, alongside populism and expansionism, there was an emphasis on order, restraint, legalism and sovereignty that affected both army and government in their attitudes to America's place in power politics. This helped to differentiate the 1830s from the more expansionist 1810s, and, in doing so, both reduced the volatility of politics and preserved peace with Britain.[53]

For a country with, by the standards of the age, a strong anti-statist ideology, America maintained a striking monopoly of public military force. For example, in October 1831, the British envoy reported: "Meetings have been convened in several parts of the United States to raise subscriptions in favour of the Poles [then in rebellion against Russia] and a proposition has been made to form battalions and go to the aid of the Poles. The President has since caused the District Attornies of the United States to publish and put in force the provisions of an act of Congress passed on the 20th April 1818 prohibiting enlistment within the US, for the purpose of serving any foreign nation or people."[54] This stance helped to contain the fissiparous consequences of American political culture, as long that is as the political system worked. The system broke down in 1861, but the characteristics of America's response to force—a ready acceptance of individual white males being armed, but not an acceptance of non-governmental organised forces—continued and helped in the reintegration of America after the Civil War.

## NOTES

1. W. Murray, "Does Military Culture Matter?", *Orbis*, 43 (1999), pp. 27–42.

2. D.E. Leach, *Arms for Empire: A Military History of the British Colonies in North America, 1607–1763* (New York, 1973); F. Anderson, *A People's Army: Massachusetts Soldiers and Society in the Seven Years' War* (Chapel Hill, 1984); E.W. Carp, "Early American Military History: A Review of Recent Work," *Virginia Magazine of History and Biography*, 94 (1986), pp. 259–84; D. Higginbotham, "The Early American Way of War: Reconnaissance and Appraisal," *William and Mary Quarterly*, 44 (1987), pp. 230–73; J.M. Dederer, *War in America to 1775: Before Yankee Doodle* (New York, 1990); W.E. Lee, "Early American Ways of War: A New Reconnaissance, 1600–1815," *Historical Journal*, 44 (2001), pp. 269–89.

3. M.A. Bellesiles, *Arming America: The Origins of a National Gun Culture* (New York, 2000). For a regional example of bellicosity, W.E. Lee, *Crowds and Soldiers in Revolutionary North Carolina: The Culture of Violence in Riot and War* (Gainesville, 2001).

4. J.R. Sellers, "The Common Soldier in the American Revolution," in S.J. Underal (ed.), *Military History of the American Revolution* (Washington, 1976), pp. 151–61; J.K. Martin and M.E. Lender, *A Respectable Army: The Military Origins of the Republic, 1763–1789* (Arlington Heights, 1982); G.T. Knouff, "Enlistment: The Complexity of Motivations," in J.W. Chambers and G.K. Piehler (eds.), *Major Problems in American Military History* (New York, 1999), pp. 87–93.

5. W.T. Hutchinson et al. (eds.), *The Papers of Alexander Hamilton* (Chicago, 1962), I, 320–23.

6. P.D. Nelson, *Anthony Wayne. Soldier of the Early Republic* (Bloomington, 1985), pp. 69–71.

7. Nelson, "Major General Horatio Gates as a Military Leader: The Southern Experience," in W.R. Higgins (ed.), *The Revolutionary War in the South* (Durham, N.C., 1979), pp. 150–51.

8. R. Middlekauff, "Why Men Fought in the American Revolution," *Huntington Library Quarterly*, 43 (1980), pp. 135–48, and *The Glorious Cause: The American Revolution, 1763–1789* (New York, 1982), pp. 496–510.

9. J. Lurie, "Andrew Jackson, Martial Law, Civilian Control of the Military, and American Politics: An Intriguing Amalgam" *Military Law Review*, 126 (1989), pp. 133–45.

10. D.J. Weber, *The Spanish Frontier in North America* (New Haven, 1992), p. 198.

11. J.R. Short, *Representing the Republic. Mapping the United States, 1600–1900* (2001), pp. 174–75.

12. G.J. Goodman and C.A. Lawson (eds.), *Retracing Major Stephen H. Long's 1820 Expedition: The Itinerary and the Botany* (Norman, Oklahoma, 1995).

13. W.H. Goetzmann, *Army Exploration in the American West, 1803–63* (New Haven, 1959); F. Schubert, *Vanguard of Expansion: Army Engineers in the Trans-Mississippi West, 1819–1879* (Washington, D.C., 1980).

14. A.G. Traas, *From the Golden Gate to Mexico City: The US Army Topographical Engineers in the Mexican War, 1846–1848* (Washington, 1993).

15. M. Warhus, "Cartographic Encounters: An Exhibition of Native American Maps from Central Mexico to the Arctic," special issue of *Mapline*, no. 7 (Sept. 1993), pp. 15–16.

16. F.C. Luebke, F.W. Kaye, and G.E. Moulton (eds.), *Mapping the North American Plains* (Norman, Oklahoma, 1987); F.G. Hill, *Roads, Rails and Waterways: The Army Engineers and Early Transportation* (Norman, Oklahoma, 1957).

17. A. Nevins, *Fremont: Pathmarker of the West* (New York, 1955).

18. J.E. Thomson, *Mercenaries, Pirates, and Sovereigns: State-building and Extra-territorial Violence in Early Modern Europe* (Princeton, 1994).

19. B.M. Downing, *The Military Revolution and Political Change: Origins of Democracy and Autocracy in Early Modern Europe* (Princeton, 1993); B.D. Porter, *War and the Rise of the State: The Military Foundations of Modern Politics* (New York, 1994).

20. J. Gommans, "The Silent Frontier of South Asia, *c.* AD 1100–1800" *Journal of World History*, 9 (1998), pp. 1–23.

21. R.J. Taylor, *Western Massachusetts in the Revolution* (Providence, 1954), pp. 128–67; D.P. Szatmary, *Shays' Rebellion: The Making of an Agrarian Insurrection* (Amherst, 1980).

22. M.A. Bellesiles, *Revolutionary Outlaws: Ethan Allen and the Struggle for Independence on the Early American Frontier* (Charlottesville, 1993); C.R. Ritcheson, *Aftermath of Revolution: British Policy Toward the United States, 1783–1795* (Dallas, 1969), pp. 152–58.

23. T.P. Slaughter, *The Whiskey Rebellion, Frontier Epilogue to the American Revolution* (1986).

24. J.R. Sharp, *American Politics in the Early Republic: The New Nation in Crisis* (New Haven, 1993); D. Waldstreicher, *In the Midst of Perpetual Fetes: The Making of American Nationalism, 1776–1820* (Chapel Hill, 1997); J. Lewis, *The Union and the Problem of Neighbourhood* (Chapel Hill, 1998).

25. H.G. Warren, *The Sword Was Their Passport: A History of American Filibustering in the Mexican Revolution* (Baton Rouge, 1943).

26. S.J. Watson, "U.S. Army Officers' Fight the 'Patriot War': Responses to Filibustering on the Canadian Border, 1837–1839," *Journal of the Early Republic*, 18 (1998), pp. 485–519. More generally, R.W. Coakley, *The Role of Federal Military Forces in Domestic Disorders, 1789–1879* (Washington, 1988) and M. Cunliffe, *Soldiers and Civilians: The Martial Spirit in America, 1775–1865* (Boston, 1968).

27. N. Furniss, *The Mormon Conflict, 1850–1859* (New Haven, 1960). For map of Deseret and Utah, D.W. Meinig, *The Shaping of America. A Geographical Perspective on 500 Years of History. III. Transcontinental America* (New Haven, 1998), p. 97.

28. D.R. Egerton, *Gabriel's Rebellion: The Virginia Slave Conspiracies of 1800 and 1802* (Chapel Hill, 1997); J. Sidbury, *Ploughshares into Swords: Race, Rebellion, and Identity in Gabriel's Virginia, 1730–1810* (Cambridge, 1997).

29. BL. Add. 49964 fol. 27.

30. H.M. Ward, *The War for Independence and the Transformation of American Society* (1999), pp. 75–76.

31. John Harriott (not Herriott as in the catalogue) to Sidmouth, 7 May 1814, DRO. 152 M/C1814/OF 13.

32. PRO. WO. 1/141, pp. 63–67. For earlier interest in threatening the Americans with support for slaves, DRO. 152M/C1813/OF3.

33. J. de Grummond, *The Baratarians and the Battle of New Orleans* (Baton Rouge, 1961).

34. D. Pickering and J. Falls, *Brush Men and Vigilantes. Civil War Dissent in Texas* (College Station, 2000).

35. B. Quarles, *The Negro in the American Revolution*, with a new introduction by G.B. Nash (Chapel Hill, 1996); J.T. Glatthaar, *Forged in Battle: The Civil War Alliance of Black Soldiers and White Officers* (New York, 1990); J.G. Hollandsworth, *The Louisiana Native Guards: The Black Military Experience During the Civil War* (Baton Rouge, 1995); R.B. Edgerton, *Hidden Heroism. Black Soldiers in America's Wars* (Boulder, 2001), pp. 21–38.

36. *Sunday Morning Chronicle*, 15 Feb. 1863.

37. D.T. Cornish, *The Sable Arm: Black Troops in the Union Army, 1861–1865* (Lawrence, 1987); E.S. Redkey, "Black Chaplains in the Union Army," *Civil War History*, 33 (1987), pp. 331–50.

38. M. Banton, *Racial Theories* (Cambridge, 1987); R. Wokler, "Anthropology and Conjectural History in the Enlightenment," in C. Fox, R. Porter, and Wokler (eds.), *Inventing Human Science: Eighteenth-century Domains* (Berkeley, 1995), pp. 31–52.

39. P.S. Onuf, *Jefferson's Empire. The Language of American Nationhood* (Charlottesville, 2000), p. 51.

40. A.F.C. Wallace, *Jefferson and the Indians: The Tragic Fate of the First Americans* (Cambridge, Mass., 1999).

41. M. Kelly, *Early Missionaries' Impact on Hawaiians and their Culture* (Honolulu, 1988).

42. J. Scofield, *Hail Columbia, Robert Gray, John Kendrick and the Pacific Fur Trade* (Portland, 1993); J.R. Gibson, *Otter Skins, Boston Ships, and China Goods. The Maritime Fur Trade of the Northwest Coast, 1785–1841* (Montréal, 1992).

43. D. Stannard, *Before the Horror* (Honolulu, 1989).

44. R.L. Webb, *On the Northwest: Commercial Whaling in the Pacific Northwest 1790–1967* (Vancouver, 1980).

45. W.B. Skelton, "The Confederation's Regulars: A Social Profile of Enlisted Service in America's First Standing Army," *William and Mary Quarterly*, 3rd ser. 46 (1989), pp. 774–79.

46. Prucha, "An Army Private and Old Fort Snelling in 1849," *Minnesota History*, 36 (1958), pp. 15–16.

47. For health and welfare, as well as institutional responses, M.C. Gillett, *The Army Medical Department, 1818–1865* (Washington, 1987).

48. Prucha, "The United States Army as viewed by British Travellers, 1825–1860," *Military Affairs*, 17 (1953), pp. 113–24, esp. 114–20.

49. BL. Add. 49964 fols. 10, 34.

50. M.A. Vargas, "The military justice system and the use of illegal punishments as causes of desertion in the U.S. Army, 1821–1835," *Journal of Military History*, 55 (1991), pp. 1–19.

51. R.L. Nicholas, "The Black Hawk War in Retrospect," *Wisconsin Magazine of History*, 65 (1982), p. 239.

52. F. Merk, *Manifest Destiny and Mission in American History: A Reinterpretation* (New York, 1963); T.R. Hietala, *Manifest Design: Anxious Aggrandizement in Late Jacksonian America* (Ithaca, 1985).

53. S.J. Watson, "U.S. Army Officers," pp. 518–19, and "Manifest Destiny and Military Professionalism: A New Perspective on Junior U.S. Army Officers' Attitudes Toward War with Mexico, 1844–1846," *Southwestern Historical Quarterly*, 99 (1996), pp. 467–98.

54. BL. Add. 49964 fol. 31.

# 8

# Conclusions

## REVIEWING EXCEPTIONALISM

The extent and importance of conflict in independent America's first century emerges clearly from this study. It is also apparent that America's military development, institutionally, operationally and doctrinally, was centrally determined by the country's political structure and culture, rather than by factors inherent to the processes of military change. The "pluralist democracy" that resulted from the interaction of president, Congress, and the public, greatly affected tasking, force structure, military preparedness and the conduct of war.[1] So also did the relationship between national and state institutions and politics. The legacy of independence was also important. The condemnation of George III in the Declaration of Independence includes "He has kept among us in times of peace standing armies without the consent of our legislatures. He has affected to render the military independent of, and superior to the civil power." The politics of independence set the parameters for American governments.

These factors helped to provide and secure a military exceptionalism that is worthy of note. This exceptionalism requires probing, however, by considering it from "within," in terms of American military development, but also from "without," in terms of the wider Western context within which America should be considered. In the latter case, it is possible to propose a lesser degree of exceptionalism than that sometimes claimed for American military development by moving from a contrast between America and a Western paradigm and, instead, underlining the variety of warfare and military organisation within the West. At a basic level, "the Western" military and "Western" warfare in 1775,

1810, 1830, or 1865 looks very different if the focus of attention is Britain, France, Prussia, Russia, Mexico or Brazil, rather than the West as a whole. The same is true if the last two are excluded and the focus is a supposed European paradigm; although most European states in this period did not face problems of the interplay of federalism and centralisation seen in Mexico, Argentina, Brazil and the United States. Within this more multifaceted context, of a pluralist Western world, it is possible to discern a myriad of exceptionalisms, and thus to downplay that of America.

It is also possible to look for important similarities and linkages between developments in America and those elsewhere in the West. Weaponry is a crucial one: American military matériel was far more similar to those of European armies, than were its Chinese or Persian counterparts. There were also linkages with American attempts to observe best practice; which was found, as far as Americans were concerned, in Europe, both for land and for naval warfare. Thus, officers were sent to European military schools, or on, official or unofficial, observer missions. American officers went overseas over 150 times in 1815–60 in order to gather military information. These included senior commanders, such as Scott, who went after the Napoleonic Wars and interviewed generals on both sides, as well as more junior officers.[2] In some cases, exposure to European forces was extensive. Philip Kearny attended the 1839–40 session of the French cavalry school at Saumur, with five other young dragoon officers. He served with the French army in Algeria in 1840, writing a book about the conflict, and, after military service in the Mexican War, served in the French army in the Italian War of 1859, seeing battle in the major clashes at Magenta and Solferino, and winning the Legion of Honour. Philip Cooke, an experienced veteran, was an observer in the Italian war and went on to command a division during McClellan's Peninsula campaign. Henry Halleck, who was sometimes known as Old Brains, updated his *Elements of Military Art and Science* (1846), the first major American textbook on war, with *Critical Notes on the Mexican and Crimean Wars* for the second (1859) and third (1862) editions. It is instructive that the Crimean War was seen as worthy of note.

However, the value of what officers learned abroad has been questioned, and it has been suggested that they were overly willing to accept the value of a European paradigm. Thanks in large part to the prestige of Napoleon I's campaigning, France served as this model before the Crimean War, but, during that war, Russia earned praise from the Military Commission to the Theater of War in Europe or Delafield Commission, especially from McClellan, who was one of its members. This claim of excessive European influence has been advanced in an important recent study of the Commission, and it has been argued that the army should have developed "a new American theory and doctrine that was useful in an American context."[3]

This would be an easier argument to make were it possible to show that there was a clear tasking for the American military. Instead, any consideration of the variety of tasks that had to be fulfilled, combined with the counterfactuals considered by contemporaries that might have enlarged this list, suggests that there was no distinctive American tasking, on land or sea. More specifically, conflict with other Western powers was a possibility through most of the period. Throughout, the longest border was with another Western state, Britain, and war with her was possible in the 1840s and 1860s, while the Mexicans also looked to the Western tradition, especially the Spanish and French armies. It was therefore appropriate for the Americans to look to Western examples, both as models and as threats.

It is reasonable today to emulate the observers of the past in looking for comparisons and contrasts in order to throw light on the extent and nature of American distinctiveness. Here the point of departure should not be the "material culture" of war, particularly weaponry, but rather how military resources were employed. This raises interrelated issues not only of force structure and doctrine, but also of strategic culture. This concept can be interpreted in a number of ways, with, in particular, varying degrees of emphasis placed on the American ability to shape military options and thus develop a distinctive culture, as opposed to a stress on the role of constraints in this development.

## GEOGRAPHICAL EXCEPTIONALISM

The latter is exemplified by John Keegan, who proposed a geographical exceptionalism for American warfare and claimed that those who did not appreciate this were doomed; in other words that geographical constraints took precedence over any independent strategic culture. Thus, for McClellan's strategy in 1862:

Its failure may be seen, in a larger sense, as intrinsic to McClellan's plan rather than as contingent on delay and mismanagement. By selecting the Peninsula as his war-winning theater of operations, McClellan chose to fight an essentially European campaign in an American landscape, confining his army to a narrow front, constricted by obstacles to left and right and closed at the bottom of corridor by his principal objective . . . that could be transformed into an obstacle, as indeed it was by energetic digging.

For Keegan, once Grant was on the job, Confederate defeat "had the force of inevitability":

. . . it had lost because it had never understood the critical dimension of space in the making of war on the American continent. Lee, in the end, lost because he allowed himself to be confined to a European-scale theater of operations, just as the French had so allowed themselves to be confined in 1759 and the British in 1781 . . . all failed by abandoning free use of space in America's enormous landscape to fight conventional campaigns of confrontation on fixed fronts.[4]

This approach to exceptionalism has serious limitations, both in general terms and, more specifically, with reference to the Civil War, a theme that can be followed in chapter six. Keegan adopts a monocausal explanation, which is always troubling, and seriously underplays the diversity of military environments in both Europe and North America. The notion of a "narrow front" and a "European-scale theater of operations" as distinct from American warfare looks surprising in light of Scott's campaign in 1847 or Grant's in 1864–65. The Napoleonic campaigns of 1805–7 do not approximate to that of McClellan in 1862, and there are other examples of European forces being able to manoeuvre across considerable spaces in order to achieve success, for example Russian campaigning against the Turks in 1736–39, 1768–74, 1787–92, 1806–12, and 1828–29, or in Poland. The suppression of the Hungarians in 1849 also saw wideranging movements by Austrian and Russian forces.

There was a distinctive geographical context to conflict in North America, but it was set rather by the relatively small number of sovereign powers (a situation that corresponded to Eastern Europe in 1795–1878 but not to Western Europe), and was transformed briefly by the Civil War which was eccentric to the politics and the geographical pattern of conflict in North America in the period 1775–1865, and certainly not integral to it.

## THE SOCIAL DIMENSION

The major point of departure in considering exceptionalism is not geographical, but, rather, the nature of American politics. This was not deferential: servitude, like slavery, was an "other." British observers had noted this from the outset. The social politics of the Continental Army was very different to that of the *Mischianza* held by the British in Philadelphia on 18 May 1778 with its mock tournament of knights, or the suggestion in 1815 that the British stabilise their North American situation by introducing a form of military feudalism:

I have understood that your Lordship is sensible of the hostile spirit which prevails in America against this country and that political rivalship which keeps it alive and that your Lordship is anxious to guard our Canadian provinces against surprize, as the Americans will not fail to strengthen their frontier and build vessels of force on the Lakes. I conceive the most economical mode would be to disband some of the young regiments that may now be in America and to induce the officers to settle there to grant lands according to their rank to be held of the crown by feudal service for themselves and heirs. You would thus have an effective and formidable militia that could be brought into immediate active service without the expense of recruiting, and commanded by officers of some experience. I think it would be politic to engage as many officers to settle as you could from any regiments as the mode of conducting war in that country is different from the tactics of Europe and requires local knowledge and experience.

In 1779, in contrast, James Harris MP recorded:

Saw Ambrose Serle, Secretary to Lord Howe, and lately returned from North America. As a sample of the Bostonian spirit, he told me 'twas a common language in that country, when they were desirous to praise a man—"that he was a good sort of man—that he had nothing of a *gentleman* in him." He added this liberal, levelling spirit went so far that even their own (mock) Governor durst [dares] not keep a valet de chambre, but went regularly to the barber's shop to be shaved; and that, the rule there being that the *first* comer should be *first* served, the Governor, if he found a cobbler before him, was obliged to wait till that worthy cobbler had been shaved first.[5]

Such attitudes provided two of the parameters of military organisation: despite the rapid rise of the American population and a conviction that Americans had a martial spirit, a system of conscription was bound to face difficulties in the face of such independence; while individualism potentially challenged the disciplinary basis of military life. Individualism interacted with a strong anti-statist tradition, seen, for example, in the hesitation about establishing an army in 1784, and in distrust of regular officers.[6] This tradition was kept alive in and by American politics and ideology. There have been suggestions that the extent of opposition to a standing army has been exaggerated,[7] but it was certainly powerful, and very much so by comparison with other states created by revolutionary war.

Indeed, it was not surprising that, despite the cross-class cohesion that helped sustain the Revolution, the belief in which formed a potent part of subsequent political culture, much of the regular army came from marginal economic groups: the successful were not willing to accept discipline, and did not need to do so.[8] This marginality was seen in terms of origins, with much of the army and navy foreign born; and also led to high rates of desertion. Whereas the officer corps in the American army was probably more reflective of the general social order than in most European armies, parallels were probably stronger between enlisted personnel on both sides of the Atlantic.

Service in the common militia (as opposed to volunteer units) was an alternative type of conscription to a conscript force of regulars, but its military value in America was limited by a number of factors. These included the dubious constitutional status of compulsory out-of-state service for the common militia, the term character of enlistments, and the state, rather than federal, nature of the militia. These factors were all aspects of a conditionality of military service. Although the militia did not normally contravene federal policies, its existence shaped those policies and also the broader cultural visions of military power. The regular troops, and their campaigns, can be held up to comparison with other Western powers, but the militia was different. The federal nature of the government combined with the role of the militia and volunteers to create a situation different to that in other major powers. The existence of the militia was imprinted on wider American notions of military power and its application, particularly until the Civil War, changing slowly thereafter, but with effects that linger to the present.

The conditionality of military service was, in many respects, an important aspect of the democratic character of American society. It was the counterpart of the language of citizen soldiers, for their soldiering was conceived of in terms of their citizenship. Recruitment and mobilisation stemmed in part from a sense of commitment to community and of idealised co-operation with fellow Americans.

## MILITARY TASKS

To draw attention to the limitations for military effectiveness of this conditionality of military service, as was done by contemporary critics, not least regular army officers, with their interest in professionalism, is to downplay the role of political context and tasking in the military. It also assumes that force structure and doctrine should be set by an abstract and universal definition of military effectiveness, and by the military, rather than with reference to these specific political criteria, and by civilian politicians who responded to and helped shape the longstanding hostility to standing armies and military pretensions in the Anglophone world. The idea of conforming to an abstract definition of military effectiveness was particularly questionable given the political geography of America's military tasking. The Americans were concerned with capability in North America, and against the opponents they might confront there, not with having an army able, for example, to prevail against the Prussians or the Brazilians.

In rough terms, there were three periods of tasking within the scope of this book. First, there were the decades of anxiety before 1815, when the new state was confronted by European powers, especially Britain, with a role in North America and willing, or apparently willing, to stir up opposition to the United States, not least among the Natives. In this period, there was urgent concern about defensiveness, which led to stress on the militia and anxiety about how best to protect coastal positions leading to an emphasis on fortifications and gunboats.

This anxiety ebbed after the War of 1812 and was followed by a more confident period in which defensiveness was of far less importance. This owed much to the attitude of the major world power, Britain, which definitely had a capability sufficient to harm America, as was shown in the War of 1812. There were a whole series of issues that could have set the two powers apart, not simply differences over trade and Canada, but also British attitudes towards American expansion. Thus, in 1811, the Spanish government, then fighting with Britain against France, sought British help against American expansion into West Florida. The British government saw this expansion as unprovoked aggression against a close ally and instructed the envoy to protest, and to do the same if East Florida was attacked, but he was also instructed to avoid hostile or menacing language and informed that the government did not want to fight.[9]

Aside from the Floridas, there was subsequent concern about British attitudes towards Texas, in particular a lack of support for American annexation, while, during the Mexican War, the British made efforts to mediate that were unwelcome to the Americans. The Mexicans sought British help, and there was also talk that the Mexican inhabitants of California might turn to Britain.[10] Nevertheless, the British did not move to block America's southward expansion. They could have wrecked America's use of naval power against Mexico, in the Gulf of Mexico and, with greater ease, in the Pacific, and forced the Americans to rely on the overland campaigning blazed by Taylor, rather than on Scott's amphibious thrust, but did not do so.

More generally, after the War of 1812, areas of vulnerability were no longer close to the centres of American power and, instead, there was concern about how best to ensure authority in areas over which American sovereignty was recognised. The only clash with a sovereign state, the Mexican War, was with a weaker military and economic power, and one that was affected by serious political division and disorder. In the period 1815–60, the focus in America was on the regular army, but this was a small force and it was supplemented when necessary by volunteers.

## CITIZEN-SOLDIERS

This remained the case until the Civil War, when the need for massive quantities of manpower and matériel forced new solutions. The most important was conscription, but its eccentric character to American public culture was shown by the rapid return to a small volunteer army thereafter. Furthermore, most of the troops raised by each side were volunteers, not conscripts. These volunteers carried many aspects of civilian life over into the army, including the election of officers, a practice that regular soldiers despised, first because it defied the precepts and practice of military life, especially the character of hierarchy, and, secondly, because popularity, rather than skill tended to be the crucial element in elections.

This account might seem to bear scant reference to events elsewhere in the West, but that was not, in fact, the case. Instead, allowing for the pronounced variety between countries, it is possible to suggest a similar tension between regular and militia forces in Europe and the United States, and a not dissimilar chronology. The French Revolutionary and Napoleonic Wars led to a rapid increase in not only the size of the military but also the development of non-regular reserves. This was especially so in Prussia where, by 1813, there was a 120,000-strong militia, the *Landwehr*.

However, after the Napoleonic Wars, fewer soldiers were required and there was a move against the militia and towards a smaller force of long-service regulars. This was seen as more politically reliable, especially in France. There, the restored Bourbons suspended conscription and cut the size of the army. The key European army in 1815–49 was the Austrian. This was a relatively small force (compared to that of Napoleonic France) that was used for counter-revolutionary operations in Italy and in the Habsburg dominions.

It was not until mid-century that the need for troops increased again, with a sequence of major conflicts involving large numbers of troops: the Crimean

(1854–56), Franco-Austrian (1859), Austro-Prussian (1866), and Franco-Prussian wars (1870–71), the last two the major struggles of the Wars of German Unification. The Prussians met the challenge by the use of large reserve forces. Conscripts served for a short period, and then entered the reserves, ensuring that substantial forces of trained men could be mobilised in the event of war, and that the state did not have to pay them in peace. This gave Prussia numerical superiority over France, which continued to rely on long-service regulars, and had a smaller and less effective reserve. In 1870, Prussia could call on nearly a million troops. Thus the raising of large numbers of men in the American Civil War was a parallel to developments in Europe, with the significant difference that it was reversed after the war in America, but accentuated in mainland Europe. This contrast owed much to political culture, but also reflected the far more competitive nature of power relationships in Europe and the extent to which the Franco-Prussian war did not provide the lasting resolution offered by the American Civil War.[11]

Britain did not introduce conscription until 1916. The extent to which American and British developments did not match those in Prussia necessarily qualifies any concept of a Western military model. Furthermore, although neither fitted into the Prussian paradigm, they were very different from each other. The Americans did not share the British emphasis on a navy, nor the large colonial army, much of it recruited from subject and allied peoples, that the British had in India. Conversely, the British lacked the American's emphasis on the militia and on volunteer units. There were comparisons. For example, the professionalism of Scott's army in Mexico in 1847 matched that of British regulars. However, after 1815 the British did not deploy large forces comparable to those in the Civil War until World War I.

The idea of the citizen soldier was not only seen in America. It was also a characteristic of republican and liberal circles in Europe, and thus throws doubt on Samuel P. Huntington's claim that "liberalism does not understand and is hostile to military institutions and the military function."[12] More generally, there was a romanticisation of military life and war throughout the West in the nineteenth century. It varied greatly in its hold, was highly unrealistic, was frequently more effective for the would-be or new soldier than for those with experience, and did not prevent desertion. Nevertheless, military life and conflict were generally presented as manly and noble. They were applauded, praised and eulogised in popular song and church service, processions and celebrations, and in print and on canvas.

## THE IMAGE OF MILITARY LIFE

America shared in this process of praising the manliness of war. Although, Americans emphasised a view of nation-creation not state-formation, and stressed the role of peaceful deliberation and voluntary consent, of constitution-making and ratification, not war, in their national myth, the War of Independence was still seen as important, while the War of 1812, the Texan War for Independence, and the Mexican War were each given an heroic sheen.[13] The romanticism of military life and combat helped sustain morale in the bloody combat conditions of the Civil War, although the role of religious conviction should not be underrated. It is also pertinent to devote due attention to a sense of community and to peer-group obligations, as well as to more defined ideological positions, such as the cause of "Southern freedom" or the Union, or of "Liberty," a cause that both sides could claim to serve, and to diverse local patterns of enlistment, which suggest the need to emphasise the variety of factors involved.[14]

Whatever the stress on manly struggle and suffering, disease in the Civil War claimed the lives of about twice as many troops as combat. Poor sanitation was a terrible problem and it exacerbated the impact of such conditions as dysentery. This reality of military service was matched by that of parlous conditions for the wounded. This was a reflection not simply of the nature of contemporary medicine and surgery, but also of the lack of surgeons, doctors and adequate facilities.[15]

In part as a result of the "patriotic" legacy of the American Revolution, manliness was associated with heroism and leadership with generalship. It was no accident that Washington became President, as did Jackson, twice, and William Henry Harrison, the hero of Tippecanoe, and Zachary Taylor; although the presidencies of the two latter were cut short by their death in office. Jefferson Davis, the President of the Confederacy, was a graduate of West Point, who had served on the Wisconsin frontier, been a colonel of Volunteers and war hero in the Mexican War, and been Secretary of War in 1853–57. Harrison beat Scott to the Whig nomination in 1840, but, in 1852, when Scott ran as the Whig candidate he was defeated by the Democrat Franklin Pierce, who had been a brigadier-general of volunteers in the Mexican War and was injured at the battle of Churubusco when he fell from his horse. Frémont was Republican candidate in 1856, but was defeated by James Buchanan. After an inglorious career as a Union general in 1861–62, Frémont challenged Lincoln unsuccessfully for the Republican nomination in 1864, and then ran as a Radical Democrat, withdrawing shortly before the election. The Democratic candidate in the election was McClellan. New wars kept past episodes of military glory, resolution and dedication alive. Thus, in 1864, Emanuel Leutze's painting *Washington Crossing the Delaware* was hung in the place of honor at the New York Metropolitan Fair, a fundraising event for relief efforts for Union troops.[16]

The conflation of military gloire and high office is a reminder of the degree to which republican, federal America had more in common with other regimes than an emphasis on exceptionalism might suggest. This can be taken further if comparisons are made with Latin America, although there militarism played a larger role in politics, and, as a consequence, politics in the military.

## THE PRESSURE OF MILITARY NECESSITY

A stress on citizen soldiery, manly leadership and the military as an instrument of the state, would correspond to idealised contemporary views, but it would also be misleading, not least because it would underrate tensions between the armed forces and civilian society. Thus, the military misgivings about civilian leadership seen in recent decades[17] have a long history. Scott clashed with Jefferson Davis when the latter was Secretary of War. Joseph Hooker, who succeeded Burnside as commander of the Army of the Potomac in January 1863, offered the Napoleonic-style dictum that America might need a dictator in order to overcome the South, to which Lincoln offered the pertinent rejoinder, "Only those generals who gain successes, can set up dictators. What I now ask of you is military success, and I will risk the dictatorship." Indeed, that year, Halleck, the General-in-Chief of the Army, circumvented Lincoln's instructions about strategy in Texas, because he did not share the President's concern about the threat posed by the French army in Mexico. Lincoln wanted Union forces built up on the Texas coast for that end. In contrast, Halleck saw deployment to Texas as part of the strategy for action against the Confederacy. This has been seen as an instance of a wider problem: the clash between the local strategic authority of military commanders and the grand strategy backed by a civilian president who had other than military considerations to address.[18]

The claims of necessity were not only pressed by generals. In the South, the Confederate government aroused concern with the expedients it adopted to gain supplies, including conscription, direct taxation, martial law in several areas, and the impressment of supplies in return for paper currency. To Democrats in the North, the Lincoln government also seemed to be spreading its power, if not tyrannical, for example with the suspension of habeas corpus in Maryland. Conscription and emancipation both aroused anger. In the Congressional elections of 1862, the Democrats won the Indiana state legislature only to find it dismissed by the Governor, Oliver Morton, who governed without it. The Democratic presidential platform, agreed on 29 August 1864, declared that "under the pretence of a military necessity, or war power higher than the Constitution, the Constitution itself has been disregarded in every part." On 10 March 1863, the British envoy reported:

The appropriation bills have sanctioned military and other expenditure on an immense scale. The act to provide ways and means for the support of the government has conferred on the Secretary of the Treasury vast powers of borrowing and of issuing paper money, and the large discretion left to him in these matters must give him enormous influences and the National Currency Act is intended to cause the government's paper money to be everywhere substituted for the notes of private banks to give the government a control over the banking interests.

Lord Lyons argued that the Conscription Act placed the male population:

without restriction at the disposal of the President. The "Act relating to Habeas Corpus" has granted the executive government an indemnity for the arbitrary arrests it has already made, and sanctioned its making arbitrary arrests in future throughout the country. The Act authorising the issue of letters of marque has gone far to transfer the war powers of Congress to the President.

All these measures appear at this moment to find favour with the people at large. Most of the newspapers announce that a dictatorship has been established, and make the announcement in a strain of exultation.[19]

## PROFESSIONALISM

In peacetime, it is inappropriate to exaggerate the divide or sense of divide between the military and civilian society, not least because to do so would be to minimise the myriad links between them, and, also, overly to emphasize the coherence of army society. In the early Republican period, the practice of commissioning men directly from civil life, rather than promoting from the ranks in peacetime, led to a stress on political affiliation, social connections and "gentlemanly" conduct,[20] all of which brought the military close to civil society, but with deleterious consequences for military effectiveness, as was seen in the War of 1812.

Jefferson hoped to use the military academy founded at West Point in 1802 as an institution for inculcating Democratic-Republican ideology within the officer corps.[21] However, especially after 1815, when, increasingly, officers were recruited from West Point, and thus provided with a new coherence of background, professionalism helped to link the military, especially the officers, to civil society; although there was also criticism of West Point as a source of aristocratic privilege. In addition, professionalism was redefined in terms of more training and theory than hitherto; correspondingly, social position and physical prowess alone became less important to professional success. A new emphasis on expertise in command led to a greater stress on formal education, seen most clearly with the role of West Point, offering a set of priorities that did not correspond directly to those of social hierarchy.

Furthermore, a warfare of scientific professionalism was implied by the formal education that was provided. An emphasis on control and training enhanced the possibilities of planned war. This led to a greater stress on publications about war. Philip Cooke published *Scenes and Adventures in the Army* (1857), as well as *Cavalry Tactics* (1859, revised 1861). This professionalism was linked to an institutionalization of military life with, for example, printed drill books. West Point ensured that professionalism was linked to validation by a state officer training school, a situation that again conformed to that across the West.

The "ideology" of the American military, with its stress on duty to the country and on professionalism, minimised an overt engagement with partisan politics.[22] The notion of a depoliticized command system, defined and organised by talent, was an aspect of American public culture, rather than, as in Europe, a construct of the notion of the impersonal state that was important to the ideology of nineteenth-century European government. In practice, in most of the West, but far more in Latin American and Europe than in the United States, political reliability was an important issue in the treatment of commanders and officers. Given the importance of the military to the domestic politics of many states, it is scarcely surprising that, rather than suggesting that political reliability might compromise efficiency, the issue could be reconceptualized so that, reliability took precedence and was seen as a prime definition of efficiency. The contrasting situation in the United States constituted a significant difference in American military culture.

## THE MILITARY AND CIVIL SOCIETY

The different situation in America reflected the limited nature of the use of the army in civilian political disputes, and the practice and possibility of changing government through elections, not insurrections or coups; a marked contrast to the situation in Latin America, but also to a number of European states, especially Spain and France. The American army was only used, or its use considered, in civilian political disputes on a few occasions. Troops were deployed in response to South Carolina's attempted nullification of a new tariff in 1832–33, while in the "Dorr War" between political groupings in Rhode Island in 1842 army intervention was planned in order to restore order. In the Dorr War, dual elections held under two rival constitutions led to conflict, with Thomas Dorr, one of the two Governors, leading an abortive attack on the state arsenal and being charged with treason. Compared to the situation in Europe, there was a reluctance to use regular forces to deal with domestic discontent. Regular troops were not in the event used in the Dorr War.

In the "Buckshot War" in Pennsylvania in 1838, the state militia was used to suppress disorder in Harrisburg. The conflict arose from a disputed election in Philadelphia County in October 1838, success in which would determine control of the state legislature. Both sides had threatened violence if they did not go their way, and Harrisburg filled with squads of men, mainly from Philadelphia. The city fell under mob rule until about 1,100 volunteer militia restored order. Governor Ritner proclaimed that the situation constituted a rebellion and applied for the use of regulars stationed at Carlisle but was refused. As with the Dorr War, the crisis remained entirely a state matter. Federal regulars could only be used as police if the breakdown of law and order was beyond state control.

The term "Buckshot War" was applied because General Robert Patterson instructed the volunteers to arm themselves with buckshot. Buckshot was large enough to bring down a buck deer, as opposed to game birds. The Buckshot War did not become as violent as had been feared, but it led to consideration of some drastic steps. Augustus Pleasonton, a militia colonel, recorded in his diary for 11 December his proposal for dealing with the "mob" holding the Senate Chamber:

Two pieces of artillery, six pounders, should be posted in the street immediate north of the Capitol and about 250 feet distant—They should be double shotted. The storming party under a proper officer, and suitably armed and equipped, should be directed to carry by force the north door of the Capitol and one of the windows of the Senate Chamber . . . while the artillery should be directed to fire upon one of the piers between the windows, farthest from the storming party, and at about eight feet above the floor of the Senate Chamber—a few discharges from these guns would soon cut away the supports of the second storey, and would let it down upon the heads of the mob, if they should not be soon driven out. By leaving the whole southern front open for the escape of the rioters, bloodshed might be avoided, and the Senate Chamber evacuated without the necessity of firing a shot.[23]

The military presence probably prevented the "Buckshot War" from becoming more serious. Equally, the authorities employed force cautiously, and this helped to keep the war bloodless. In the second respect, there is a parallel with the passage of the British First (Parliamentary) Reform Act in 1832.

In the Nullification Crisis, John C. Calhoun of South Carolina claimed that the tariff was unconstitutional as well as unfair, and that individual states could protect themselves from such acts by interposing their authority, and thus nullifying the federal law. In November 1832, the South Carolina convention passed an ordinance of nullification, and the state raised an enthusiastic army of over 25,000 men and purchased arms. The nullifiers threatened secession from the Union if the federal government sought to enforce the tariff. However, the federal government did not give way and the garrison in Charleston was reinforced by Winfield Scott, who then proved an adept manager of local sensitivities. South Carolina was not supported by the remainder of the South, and there was also opposition to nullification from within the state. In the end, South Carolina had to abandon the threat of nullification and to accept a settlement of the tariff issue which did not meet its goals.[24] To the British envoy, the dispute showed America as weakened by its political system and public culture: "Every public measure takes the colour of party in the U.S., a constant excitement being kept up in the public mind by the frequent recurrence of elections."[25]

This approach threatened confidence in the fixity as well as the strength of American power. Thus, in 1796, Edward Thornton, British Secretary of Legation, noted American support for Britain, but added "an opinion so fickle and inconstant is scarcely to be relied upon for any length of time," while, in 1833, a British government memorandum on frontier negotiations commented, "it is especially essential that His Majesty [William IV] should be previously assured that the President of the United States will possess the power of carrying into full effect his part of any engagement which may be concluded betwixt the plenipotentiaries of the two governments."[26]

In practice, with both the military and with foreign policy, the Americans avoided the fissiparous consequences of a federal system, by giving the key power to federal, not state, government. In 1778, Congress banned individual congressmen from talking to the Carlisle Commission. In part as a result of the Longchamps affair in 1784, in which a French diplomat was attacked, the Supreme Court was given jurisdiction over international law and the authority of the individual states was subordinated, although the authority of the Supreme Court in international cases (expressed in the Constitution in 1787) also drew on broader cases and considerations.[27] Individual states lacked the right to negotiate "foreign" treaties or to make war; although their relations with Native Americans initially threatened to permit both. Thus, for example, in the mid-1780s, Georgia raised state forces for duty against the Cherokee. In 1839, frontier disputes between Maine and Canada over land and timber cutting seemed about to lead to war, and the Governor of Maine called up the militia, but, helped by British restraint, Scott kept the peace.[28] Texas followed its own policies as an independent country and, although it surrendered this right when it joined the union, differences over policy towards the Natives were a major problem in the 1850s. In 1858, Texas Rangers operated independently of the regulars against the Comanche. Six years earlier, the Governor of Texas called out the Rangers without the authorisation of the Secretary of War and against his wishes.

The integrating range of the federal perspective, and its capacity to provide a measure of consistency to frontier policy can be seen in the case of individual careers. Thus, Zachary Taylor, born in Kentucky, served on the northwest frontier in the War of 1812 and in command of Fort Winnebago in 1817–19, before being transferred to Louisiana. He moved back north, serving at Fort Snelling (Minnesota) as an Indian superintendent, before fighting the Seminole and moving, in succession, to Louisiana, Arkansas and Texas. This helped give him a national perspective that put him at variance to more sectional politicians.[29]

The ability of the federal government to take advantage of its key role in military and foreign policy was limited due to the nature of politics and of public ideology. Thus, Benjamin Lincoln, who served in 1781–83 as the first Secretary at War, was elected in large part because he was acceptable to all the factions in Congress and had a reputation for observing the line between military and civil powers. National feeling in the early-nineteenth century could not easily be focused on government demands and agencies: "Repudiating the Federalists' version of a consolidated, 'energetic' postimperial regime, ascendant Republics promoted a radically diffuse and decentered national identity, constantly refreshed by electoral mobilizations that reenacted the Revolution for rising generations of patriots."[30]

The Nullification Crisis, in which President Jackson personally directed military preparations, and, far more clearly, the Civil War, showed that, in the last resort, the army was the arm of the federal government and would be employed to enforce government authority.[31] Nevertheless, the character of American society made the nature and goals of this employment different to those in Latin America or Continental Europe, and such intervention by federal forces was rare. The military was not in a position to prevent change, nor was expected to do so, unlike in much of the West where the military was designed to support prevailing political, social and ideological practices and norms. In addition, the separatism that led to the Civil War originated in political circles, not the military: political revolt led to military separatism, not vice versa.

On 4 December 1861, the front page of the *New York Times* offered "The National Lines before Washington. A Map exhibiting the defences of the national capital, and positions of the several divisions of the Grand Union army." The accompanying text began,

The interest which attaches to the military operations of the National army on the line of the Potomac, has induced us to present the readers of the Times with the above complete and accurate map of the impregnable lines on the Virginia side of the National Capital . . . The principal permanent fortifications, which the rebels, if they attempt them, will find to be an impassable barrier to their ambitious designs upon the Capital, have been enumerated by title and position in the General Orders of General McClellan, but are, for the first time, located and named upon the present map . . . Another novel and useful trait of our present map is its geographical definition of the territory occupied by each of the eight divisions constituting the grand defensive army.

McClellan furiously demanded that the paper be punished for aiding the Confederates. The Secretary of War restricted himself to urging the editor to avoid such action in the future. The following spring, however, the War Department established a voluntary system to prevent journalists with the Army of the Potomac from publishing compromising maps. The situation was very different in more autocratic Prussia, which between 1864 and 1871 became the most influential European military power.[32]

If the character of American public culture affected the response to war, then war also affected the development of this culture. Conflict during the colonial period had led to economic problems and social tension, helping weaken imperial links.[33] In the American Revolution, military service and the burdens of supporting the struggle encouraged the development of a more democratic political culture: "Military service legitimated claims to petition the legislature for the repeal of exemption laws, draft laws, and unequal recruiting laws. . . . The war politicized men,"[34] although, in addition, the social and cultural development of the colonies produced men who took specific political expectations of contractual service with them into the military. The experience of war tended to reinforce those expectations. These men also carried into service a set of ideals about the appropriate use of military force, that, in part, prevented them from being used against the civilian population the way French Revolutionary soldiers were. This process of politicization was also seen clearly in the Civil War, while the widespread participation of volunteers in intervening conflicts encouraged a sense of the country as an active and participatory democracy with an obligation to heed the citizenry. In America, war led to pressure for a more powerful state, but much of this pressure proved short-term, while the consequences in terms of politicisation proved to be more enduring. It is clear that accounts of American political and social development have to give due weight to its military history, just as the latter cannot be understood in isolation from these developments.

## NOTES

1. M.D. Pearlman, *Warmaking and American Democracy: The Struggle over Military Strategy, 1700 to the Present* (Lawrence, Kansas, 1999).

2. M. Moten, *The Delafield Commission and the American Military Profession* (College Station, Texas, 2000), pp. 83–86.

3. *Ibid.*, pp. 86, 209–10.

4. J. Keegan, *The Military Geography of the American Civil War* (Gettysburg, 1997), pp. 23–24, 26–27. See also his *Fields of Battle: The Wars for North America* (1996). For a more successful use of geography, D.C. Skaggs, "The Sixty Years' War for the Great Lakes: An Overview," in Skaggs and L.L. Nelson (eds.), *The Sixty Years' War for the Great Lakes, 1754–1814* (East Lansing, 2001), pp. 1–18.

5. Colonel Stephenson to Sidmouth, 29 Aug. 1815, DRO. 152M/C1815/OC1; Harris memoranda, Jan. 1779, London, History of Parliament transcripts, Malmesbury papers.

6. M. Cunliffe, *Soldiers and Civilians: The Martial Spirit in America, 1775–1865* (Boston, 1968; 2nd ed., New York, 1973); C. Royster, *A Revolutionary People at War: the Continental Army and American Character, 1775–1783* (New York, 1979).

7. D. Higginbotham, "The Early American Way of War: Reconnaissance and Appraisal," in Higginbotham (ed.), *War and Society in Revolutionary America* (Columbia, South Carolina), pp. 290–91; J. Resch, *Suffering Soldiers: Revolutionary War Veterans, Moral Sentiment, and Political Culture in the Early Republic* (Amherst, Mass., 2000), p. 38.

8. E.C. Papenfuse and G.A. Stiverson, "General Smallwood's Recruits: The Peacetime Career of the Revolutionary War Private," *William and Mary Quarterly*, 3rd ser. 30 (1973), pp. 117–32; M.E. Lender, "The Social Structure of the New Jersey Brigade: The Continental Line as an American Standing Army," in P. Karsten (ed.), *The Military in America from the Colonial Era to the Present* (New York, 1980), pp. 27–44; R.H. Kohn, "The Social History of the American Soldier: a review and prospectus for research," *American Historical Review*, 86 (1981), pp. 553–67; C.P. Neimeyer, *America Goes to War: A Social History of the Continental Army* (New York, 1996).

9. BL. Add. 49990 fols. 17–20.

10. BL. Add. 49968 fol. 7.

11. J.M. Black, *Western Warfare 1775–1882* (Bloomington, 2001).

12. S.P. Huntington, *The Soldier and the State: The Theory and Politics of Civil-Military Relations* (New York, 1964), p. 144.

13. R.W. Johannsen, *To the Halls of the Montezumas: The Mexican War in the American Imagination* (Oxford, 1985).

14. D. Faust, "Christian Soldiers: The Meaning of Revivalism in the Confederate Army," *Journal of Southern History*, 53 (1987), pp. 63–90; S.J. Watson, "Religion and Combat Motivation in the Confederate Armies," *Journal of Military History*, 58 (1994), pp. 29–56; E.J. Hess, *The Union Soldier in Battle: Enduring the Ordeal of Combat* (1997); J.M. McPherson, *For Cause and Comrades: Why Men Fought in the Civil War*

(New York, 1997); J.A. Frank, *With Ballots and Bayonet: The Political Socialization of American Civil War Soldiers* (Athens, Georgia, 1998). For religion, see, more generally, R.M. Miller, H.S. Stout and C.R. Wilson (eds.), *Religion and the American Civil War* (Oxford, 1999). On diversity, K. Hackemer, "Response to War: Civil War Enlistment Patterns in Kenosha County, Wisconsin," *Military History of the West*, 29 (1999), pp. 31–62.

15. G. Linderman, *Embattled Courage: The Experience of Combat in the American Civil War* (New York, 1987).

16. M. Thistlethwaite, "Washington Crossing the Delaware. Navigating the Image(s) of the Hero," in K.L. Cope (ed.), *George Washington in and as Culture* (New York, 2001), p. 53. See also, M. Kammen, *A Season of Youth: The American Revolution and the Historical Imagination* (New York, 1978) and Thistlethwaite, *The Image of George Washington: Studies in Mid-Nineteenth-Century American History Painting* (New York, 1979).

17. R.F. Weigley, "The American Military and the Principle of Civilian Control from McClellan to Powell," and "The Soldier, the Statesman and the Military Historian," *Journal of Military History*, 57 (1993) and 63 (1999); R.H. Kohn, "Out of Control: The Crisis in Civil-Military Relations," *National Interest*, 35 (1994); A.J. Bacevich, "The Paradox of Professionalism: Eisenhower, Ridgway and the Challenge to Civilian Control, 1953–1955," *Journal of Military History*, 61 (1997).

18. K. Hackemer, "Strategic Dilemma: Civil-Military Friction and the Texas Coastal Campaign of 1863," *Military History of the West*, 26 (1996), pp. 187–214, esp. pp. 212–14.

19. PRO. FO. 5/879 fols. 162–63.

20. R. Gough, "Officering the American Army, 1798," W.B. Skelton, "The Confederation's Regulars: A Social Profile of Enlisted Service in America's First Standing Army," *William and Mary Quarterly*, 3rd series, 43 (1986), pp. 460–71 and 46 (1989), p. 783.

21. T.J. Crackel, *Mr. Jefferson's Army: Political and Social Reform of the Military Establishment, 1801–1809* (New York, 1987).

22. A.R. Millett, *Military Professionalism and Officership in America* (Columbus, Ohio, 1977); Skelton, "Officers and Politicians: The Origins of Army Politics in the United States Before the Civil War," *Armed Forces and Society*, 6 (1979), pp. 22–48.

23. Historical Society of Pennsylvania, Diary of Augustus Pleasonton, f. 272. For a recent account see H.L. Trefousse, *Thaddeus Stevens: Nineteenth-Century Egalitarian* (Mechanicsburg, 2001), pp. 58–60. I am most grateful to Dennis Rubini for his advice about this conflict.

24. W.W. Freehling, *Prelude to Civil War: The Nullification Controversy in South Carolina, 1816–1836* (New York, 1965); R.E. Ellis, *The Union At Risk: Jacksonian Democracy, States' Rights, and the Nullification Crisis* (New York, 1987); D.J. Ratcliffe, "The Nullification Crisis, Southern Discontents, and the American Political Process," *American Nineteenth Century History* 1, no. 2 (2000), pp. 1–30.

25. BL. Add. 49964 fol. 11.

26. Oxford, Bodleian Library, Bland Burges papers vol. 21; BL. Add. 49963 fol. 5.

27. G.S. Rowe and A.W. Knott, "The Longchamps Affair (1784–1786). The Law of Nations, and the Shaping of Early American Foreign Policy," *Diplomatic History*, 10 (1986), pp. 199–200. See also J.N. Rakove, "Solving a Constitutional Puzzle: The Trea-

tymaking Clause as a Case Study," *Perspectives in American History*, new ser., 1 (1984), pp. 233–81.

28. F.M. Carroll, *A Good and Wise Measure. The Search for the Canadian-American Boundary, 1783–1842* (Toronto, 2001), pp. 208–12.

29. Wooster, "Military Strategy . . .", *Military History of Texas and the Southwest*, 15, 2 (1979); K.J. Bauer, *Zachary Taylor: Soldier, Planter, and Statesman of the Old Southwest* (Baton Rouge, 1985).

30. P.S. Onuf, *Jefferson's Empire. The Language of American Nationhood* (Charlottesville, 2000), p. 79.

31. R.W. Coakley, *The Role of Federal Military Forces in Domestic Disorders, 1789–1878* (Washington, 1988).

32. For criticism by the British envoy of the press in February 1863, PRO. FO. 5/877 fol. 12.

33. W. Pencak, *War, Politics and Revolution in Provincial Massachusetts* (Boston, 1981).

34. M.A. McDonnell, "The Politics of Mobilization in Revolutionary Virginia: Military Culture and Political and Social Relations, 1774–1783," (D.Phil., Oxford, 1995), pp. 289, 298.

# Further Reading

E.W. Carp, "Early American Military History: A Review of Recent Work," *Virginia Magazine of History and Biography*, 94 (1986), pp. 259–84.

J.W. Chambers II (ed.), *The Oxford Companion to American Military History* (Oxford, 1999).

E.M. Coffman, *The Old Army: A Portrait of the American Army in Peacetime, 1784–1898* (New York, 1986).

J.C. Fredriksen, *Shield of Republic, Sword of Empire: A Bibliography of United States Military Affairs, 1783–1846* (Westport, 1991).

D. Higginbotham (ed.), *War and Society in Revolutionary America* (Columbia, 1988).

P. Karsten, *The Military in America: From the Colonial Era to the Present* (New York, 1980).

P. Karsten, "The New American Military History: A Map of the Territory, Explored and Unexplored," *American Quarterly 36* (1984), pp. 389–418.

A. Millett and P. Maslowski, *For the Common Defense: A Military History of the United States of America* (2nd ed., New York, 1994).

R.F. Weigley, *The American Way of War: A History of United States Military Strategy and Policy* (Bloomington, 1973).

R.F. Weigley, *History of the United States Army* (2nd edn., Bloomington, 1984).

R.F. Weigley, *Towards an American Army: Military Thought from Washington to Marshall* (New York, 1962).

# Index

Harrison, William H., 86, 215
Hawaii, 67, 133, 172, 200
Hayes, Rutherford B., 171
Holland. *See* United Provinces
Hooker, Joseph, 160, 187, 216
Houston, Sam, 117–18, 132
Howe, General William, 13–16, 19
Hudson's Bay Company, 62

Idaho, 102
Illinois, 80
India, 18, 30
Indiana, 80
Iowa, 40, 94
ironclads, 153–55
Italy, 20, 100, 111, 138, 153

Jackson, Andrew, 55, 69, 87–88, 94, 114, 119, 220
Jackson, General Stonewall, 138, 147, 161
Jacobites, 27
Jamaica 10, 55
James II (of England), 7
Japan, 172
Java War of 1825–30, 91
Jay's Treaty, 43, 85
Jefferson, Thomas, 42–43, 46–47, 181, 199
Johnston, Albert Sidney, 158
Johnston, General Joseph E., 142, 146, 169

Kamehameha III (King of Hawaii), 67
Kansas, 40, 93, 141, 192, 194
Kearny, Colonel Stephen, 124
Kentucky, 41, 78, 81–82, 84, 140, 142, 146, 159
Knox, Henry, 81, 185

Latin America, 34–36, 61, 65, 82, 115, 173, 202, 218, 220
Latin American Wars of Liberation, 26, 34, 60, 119, 138, 191, 217
Lee, General Robert E., 131, 139, 141–42, 149, 155, 158–60, 162–63, 165, 167–69, 171, 209
Lee, Major General Charles, 29

Lewis and Clark Expedition, 185
Lincoln, Abraham, 94, 139, 141, 157, 165, 170, 194, 215–16
Lincoln, Benjamin, 21–22, 28, 45, 190, 220
Lone Star Republic. *See* Texas
Louisiana, 39–41, 58, 66, 69, 92, 140, 157, 171, 195, 196
Louisiana Purchase, The, 39–40, 45, 85, 88–89, 185–86, 189
loyalists, 13–14, 18, 23–25, 27, 30–31, 34, 43, 50, 62, 77–78, 184

Macomb, Alexander, 62, 114
Madison, James, 46, 48, 69
Maine, 44, 51, 62, 64
Manifest Destiny, 61, 81, 96, 113, 203
Maryland, 22, 140, 142, 183, 191, 196
Massachusetts, 28, 53, 67, 130, 190–91
Mauritius, 58
McClellan, Major-General George B., 142, 147, 157–59, 165–66, 173, 187, 209, 215, 221
Mexican-American War (1846–48), 2, 109–34, 139, 142, 145, 152, 160, 208, 212–13, 215
Mexico, 34, 40, 61, 63, 65–68, 88, 95–96, 100, 109, 115–18, 120, 122–23, 126, 128–29, 131, 134, 171–73, 187, 189, 192, 203
Michigan, 80
militias, 7, 12, 22–24, 31, 47, 59, 77–78, 82, 112, 114, 180, 182, 190
Minnesota, 40, 64, 98–99, 101
Mississippi, 39, 41, 80, 87, 92–94, 96, 99, 140, 157, 169, 174
Missouri, 40, 92–93, 102, 112, 125, 140, 142–43
Moltke, Count Helmuth von, 153, 157, 159, 162–65
Monroe Doctrine, 61, 65
Monroe, James, 64, 66
Montana, 40, 102–3
Montgomery, Richard, 11

Napoleon I, 34, 39, 48, 56, 59–60, 110, 126, 145, 157, 208
Napoleon III, 129, 157, 159

**About the Author**

JEREMY BLACK is Professor of History at the University of Exeter. His books include *War and the World, 1450–2000* (1998), *Maps and History* (1997), and *The Politics of James Bond* (2001). He was 1997 Distinguished Visiting Speaker at West Point.